SUNDAY SUPPERS

Informal American Home Cooking

Melanie Barnard and Brooke Dojny

PRENTICE HALL PRESS

New York   London   Toronto   Sydney   Tokyo

The following publishers have generously given permission to use quotations from copyedited works: from *Eat This . . . It'll Make You Feel Better* by Dom DeLuise (Simon & Schuster, 1988); from *Beard on Pasta* by James Beard (Knopf, 1983); from *Julia Child & Company* by Julia Child (Knopf, 1979); from *White Trash Cooking* by Ernest Matthew Mickler (Ten Speed Press, 1986); from *The Best of Shaker Cooking* by Amy Bess Miller and Persis Fuller (Macmillan, 1985); from *Buster Holmes Handmade Cookin'* (self-published, 1980); from *Alice, Let's Eat* by Calvin Trillin (Random House, 1978); from *Winnie-the-Pooh* by A. A. Milne (E. P. Dutton & Co., 1926).

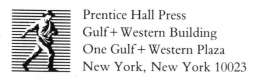

Prentice Hall Press
Gulf + Western Building
One Gulf + Western Plaza
New York, New York 10023

PRENTICE HALL PRESS and colophon are registered trademarks of Simon & Schuster, Inc.

Library of Congress Cataloging-in-Publication Data

Barnard, Melanie.
Sunday suppers.

1. Cookery, American.   2. Suppers.   I. Dojny, Brooke.
II. Title.
TX715.B4377   1988   641.5′3   87-36620
ISBN 0-13-875832-8

Designed by Laurence Alexander and Patricia Fabricant

Manufactured in the United States of America

1   3   5   7   9   10   8   6   4   2

First Edition

For Richard and Scott
David, Jeffrey, and Matthew
Matthew and Maury

ACKNOWLEDGMENTS

First, we pay tribute to our mothers: Hester, Brooke's mother, whose honesty and strength show in her good American cooking. And Marianne, Melanie's mother, who had the guts to marry a Sicilian and who cooks from her own heart and from an Italian soul—and passed on the passion. Also, of course, our fathers, Henry Maury and the late Joseph Faso, who always bestowed unqualified support and love.

And another mother of a sort is Julia Child. We were in our early twenties, newly married, and excited about the limitless world of food and entertaining that lay before us, when Julia Child, on her television series, *The French Chef,* showed that everything was possible. So, along with an entire nation of new cooks, we learned the intricacies of French cuisine, our chocolate-flecked and bechamel-spattered copies of *Mastering the Art of French Cooking* guiding us every single inch of the way. Likewise, James Beard, with whom Melanie studied. His was the most eloquent and powerful voice calling for high standards in American cooking, and his influence continues through this generation of cooks, to whom he bequeathed those standards.

Thank you to Susan Friedland, our editor, who planted the seed for *Sunday Suppers* and who nurtured us with great kindness and professionalism through the writing process. Also to Bob Cornfield, agent extraordinaire, who kept the faith even when we faltered.

In Berkeley, California, Carol Adrienne fed Brooke's newly awakening taste buds with food so wonderful that she *had* to go home and do it herself. Carol's cooking represents an ideal that has been a lifelong goal.

Also, heartfelt thanks to Jane and Michael Stern, who have been our mentors and generous friends. Their call for a return to simplicity and honesty in American food and their inquiry into some of our most interesting culinary roots truly helped to inspire *Sunday Suppers.*

We are also indebted to Martha Stewart, whose sense of style and freedom with the best raw ingredients will always be an inspiration—and whose faith in us both led us to the certainty that we could tackle a book of our own.

While she was culinary director of *COOK'S* magazine, Susy Davidson patiently shared her high standards for accuracy and attention to detail and taught us both about developing and testing recipes using those criteria.

Thanks to Richard Sax and Mary Goodbody for their steadfast encouragement; to Janet Baker for her unfailing competency, generosity, and good humor; to Sue Mills and Cathe Ryan; and to all the family and friends, especially Piotre, Andrzej, and Adam, who willingly (and almost always enthusiastically) helped us consume countless Sunday suppers.

To all of you, we are deeply grateful.

CONTENTS

FOREWORD

Fifty-Two Sunday Dinners, an earnest old cookbook popular in the 1930s, aimed to answer what it called "the eternal feminine question: WHAT SHALL WE HAVE FOR DINNER TODAY?" Its author, Elizabeth O. Hiller ("Founder and Principal of the Chicago Domestic Science School"), commiserated with readers: "It is not always the easiest thing in the world to think of a seasonable menu, nor to determine just the right combination that will furnish a meal appetizing and well-balanced in food values."

Gastronomy has changed since that book was written seventy-five years ago. Men worry about what we shall have for dinner nearly as fervently as women. To most moderns, formal meals such as those in Mrs. Hiller's book are not a necessary ritual each Sunday. Her antiquated recipes—for the likes of consommé with egg balls, calves' hearts stuffed with salt pork, and cornstarch cake—are positively frightening compared to contemporary cookery.

Fifty-Two Sunday Dinners is a quaint collectable; however, its point is not obsolete. Despite our lofty newfound culinary standards, we of the late twentieth century still must eat, and we still must eat every Sunday. Mrs. Hiller's "eternal . . . question" endures.

That is why Melanie Barnard and Brooke Dojny's *Sunday Suppers* is such a treasure. It fills a need. It is a book that demands to be pored over and used. Come see us a year from now, and we guarantee our copy will have cornmeal and cracker crumbs burrowed down to its spine, and its pages will be splattered with oil and mustard and salsa. Unlike overly glamorous cookbooks designed for coffee-table display, this one belongs in the kitchen. It is a collection of recipes that share a rare quality: they make you want to cook.

Don't you just love the title? Suppers are ever so much friendlier than dinners. And Sunday has such nice implications. It's the day for friends and family to gather at the table (or in the TV room where they can watch the game and eat pigs in blankets). Sunday suggests square meals and comfort food, hearty things to eat. It is a free day, when anything goes; when dad decides to cook Reuben sandwiches and someone gets the bright idea to make old-fashioned Tin Roof Sundaes (the recipes for both of which are here on pages 59 and 270).

The dishes that constitute *Sunday Suppers* make only the most ingenuous demands on those who want to cook them. This is a collection of handy fare, with no delusions of grandeur and no promises you will seem like a *cordon bleu* gourmet if you do as the book tells you. What you will be, if you make and serve and eat what's here, is well liked by guests and well fed yourself.

No one will have trouble turning these clearly written recipes into wonderful meals. Nor is the pleasure of cooking in any way diminished just because the recipes are easy. These are real recipes, not "I hate to cook" miracle methods of creating something from nothing. This book is for people who enjoy the sputter of bacon in the pan heralding Baked Spaghetti Carbonara (see page 93), the smell of chocolate and butter melting together—soon to become Hot Brownies with Brandy–Ice Cream Sauce (see page 265), and the frailty of Sky-High Popovers (see page 222), too hot to hold.

Melanie and Brooke's *Sunday Suppers* require no fuss or frippery. These congenial authors do not expect readers to spend all day in the kitchen worrying over complicated instructions, or all morning at the market hunting for exotic ingredients. They are the companions you want with you when you plan and prepare a meal. They brim with good sense, helpful suggestions, and a vast repertoire of dishes unbounded by either a parochial or an elitist palate.

This point must be made: These recipes work. Those we have cooked turned out perfectly—no surprise, considering Brooke Dojny and Melanie Barnard's reputations as recipe testers. They have proofed some of the finest modern cookbooks. Food writers know that if Brooke and Melanie say something works, it works.

So isn't it grand that these two now have a book of their own? What many of us have always appreciated about their work as food consultants—their probity, efficiency, and good cheer—gives *Sunday Suppers* a singular glow.

In particular, the thing that has always set them apart from others who write recipes is their ability to take a blah set of ingredients and adjust them, sometimes in subtle ways, to give the recipe clarity and force. In other words, Brooke Dojny and Melanie Barnard have a way of making food taste good. We thank them for sharing that gift with those of us who will read and use this book.

—Jane and Michael Stern
West Redding, Connecticut

INTRODUCTION

Sunday used to be a day quite separate from the other six. We slept late and our senses were awakened by the aroma of brewing coffee and the sizzle of frying bacon. We lazed over the hefty copy of the Sunday paper and began an all-day family affair with the crossword puzzle. Later, depending upon the season, we may have had an afternoon picnic at the beach or an excursion to a local farm for apple picking. But always there was the ritual long walk through the neighborhood and ultimately to Grandma's house. Inevitably, she would lean out the window and call, "You'll come for Sunday supper, y'hear?" And of course we would, for that was why we walked by in the first place.

Grandma cooked enough to feed a small army, for she was never quite sure just how many people would wander by in the afternoon, or how many times she would lean out and call, "You'll come for Sunday supper, y'hear?" Usually, there were the relatives, plus a few neighbors and assorted stragglers who had been lucky enough to catch her eye. Grandma never, never invited anyone in advance. She thought that wasn't quite proper. If she wanted to actually entertain or have a party, then she had a dinner, which, according to Grandma, wasn't the same thing at all. She sometimes had dinners, of course, but they were always on Saturday nights and we never sidled up ahead of time to be included.

Dinner meant donning your "best" dress and those tight shoes. First you sat for hours with only a bowl of nuts and a minuscule plate of hors d'oeuvres. And then you had to worry about what sort of fancied-up oddities would be put on the plate that you were expected to eat smilingly and delicately with the right fork. As a final trial, there was always a fluffy dessert.

But Sunday supper, now that was a meal to get ready for. We washed up, of course, but Grandma didn't run an inspection. We ate in the kitchen, unless there were too many people, and then we moved the meal into the dining room. Grandma knew just what we liked, and she always made it. In winter, it was a juicy glazed pork roast with a pitcher of pan gravy or a big pot of stewed chicken and dumplings. In summer, she cooked only from the garden, so supper was a bounty of tomatoes, peppers, and squash in every preparation imaginable. There would surely be a fruit pie, a plate of giant sugar cookies, and possibly even a strawberry shortcake if anyone was to have a tough week, like maybe an algebra test.

Grandma is gone now, and the hazards of modern-day life have all but wiped out Sundays as well. Now, instead of a big breakfast, a quick trip to the deli will yield a bagful of bagels. The repeal of Sunday blue laws can make it too easy to trade in a picnic at the beach for a sale at the mall.

But we are determined to keep Sunday supper, for it is the anchor upon which we build our week. Cooking is both our profession and our joy. Most weekdays, we develop recipes, testing and retesting. We make quickly prepared suppers for our families, who are constantly on the run. But we never work on Sundays. We cook then for the pure joy of it.

Like Grandma, we like simple meals filled with fresh and seasonal ingredients. Roasts and stews with winter vegetables fill our cool-weather kitchens with good smells and our own gardens provide enough inspiration for a summer's worth of Sundays. Grandma was always impressed with newfangled contraptions, and she would certainly have approved our use of food processors and microwave ovens. She wouldn't mind frozen green peas, canned chicken stock, or tinned plum tomatoes either, now that some really good brands are available. Like her, we always use unsalted butter because we prefer the taste, but we think that only a few recipes (and we have specified which ones) absolutely require it.

We agree with Grandma that a dish is only as good as its ingredients, and we think it is quite worthwhile to make friends with good butchers, fishmongers, and greengrocers— be they owners of small shops or the managers of supermarket departments. Then shop selectively and shop creatively. Rather than stick doggedly to a menu that calls for zucchini, we can easily be swayed by a few perfect green beans. In our recipes, we have often given options as to ingredients, and our menu suggestions are to be taken only as guidelines. Let your taste and your daily marketplace make the final decision.

Because we use our recipes every day in our own homes, we have developed, tested, and written them to be as easy to read and to follow as we possibly can. We want you to savor the food, not spend exhausting hours laboring over a stove.

Yes, this is a book of recipes for Sunday suppers, but it is also a collection of our favorite foods that we cook anytime we want to serve an informal, warm, inviting meal to very special people—our families and our good friends. Please use it in the same spirit. And if you are ever in our neighborhood on a Sunday afternoon and happen to catch our eye, "You'll come over for Sunday supper, y'hear?"

HEARTY SOUPS

"Soup of the evening, beautiful soup!"

—*LEWIS CARROLL*

Alice's Adventures in Wonderland (1866)

"Soup is good food."

—*THE CAMPBELL KIDS*

"If a food can be friendly, this is one of the 'friend-liest'."

—*DOM DELUISE*

Chicken Stock

This is our simple chicken stock. We accumulate chicken backs and necks in the freezer and then make a batch of stock. Quantities can be increased if you want a larger yield.

3 pounds chicken backs, necks, wing tips—or any other chicken parts except the livers
12 cups water
1 large onion, quartered
1 rib celery with leafy tops, cut into 5 pieces
1 large carrot, peeled and cut into 5 pieces

A handful of parsley stems
1 branch fresh thyme or ½ teaspoon dried thyme
1 bay leaf
5 peppercorns
Salt to taste

1. Rinse the chicken, place it in a large soup pot, and cover it with the water. Bring to a boil and simmer for 20 minutes, skimming off the foam as it rises to the surface.
2. Add all the remaining ingredients except the salt. Cook, uncovered, at a gentle simmer for 1½ hours. Strain, discarding the vegetables and chicken.
3. Spoon off the excess fat or refrigerate the stock and lift the fat off after it has congealed on the top. Add salt to taste.

YIELD: APPROXIMATELY 8 CUPS.

NOTE: If it is to be frozen, boil it for another 30 minutes or so, until the volume has been reduced to about 4 cups. Then reconstitute it with an equal amount of water when ready to use. (This saves space in the freezer.)

The discarded, cooked chicken meat, if any remains, may be used in salads or soups, but much of the flavor will have cooked out of it.

Corn and Chicken Chowder

We first had a corn and chicken chowder when a spell of stormy weather on Martha's Vineyard kept us indoors. We craved something hot like chowder, but since there was a clam-hater in the group we searched through old cookbooks in the rental cottage and found an old New England recipe for a chowder using corn and chicken instead of the bivalve. It's been a regular part of our repertoire ever since. Serve with pilot biscuits or common crackers, Classic Creamy Coleslaw (see page 223), and Georgia Peach-Pecan Skillet Cake (see page 234).

3 slices bacon
1 large onion, chopped
3 ribs celery, thinly sliced
1½ pounds (about 4 medium) boiling potatoes, peeled and diced
3 cups good-quality canned or homemade (see page 2) chicken stock
1½ cups water

1½ pounds chicken thighs
4 cups corn kernels, cut from the cob or frozen
3 cups half-and-half
1½ teaspoons dried thyme
¼ teaspoon freshly ground black pepper or more to taste
Salt to taste

1. Cut the bacon into ¼-inch pieces and cook it with the onion in a large, heavy saucepan or soup pot over medium heat until both are beginning to turn a very light brown, about 10 minutes.
2. Add the celery and the potatoes to the pot along with the chicken stock and water, bringing to a simmer, and add the chicken. Partially cover and cook over low heat for about 15 to 20 minutes, or until the chicken is cooked through.
3. Remove the pieces of chicken with tongs and set aside. Add the corn, half-and-half, thyme, and pepper and simmer, uncovered, for 5 to 8 minutes.
4. Remove meat from chicken bones, discarding skin. Chop the chicken into ½-inch pieces and return it to the pot. Season the chowder with salt to taste. (Salt may not be needed since both the bacon and the chicken stock can be salty.) Serve it hot in wide, shallow soup bowls with common crackers or saltines and butter.

YIELD: 6 SERVINGS.

NOTE: This chowder is delicious if eaten the day it is made but is even better if kept overnight in the refrigerator. Reheat slowly.

Saffron Cream of Chicken Soup

We wouldn't want to say too many nasty things about canned soups—we are, after all, patriotic Americans! But we really think that they've made life just a little too easy and lowered standards just a little too far. By now, two entire generations in this country have grown to adulthood, many never having ever tasted genuine homemade cream of chicken soup. What a pity! It's so simple, it doesn't take that long (no more than 1½ hours), and cooking the chicken in chicken stock yields a doubly delicious flavor. Ours is fairly classic, though we add a little saffron and turmeric, which give an exciting, subtle edge to the soup's flavor and turn it a beautiful pale orange-gold color. Though the saffron is expensive, its flavor is distinctive. However, if it doesn't seem worth the price to you, omit it.

Serve with a salad of hearty lettuces or Roasted Vegetables using broccoli and peppers (see page 218), and perhaps Plain Muffins (see page 219). Offer something fruity or chocolate for dessert—such as Mixed Fruit–Chocolate Pan Soufflé (see page 264), or Pear Strudel (see page 250).

1 chicken (about 3 pounds), quartered or cut in eighths, excess fat removed and discarded
6 cups water
6 cups good-quality canned or homemade (see page 2) chicken stock
1 large rib celery with leafy tops, cut in 5 pieces
1 large onion, quartered, and stuck with 2 cloves
1 bay leaf

6 whole peppercorns
2 cups half-and-half or light cream
1 rib celery, thinly sliced for the soup
½ teaspoon saffron threads
¼ teaspoon turmeric
4 tablespoons all-purpose flour
4 tablespoons butter, at room temperature
½ teaspoon white pepper
Salt to taste

1. Place the chicken in a large soup pot. Cover with the water and chicken stock and add the celery, onion, bay leaf, and peppercorns. Bring to a boil, reduce heat, and simmer, uncovered, for 20 minutes, skimming any scum and particles that rise to the surface. Partially cover the pot and simmer on low heat for another 25 minutes, or until the chicken is quite tender.

2. Strain the chicken and liquid into a large bowl. Return the cooking liquid to the pot and spoon any excess fat off the surface. Discard the vegetables and set the chicken aside for a few minutes until it is cool enough to handle.

3. Preheat oven to 350 degrees. Add the half-and-half or cream to the chicken broth and bring to a simmer. Add the sliced cel-

ery. Place the saffron threads on a sheet of aluminum foil and toast in the preheated oven for 4 minutes, or until the saffron turns one shade darker and begins to smell fragrant. Watch carefully to make sure it doesn't burn. Crush it with the back of a spoon and add it along with the turmeric to the soup.

4. Strip the skin off the chicken and pull the meat off the bones. Chop the chicken meat quite fine and add it to the soup. (There should be about 3 cups of meat.)

5. Work the flour and butter together with your fingertips to form a smooth paste. Drop about ½ teaspoon at a time into the simmering soup and cook, stirring frequently, until all the butter-flour paste has dissolved, the soup has thickened, and the flour has cooked, about 5 minutes. Season with the white pepper and salt to taste.

YIELD: 6 TO 7 SERVINGS.

NOTE: This soup will keep well, refrigerated, for 3 days. Any leftover soup can be frozen but should be thawed and reheated very slowly to avoid its separating.

Portuguese Linguisa and Lentil Soup

Linguisa (or linguica) is a pork sausage highly spiced with garlic and paprika. Spanish or Portuguese chorizo (or chourico) is a fine substitute. Both of these sausages are available in Spanish markets and increasingly (because people have discovered that they taste marvelous) in butcher shops where customers persistently ask for them. Our advice is to persevere. However, if you should fail in your immediate attempts to obtain linguisa or chorizo, this soup is quite savory made with any good, garlicky sausage links.

Soups made with legumes are usually daunting since the beans often require overnight presoaking and long hours of cooking. Lentils, however, are the harried cook's dream since they simmer to a delectably tender state in just about an hour. So this very hearty, very warming soup takes little time or effort. However, it suffers not at all if made a day ahead and reheated. Serve it with some crusty bread and a green salad. Baked Ginger–Bay Leaf Apples (see page 262) or Double Crust Apple-Quince Pie (see page 248) would be ideal desserts.

Portuguese Linguisa and Lentil Soup (cont.)

1 large onion, chopped
1 large rib celery, chopped
1 clove garlic, minced
4 tablespoons olive oil
8 cups water
4 cups good-quality canned or homemade (see page 2) chicken stock
2 cups canned tomatoes with their juices
1 pound (about 2½ cups) lentils, rinsed and picked over

1 bay leaf
¼ teaspoon red pepper flakes
½ pound kale
1 pound linguisa or other uncooked garlicky sausage links, such as chorizo or Italian sausage
1 cup red wine
Freshly ground black pepper to taste
Salt to taste

1. In a large kettle or stockpot, sauté the onion, celery, and garlic in the oil over medium-low heat until the vegetables begin to soften, about 3 minutes. Add the water, stock, tomatoes, lentils, bay leaf, and red pepper flakes. Bring to a boil, breaking up the tomatoes with the back of a spoon. Lower the heat and simmer, partially covered, until the lentils are tender, about 1 hour.

2. Meanwhile, wash the kale, discarding the stems and trimming the leaves from tough ribs. Thinly slice or coarsely chop the kale leaves. You will have 8 to 10 cups of kale. Reserve.

3. Prick the sausages and place in a skillet large enough to hold them comfortably. Add the wine, bring to a boil, and simmer, partially covered, for about 15 minutes, turning the sausages occasionally until cooked through. Drain the sausages and cut them into ¼-inch slices. If there is wine left in the pan, skim off any fat and add the wine to the soup.

4. When the lentils are tender, add the kale and sausage slices to the soup. Simmer, covered, for 5 minutes. Season with pepper and add salt to taste. (You may not need any salt since canned stock, if you are using it, is salty.)

YIELD: 6 TO 8 SERVINGS.

Buttermilk, Bacon, and Collards Soup

Inspired by traditional and humble southern components, this soup is actually rather sophisticated and quite contemporary, and it takes very little time to make. Although neither of us have ever developed a taste for drinking buttermilk, we think it is a terrific ingredient. In baking, the acid tenderizes, and in soups, buttermilk adds thickness and tangy flavor without the guilt of fat and calories. Collards, like any deep green leafy vegetable, overflow with vitamins as well as great flavor. The smaller, younger greens are the most tender.

We would serve this with lots of warm corn bread and end the meal with Green Tomato Cobbler (see page 260) or Double Crust Apple-Quince Pie (see page 248).

1⅓ pounds young collard greens
8 slices heavily smoked bacon
2 medium onions, chopped
About 1 pound (2 large) all-purpose potatoes, peeled and coarsely diced

6 cups good-quality canned or homemade (see page 2) chicken stock
2 cups buttermilk, at room temperature
¼ teaspoon cayenne pepper
Salt to taste

1. Thoroughly wash the collards, trim off the tough stalks and ribs, and slice or tear the leaves into small pieces. Reserve the leaves.
2. In a heavy saucepan, fry the bacon until crisp. Remove with a slotted spoon, drain, crumble, and reserve. Pour off all but 3 tablespoons drippings. Add the onion and sauté until softened, about 4 minutes. Add the potatoes, collard leaves, and chicken stock. Cover and bring to a boil. Lower the heat and simmer until the potatoes and collards are tender, about 12 to 15 minutes.
3. Purée the mixture in a food processor or blender. (The mixture will not be completely smooth.) Pour it back into the saucepan, add the buttermilk and cayenne pepper, and gently heat but do not boil it. Season with salt to taste. (No salt may be needed if using canned chicken stock since it is already salted.)
4. Serve the soup while hot, garnished with the reserved bacon.

YIELD: 4 TO 6 SERVINGS.

Nana's Chicken Noodle Soup

Chicken and pasta soup seems to be such a stellar concept that most major cuisines present some version in their classic repertoire. There are the wonton soups of China, the lemon-flavored chicken and orzo soups of Greece, the chicken and dumpling soups of Middle Europe, and the many different pastas dropped into chicken stock throughout Italy. Many Americans seem to think that chicken noodle soup was the amazing invention of a large company that had the good sense to put it in cans. This recipe, handed down by Melanie's Sicilian grandmother, is simple goodness itself. She always had chicken stock on hand, and we have updated our method to enrich a quick homemade broth with some good canned stock. But we have kept the wonderfully flavored and easily made noodles since they were her justly famous signature. The noodles are quite sturdy, so the soup keeps well in the refrigerator for several days and can also be frozen.

Chicken soup has been proven to be good for whatever ails you. If you have Hot Brownies with Brandy–Ice Cream Sauce (see page 265) for dessert, a cure is guaranteed.

1 3- to-3½-pound chicken, cut up, with back
    and neck reserved
10 cups water
1 onion, quartered
1 carrot, peeled and cut in 5 pieces
1 rib celery, cut in 5 pieces
¼ cup parsley stems (reserve sprigs)
3 whole peppercorns
3 whole cloves
1 tablespoon minced fresh thyme or 1 teaspoon
    dried thyme leaves
4 cups good-quality canned or homemade
    (see page 2) chicken stock
2 carrots, peeled and thinly sliced
½ cup frozen green peas, thawed
2 tablespoons minced parsley sprigs

¼ cup freshly grated Parmesan cheese, plus
    more grated cheese to pass at the table
Generous grindings of black pepper
Salt to taste

NOODLES:

1½ cups all-purpose flour
2 eggs
2 teaspoons olive oil
2 teaspoons water
2 tablespoons minced fresh oregano or
    2 teaspoons dried oregano
2 tablespoons freshly grated Parmesan cheese
½ teaspoon salt

1. To make the stock, trim and discard any excess fatty skin from the chicken and place all the chicken parts except the breasts in a large kettle or stockpot. Add the water, onion, carrot, celery, parsley stems, peppercorns, and cloves. Bring to a boil, skim off any foam on the top, and then add the thyme. Simmer 20 minutes and then add the chicken breasts. Simmer 20 to 25 minutes more, until all of the chicken is tender.

2. With tongs or a slotted spoon, remove the chicken wings, thighs, legs, and breasts from the broth. Continue to gently simmer the broth. As soon as the chicken is cool enough to handle, remove the meat from the bones in chunks and reserve. Return the bones to the pot and simmer an additional 20 minutes.

3. While the chicken and stock are simmering, make the noodles. Place the flour, eggs, oil, water, oregano, cheese, and salt in a food processor and process for about 45 to 60 seconds to mix and knead the pasta. (If you are making the pasta by hand, place the flour on a work surface and make a well in the center. Add the remaining ingredients to the well and mix with your hands to form a dough. Knead on a floured surface for about 10 minutes.) Place the pasta dough on a lightly floured surface, cover with a towel, and let rest for 10 to 20 minutes. Divide the pasta dough in half and roll each half as thin as possible to form a square of approximately 14 inches. Trim the edges of each pasta square to make straight sides and lightly flour the surface of the pasta. Roll up each square loosely as for a jelly roll. Cut each roll with a sharp knife into ¼-inch slices. Shake the slices open and lay in an overlapping mound. Cut the mound of pasta slices into roughly 2-inch lengths and then spread them out to dry for about 15 minutes before using.

4. To make the soup, strain the broth and return it to the kettle. Add the chicken stock and bring to a boil. Add the carrots and cook 2 minutes. Add the peas and pasta and cook about 2 minutes. Add the chicken meat and parsley and stir in the Parmesan cheese. Season with pepper and salt to taste. (You may not need any salt since canned stock and cheese are both salty.)

5. Serve in large bowls and pass additional cheese to stir into the soup.

YIELD: 6 SERVINGS.

Savory Pumpkin and Bean Soup

Look for small sugar pumpkins for cooking. Their flesh is firm and sweet and their flavor is the essence of autumn. Butternut or Hubbard squash is a good substitute.

This quick and easy soup needs only a green salad and a crusty loaf of bread to turn it into a complete meal. Serve Hot Brownies with Brandy–Ice Cream Sauce (see page 265) for dessert.

4 tablespoons olive oil
1 large onion, chopped
2 cloves garlic, minced
1½ pounds pumpkin or such winter squash as butternut or Hubbard
4 cups good-quality canned or homemade (see page 2) chicken stock
1 cup water
2½ teaspoons dried savory

½ teaspoon curry powder
¼ teaspoon freshly ground black pepper
1 bay leaf, broken in half
12 ounces plum tomatoes or 1 1-pound can plum tomatoes, with liquid
12 ounces smoked ham, sliced ¼ inch thick
2 10½-ounce cans white beans, drained
½ cup chopped Italian parsley
Salt to taste

1. In a large soup pot, heat the olive oil over low heat. Add the onion and garlic and cook gently until softened but not browned, about 5 minutes.
2. Peel the pumpkin or squash with a vegetable peeler, slice open, and discard any seeds. Cut into ¾-inch chunks and add to the pot, along with the chicken stock, water, savory, curry, pepper, and bay leaf. Bring to a boil, reduce the heat, and simmer, partially covered, for 8 minutes.
3. Core the plum tomatoes and cut into ½-inch cubes, or coarsely chop the canned tomatoes. Cut the ham into thin, ¾-inch-long strips. Add the tomatoes, ham, and beans to the pot. Simmer, uncovered, for 15 minutes or until the pumpkin is tender. Stir in the chopped parsley, add the salt to taste, and correct the seasoning if necessary. Remove the bay leaf and serve.

YIELD: 6 SERVINGS.

NOTE: This soup will keep in the refrigerator for 3 days and also freezes well.

Brussels Sprouts, Cheddar, and Ale Soup

We love cheese soup on a winter evening. Since a glass of beer or ale is the perfect beverage accompaniment, we added it to the soup. Then we got adventurous and added a handful of leftover cooked Brussels sprouts and found that the combination appealed even to our families, who usually won't eat Brussels sprouts. You can, of course, change the vegetable to green beans or broccoli or leave it out entirely if you wish. If you make the soup a day or two ahead, reheat it very carefully over low heat or in the top of a double boiler to prevent the cheese from becoming stringy.

The Absolute Best Buttermilk Biscuits (see page 220) or crunchy breadsticks and a spinach salad are wonderful here along with Pear Strudel (see page 250) or Purple Plum Crumble (see page 258) for dessert.

1 pound small Brussels sprouts, trimmed
6 tablespoons butter
1 large onion, chopped
1 red bell pepper, diced
1 green bell pepper, diced
1 large rib celery, chopped
2 carrots, peeled and chopped
1 large clove garlic, minced
6 tablespoons all-purpose flour

2 teaspoons dry mustard
24 ounces flat ale or beer
6 cups good-quality canned or homemade (see page 2) chicken stock
1½ pounds cheddar cheese, grated
1½ cups milk or half-and-half
¼ teaspoon cayenne pepper or to taste
Salt to taste

1. Cook the Brussels sprouts in boiling, salted water until just tender, about 6 to 8 minutes. Drain, cut the sprouts in half, and reserve.

2. Heat the butter in a heavy 4-quart saucepan and sauté the onion, bell peppers, celery, and carrots over medium-low heat until the vegetables are softened, about 5 to 8 minutes. Add the garlic and sauté 1 minute.

3. Add the flour and mustard and cook, stirring, over low heat for about 2 minutes. Whisk in the beer and cook over medium-low heat, stirring constantly, until thickened and bubbly. Stir in the stock, bring to a simmer and cook, uncovered and stirring often, over low heat for about 5 minutes.

4. Remove the pan from the heat and stir in the cheese, ¼ at a time, stirring until each addition is melted before adding another. Place the pan over the lowest possible heat, add the milk and Brussels sprouts and stir until the vegetables and the soup are hot, about 1 to 2 minutes. Season with cayenne pepper. Add salt to taste. (If you are using canned chicken stock, no salt may be needed since both stock and cheese are salty.)

YIELD: 6 SERVINGS.

Duck Soup

Here is a delicious soup that is at once hearty yet quite elegant by virtue of its stellar main ingredients—duck, wild mushrooms, and wild rice. We owe our inspiration for this to chef Larry Forgione.

If the list of ingredients seems daunting, don't be put off. This recipe is very simple to make. And since this soup is one that really improves in taste if allowed to age overnight in the refrigerator, it can be completed a day before serving.

Serve with breadsticks or warm French bread and a salad of Roasted Vegetables (see page 218). Either Pumpkin Custard (see page 255) or Double Crust Apple-Quince Pie (see page 248) would be a lovely dessert.

1 duck, cut in quarters if possible
6 cups water
4 cups beef stock (canned is fine, but do not use bouillon)
1 cup white wine
1 onion, quartered and stuck with 2 cloves
1 leek, including 2 inches of green leaves, washed and coarsely chopped
1 large rib celery, coarsely chopped
1 clove garlic, crushed
6 peppercorns
6 parsley stems

1 teaspoon dried thyme
1 bay leaf
3 carrots, peeled and thinly sliced
1 cup wild rice
4 ounces fresh mushrooms, such as oyster mushrooms or shiitake, sliced
1 cup heavy cream
¼ cup chopped flat-leaf parsley
2 teaspoons Worcestershire sauce
½ teaspoon freshly ground black pepper
Salt to taste
3 tablespoons Madeira or medium-dry sherry

1. Pull off or trim and discard all the removable fat from the duck. Place the duck in a large soup pot. (It's easier to manage if you've had the duck cut in quarters at the market, but if yours is whole, just be sure to use a deep enough pot so the duck is submerged in the liquid.) Add the water, beef stock, and white wine to the pot and bring to a boil over high heat. Cook over medium heat for 20 minutes, skimming off the fat and foam that rise to the surface.
2. Add the onion, leek, celery, garlic, peppercorns, parsley stems, thyme, and bay

leaf to the pot. Cook, uncovered, at a gentle simmer for 45 minutes to 1 hour or until the duck is tender. (Duck pieces will cook faster than the whole duck.)
3. Strain through a colander. Return the stock to the pot. Discard the vegetables and set the duck aside until cool enough to handle.
4. Place the pot of duck stock over medium heat, steadily balanced half on and half off the burner. The fat on the surface will accumulate on the side of the pot that is off the heat, making it easier to spoon it

off. Remove as much of the fat as possible (or chill the pot of stock and lift the hardened fat off the surface).

5. Add the carrots and the wild rice to the stock and simmer, uncovered, for 30 minutes.

6. Meanwhile, strip the duck meat off the bones, discarding the bones and fat. Cut the meat into thin slivers. Add the duck to the soup along with the mushrooms and the cream and simmer for another 20 minutes or until the rice is tender.

7. Stir in the chopped parsley, Worcestershire sauce, pepper, and salt to taste.

8. Just before serving, stir in the Madeira or sherry.

YIELD: 6 SERVINGS.

NOTE: The soup may be made ahead and refrigerated for 3 days or frozen. Reheat before serving.

Jamaican Seafood Stew

The Caribbean Islands are among our closest neighbors, yet few of us know very much about the complex and exciting cuisine enjoyed by the talented native cooks. The cuisine varies from island to island, but there are several common threads. The food uses the marvelous tropical fruits and vegetables that grow there in lush profusion. Seasonings are a rich combination of spicy creole and a sprinkling of influence from whatever country (or countries) claimed the islands over the course of the last several centuries. The result is a thoroughly delightful blend of ingredients and seasonings with a sweet/hot/spicy/smooth character.

This is an adaptation of a wonderful seafood stew that Melanie once enjoyed while on holiday. Canned cream of coconut lends a sweet touch offset by the fresh, tart flavor of good limes. Limes are available throughout the year, but their flavor and acidity vary according to the season, so you may need a little less or a little more juice depending upon the limes and your personal taste. We have used seafood typical of the Caribbean waters, but you can choose almost any fresh seafood that you like. Clams are not usually used, but we think they are quite tasty in the stew. Almost any firm, white fish is good and we especially like monkfish, although they swim in colder waters. If you want to be thoroughly authentic, you might want to add turtle or conch meat.

We like this with a loaf of good Cuban bread and a salad of cooked, sliced sweet potatoes on a bed of greens dressed with a light vinaigrette. Luscious Pecan Pie Bars (see page 266) and vanilla ice cream drizzled with golden rum would be a fitting dessert.

Jamaican Seafood Stew (cont.)

2 tablespoons butter
2 tablespoons vegetable oil
1 large onion, chopped
1 large green bell pepper, chopped
2 cloves garlic, minced
2 jalapeño peppers, with seeds and ribs removed, finely minced (note: wash your hands carefully after working with hot peppers)
2 teaspoons curry powder
½ cup canned cream of coconut
1 cup fish stock or bottled clam juice
1 16-ounce can plum tomatoes with liquid, coarsely chopped

4 tablespoons lime juice
1 pound firm fish fillets, cut into 2-inch pieces (use red snapper, monkfish, redfish, or dolphin)
½ pound medium shrimp, peeled, and deveined
½ pound lump crabmeat, picked over to remove cartilage
2 tablespoons minced cilantro or flat-leaf parsley
Salt and freshly ground black pepper to taste
2 cups cooked rice

1. Heat the butter and oil in a large, heavy, nonreactive saucepan. Sauté the onion and green pepper over medium-low heat until just softened, about 5 minutes. Add the garlic, minced jalapeños, and curry powder and sauté about 1 minute. Stir in the cream of coconut, fish stock, and tomatoes with their liquid. Bring to a boil, then lower the heat and simmer, partially covered, for 10 minutes.

The soup base can be made a day ahead up to this point. Let it cool and then refrigerate. Reheat it before continuing with the recipe.

2. Stir in the lime juice and then add the fish fillets and shrimp. Simmer until the fish and shrimp are just cooked through, about 2 to 3 minutes. Gently stir in the crabmeat and cilantro. Simmer about 1 minute. Add salt and pepper to taste.

3. To serve, pack a ⅓-cup measure with rice and unmold it onto the bottom of a wide shallow soup bowl. Ladle the hot stew over the rice. Serve immediately.

YIELD: 6 SERVINGS.

Simple Szechuan Chicken Soup

This is simple and quick chicken, rice, and greens soup with oriental overtones.

Serve with Sky-High Popovers (see page 222) and a plate of raw vegetables such as radishes, pepper strips, and chunks of cucumber accompanied by a mixture of yogurt and herbs for dipping. Baked Ginger–Bay Leaf Apples (see page 262) are a nice finish.

6 cups good-quality canned or homemade
    (see page 2) chicken stock
6 cups water
2 pounds chicken breasts, split
¾ cup raw long-grain rice
1½ pounds escarole or chicory
6 scallions, including the green tops,
    thinly sliced

1 teaspoon grated fresh ginger
1 tablespoon sesame oil
¼ teaspoon freshly grated nutmeg
¼ teaspoon freshly ground black
    pepper
Salt to taste

1. Bring the chicken stock and water to a boil in a large soup pot. Add the chicken breasts and the rice and simmer over low heat, partially covered, for 15 minutes, or until the chicken is just cooked through. Remove the chicken with tongs and set it aside until it is cool enough to handle.

2. Meanwhile, wash the escarole or chicory, removing any discolored leaves and tough stems, and slice the greens crosswise ¼ inch thick. Add the greens to the soup and simmer, uncovered, for 10 minutes.

3. Pull off and discard the chicken skin and bones and cut the meat into ¾-inch chunks.

4. Return the chicken to the pot along with the sliced scallions, ginger, sesame oil, nutmeg, pepper, and salt to taste. Simmer for 5 minutes to blend the flavors. Correct the seasoning, if necessary.

YIELD: 6 SERVINGS.

Spicy Seafood and Sorrel Gumbo

As the arguments about what *exactly* and *officially* constitutes a gumbo—that coastal Louisianan soup/stew—rage all about us, we happily present this version. We think it strikes just the right balance: it uses a roux as the base (but one that calls for a minimum of oil and flour), both okra and filé powder as thickeners (possible heresy, we realize, but we don't want to do without either of those wonderful ingredients), sorrel to add a fresh herbal tang, and judicious amounts of pepper to give it zip without drowning out the flavors of the seafood. The types and proportions of seafood can be varied and adjusted according to their availability in your region and your own preferences.

Since gumbo contains so many vegetables already, it doesn't need a salad—unless you really want one. Squares of cornbread or corn sticks are a great accompaniment. To carry through with the feeling of the meal, serve either Cranberry Bread Pudding with Whiskey Sauce (see page 252), Miss Hulling's Banana-Coconut Cream Pie (see page 246), or Maggie Valley Buttermilk Pie (see page 244) for dessert. This is, indeed, a truly memorable meal!

¾ **pound medium shrimp**
4 cups water
3 tablespoons vegetable oil
3 tablespoons all-purpose flour
1 large onion, chopped
1 green pepper, chopped
1 large rib celery, finely chopped
2 cloves garlic, minced
½ **pound okra, thinly sliced (about 2 cups)**
6 cups good-quality canned or homemade (see
    page 2) chicken stock

1 1-pound can plum tomatoes with their liquid
1 bay leaf
1 teaspoon dried thyme
½ **teaspoon cayenne pepper**
About 6 ounces sorrel or spinach leaves
½ **teaspoon freshly ground black pepper**
1½ **tablespoons filé powder**
¾ **pound crabmeat (fresh, frozen, or canned),**
    picked over to remove cartilage
Salt to taste
3 cups hot cooked rice

1. Shell and devein the shrimp and refrigerate the shrimp until ready to use. Rinse the shells and place them in a saucepan with the water. Simmer, partially covered, for 20 minutes. Strain, discard the shells, and use this broth later as part of the liquid in the gumbo.

2. Heat the oil in a heavy 4-quart saucepan. Add the flour and cook over medium-high heat, stirring almost constantly, until the mixture turns a brown shade the color of pecan shells, about 5 minutes. This is the roux.

3. Remove the pan from the heat and stir

in the onion, pepper, celery, garlic, and okra. Return to the heat and stir in the chicken stock, plum tomatoes, and their liquid, the reserved shrimp broth, bay leaf, thyme, and the cayenne and black peppers. Bring to a simmer, stirring and breaking up the tomatoes with the back of a spoon. Simmer gently, uncovered, for 20 minutes, stirring occasionally.

The gumbo may be made ahead up to this point and held in the refrigerator overnight. Add the shrimp and remaining ingredients the next day.

4. Slice the sorrel or spinach crosswise into thin slivers. Add it to the pot along with the shelled shrimp and filé powder. Simmer over low heat for 3 minutes, stirring frequently. Add the crabmeat, stirring it in gently so some of the larger chunks remain. Season with salt to taste. Discard the bay leaf.

5. For each serving, ladle the gumbo around and over a small mound of cooked rice in a shallow bowl.

YIELD: 6 TO 8 SERVINGS.

NOTE: Leftover gumbo may be stored in the refrigerator for up to 3 days. Reheat very gently since prolonged boiling can cause the filé powder to become stringy. Filé powder (ground sassafras leaves) is available in specialty stores and most supermarkets.

Summer Garden Minestrone

Minestrone is one of Italy's best vegetable soups. It is usually a hearty mixture of wintertime vegetables, white beans, and pasta in a long-simmered and richly seasoned beef broth. Our version substitutes the bounty from the summer herb and vegetable gardens and, in spite of the frighteningly long ingredient list, takes far less time to make—a boon for wilted, hot-weather cooks. It can also be made a day or two ahead and reheated.

We particularly like this vegetable combination, but other produce can be added whenever it looks good in your garden or at the local stand. Be sure to include the lima or fava beans and the pasta since the duet makes this meatless meal complete in protein.

Our favorite accompaniments are toasted Italian bread slices brushed with garlic-imbued olive oil and Double Lemon Loaf (see page 236) or Georgia Peach-Pecan Skillet Cake (see page 234) for dessert.

Summer Garden Minestrone (cont.)

6 tablespoons olive oil

2 leeks, white part only, thinly sliced

2 ribs celery, thinly sliced

2 carrots, thinly sliced

1 small green or yellow bell pepper, seeded and diced

1 small red bell pepper, seeded and diced

2 cloves garlic, minced

12 cups good-quality canned or homemade (see page 2) chicken stock

1 cup white wine or water

1 pound (8 or 9) fresh plum tomatoes, peeled, seeded, and diced or 1 28-ounce can plum tomatoes, drained

10 ounces fresh shelled lima or fava beans or 1 10-ounce package frozen lima beans

½ pound string beans, trimmed and cut diagonally into 1-inch lengths

2 small zucchini, sliced

2 small crookneck squash, sliced

1 small head (1 pound) savoy cabbage, thinly sliced or shredded

6 ounces broken vermicelli

2 tablespoons minced fresh basil or 2 teaspoons dried basil

2 tablespoons minced fresh marjoram or 2 teaspoons dried marjoram

2 teaspoons minced fresh thyme or 1 teaspoon dried thyme

Salt and freshly ground black pepper to taste

About ¾ cup freshly grated Parmesan cheese for passing at the table.

1. Heat the oil in a large kettle or soup pot. Add the leeks, celery, carrots, and both bell peppers and sauté over medium–low heat until vegetables are softened, about 5 to 7 minutes. Add the garlic and sauté 1 minute.

2. Add the chicken stock, wine, tomatoes, and lima beans. Bring to a boil, then lower the heat to medium and simmer until the beans are tender, about 10 to 15 minutes. (Cooking time will vary according to the size and freshness of the beans.)

3. Bring the soup to a boil and add the string beans, zucchini, crookneck squash, cabbage, and vermicelli. Return to a boil, add the dried herbs if you are using them, and cook until the pasta is tender, about 5 minutes. Stir in the fresh herbs. Add pepper generously and salt to taste. (No salt may be needed if using canned chicken stock since it is already salted.)

4. Ladle the hot soup into bowls and pass the Parmesan cheese to sprinkle over each serving.

YIELD: 6 TO 8 SERVINGS.

Avocado Soup with Salsa Arizona

On particularly sultry summer evenings, we favor cool, light suppers. This soup is completely meatless and needs absolutely no cooking, yet the richness of the ripe avocados puréed to a pastel smoothness makes it an utterly satisfying and very beautiful main course. We think it is a perfect meal with Peppery Corn Bread (see page 228) and Purple Plum Crumble (see page 258), but a plain chicken sandwich on the side would make the carnivores in your party feel satiated.

Fresh coriander, sometimes called cilantro or Chinese parsley, is essential to the success of the salsa. Most well-stocked supermarket produce sections carry it, and it is worth seeking out. At the same time, be sure to choose the reddest and ripest of fresh tomatoes. The salsa ingredients can be chopped together in a food processor, and, although the soup should be chilled, it is best served on the day it is made.

SALSA:

10 to 12 ounces (about 3 medium) tomatoes, peeled, seeded, and coarsely chopped
1 small cucumber, peeled, seeded, and coarsely chopped
1 small onion, chopped
2 scallions, including about 2 inches of the green tops, thinly sliced
1 medium green bell pepper
2 fresh or canned jalapeño peppers, seeded and finely minced (note: wash your hands carefully after working with hot peppers)
1 large clove garlic, minced
3 tablespoons minced fresh coriander
Salt to taste

SOUP:

4 ripe avocados
2 tablespoons lemon juice
3 tablespoons lime juice
4 cups good-quality canned or homemade (see page 2) chicken stock
3 cups half-and-half or light cream
1/8 teaspoon ground cumin
1/4 teaspoon white pepper
Salt to taste

1. To make the salsa, combine the tomatoes, cucumber, onion, scallions, green pepper, jalapeño peppers, garlic, and coriander. Let stand 5 minutes, then taste and add salt as desired. Let stand another 10 minutes, taste again, and correct the saltiness if necessary.

The salsa may be made a few hours ahead, covered, and refrigerated.
2. To make the soup, peel and pit the avocados. Purée in a food processor along with the lemon and lime juices. Add the stock and half-and-half and blend until smooth. Add the cumin, white pepper, and salt to taste. Pour the mixture into a bowl, cover, and chill at least 1 hour or up to 6 hours.
3. To serve, ladle the soup into shallow bowls and add a spoonful of salsa to each. Pass any remaining salsa in a small dish.

YIELD: 6 servings.

Gloucester Baked Cod Chowder

Unlike many of the other New England seaport fishing villages, Gloucester has never become a slick and trendy, natty and suave getaway for the yachting crowd. It remains much as it was—a quiet town of whitewashed houses and hardworking fishermen. In fact, a large percentage of the fresh Atlantic fish we see in markets has come through the port of Gloucester, hauled off family-owned boats and shipped out through small companies that have been there for generations.

It is no surprise, then, that the cooks of Gloucester know their chowder. Although the word is derived from *chaudière,* the pot used to cook fish stew in coastal France, New Englanders firmly believe that chowder means a creamy soup fragrant with fresh fish (usually cod) or shellfish (usually clams), potatoes, celery, salt pork, and a little thyme. To add much else is heresy.

But tradition does not limit chowder to stove-top preparation. And we think that this old-fashioned method of simmering the fish bones in milk to extract their wonderful essence and then "baking" the chowder in the oven gives an extraordinarily flavorful result. Like any Yankee cook, we have added a few personal touches to the classic soup.

Chowder is excellent when reheated, but we think the fish should be added only for the last few minutes of the reheating time to avoid overcooking it. Try to get the kind of common crackers that are sold in tins—they are harder, crunchier, and tastier. In summer serve Red, White, and Blueberry Shortcakes (see page 232) for dessert, and in winter try Cranberry Bread Pudding with Whiskey Sauce (see page 252).

3 pounds fish bones (preferably cod or other
    lean white fish)
2 quarts whole milk
½ cup white wine
4 ounces salt pork, cut in ¼-inch cubes
1 large onion, thinly sliced
2 ribs celery, thinly sliced
1¼ pounds (about 4) potatoes, peeled and
    thinly sliced
¼ teaspoon freshly ground black pepper or
    more to taste

1 tablespoon minced fresh thyme or 1 teaspoon
    dried thyme
1 bay leaf, broken
2 cups bottled clam juice or fish stock
2 pounds cod or haddock fillets, cut in large
    serving pieces
1 tablespoon minced parsley
Salt to taste
1 to 2 tablespoons unsalted butter
Common crackers

1. Place the fish bones in a kettle and cover with the milk and wine. Simmer gently, uncovered, for 20 minutes. Strain and reserve the liquid, keeping it warm.

2. Preheat the oven to 400 degrees.

3. While the liquid is simmering, fry the salt pork in a 6-quart Dutch oven or heavy ovenproof casserole over medium-low heat until it is browned and the fat is rendered, about 10 minutes. Remove the salt pork bits with a slotted spoon and reserve. Sauté the onion and celery in the drippings over medium-low heat until the vegetables are softened, about 4 minutes.

4. Remove the Dutch oven from the heat, layer the potatoes over the vegetables and sprinkle with the pepper and thyme. Add the bay leaf, milk mixture, and clam juice.

Stir the liquid gently, but do not disturb the layers.

5. Bake, uncovered, until the potatoes are nearly tender, 30 to 35 minutes. Arrange the fish over the potatoes and submerge in the liquid. Bake until the fish is just cooked through, an additional 5 to 8 minutes. Add the parsley and swirl gently.

6. Use a large serving spoon to transfer the fish, vegetables, and broth to shallow soup bowls. Avoid breaking up the fish pieces. Swirl a teaspoon of butter into each serving and sprinkle with the reserved salt pork bits, if desired. Serve with common crackers.

YIELD: 6 SERVINGS.

Martha's Mother's Polish Mushroom Soup

When Brooke worked for Martha Stewart she discovered that they shared a common link: Both Martha herself and Brooke's husband come from a Polish background. Brooke searched for years for the right version of wild mushroom soup to serve at their traditional meatless Christmas Eve–Polish dinner, but it wasn't until she made Martha's mother's soup that all the family around the table said, "This is right! This tastes just like the one we remember our mothers and grandmothers making!"

Martha published her mother's recipe in *Entertaining* (Clarkson N. Potter, 1982), and Brooke has adapted and changed the recipe over the years so that it's now somewhat different. The dried wild mushrooms are absolutely necessary. This soup is meatless, but the mushrooms contribute a haunting, intensely wild woodsy taste and aroma that reminds us of a primeval forest.

Serve on a cold winter's day with thickly sliced rye bread and butter, a cucumber salad, and Classic Rice Pudding (see page 243) or Candied Gingerbread with Vanilla Cream (see page 256) for dessert.

Martha's Mother's Polish Mushroom Soup (cont.)

1½ ounces dried Polish mushrooms, dried
    cèpes, or porcini
8 cups beef stock, canned or homemade
2 onions, chopped
4 carrots, peeled and cut into small cubes
2 ribs celery with leafy tops, finely chopped
2 tablespoons chopped parsley
8 ounces shiitake mushrooms, stems chopped,
    caps sliced
1 pound domestic, cultivated mushrooms,
    sliced

⅓ cup very small dried pasta (squares, orzo,
    bows, or tiny tubes)
3 tablespoons chopped fresh dill
½ teaspoon freshly ground black
    pepper
1½ tablespoons butter
1½ tablespoons all-purpose flour
¾ cup sour cream
Salt to taste

1. Soak the dried mushrooms in 2 cups boiling water for 1 hour. Lift the mushrooms out of the liquid and rinse them gently under running water to remove any remaining grit or debris. Chop and set aside to use later in the soup. Strain the mushroom soaking liquid through a coffee filter or a double layer of cheesecloth.

2. Combine the mushroom liquid in a large pot with 3 cups water and the beef stock. Bring to a simmer and add the chopped onion, carrots, celery, and parsley. Simmer, partially covered, for 20 minutes. Add the sliced fresh mushrooms and the reconstituted dried mushrooms and simmer, partially covered, for an additional 15 minutes.

The soup may be made ahead up to this point and refrigerated or frozen.

3. Bring the soup to a full boil and add the pasta. Cook, uncovered, for 4 to 7 minutes, or until the pasta is almost tender. Add the chopped dill and the pepper.

4. In a small saucepan, melt the butter and stir in the flour. Cook over medium heat, stirring, for 2 minutes. Remove the pan from the heat and whisk in the sour cream. Whisk the sour cream mixture into the soup and cook, stirring occasionally, over low heat for 3 minutes. Since the sour cream has been stabilized with the flour it is not likely to curdle, but it is best not to let it come to a full boil.

5. Add salt and perhaps some additional pepper to taste.

YIELD: 6 TO 8 SERVINGS.

NOTE: This soup will keep well in the refrigerator for several days. Reheat gently.

Minted Green Pea and Smoked Ham Vichyssoise

This is a lovely soup for a supper in the spring. Serve with a salad of light lettuce and slivered radishes and a basket of Plain Muffins (see page 219). Sliced ripe strawberries tossed with sugar and served over vanilla ice cream is the perfect accompanying springtime dessert.

3 tablespoons butter
2 leeks
1 onion, coarsely chopped
1 clove garlic, chopped
6 cups good-quality canned or homemade (see page 2) chicken stock
1 pound (2 or 3 large) all-purpose potatoes
3 cups green peas (freshly shelled or frozen peas, thawed)

¼ cup chopped fresh mint or 2 teaspoons dried mint
2 cups half-and-half or light cream
8 to 10 ounces smoked ham, sliced ¼ inch thick
¼ teaspoon freshly ground black pepper
¼ teaspoon Tabasco
Salt to taste
2 tablespoons chopped mint for garnish

1. Melt the butter in a large saucepan or soup pot. Trim off the tough green leaves of the leeks, leaving only the white and tender pale green parts. Split the leeks from the top almost to the root end and wash well under running water to remove all dirt and grit. Thinly slice the leeks crosswise and add to the pot along with the chopped onion and garlic. Cook the vegetables over medium heat in the butter until they begin to soften, about 5 minutes.

2. Add the chicken stock to the pot. While it is heating, peel and thinly slice the potatoes. Add the potatoes to the soup, bring it to a boil, lower the heat, and simmer, uncovered, for 10 minutes. Add the peas and simmer for 8 minutes more, or until the potatoes and peas are tender. Stir in the mint.

3. Purée the soup (in several batches if necessary) in a food processor or blender and return it to its original pot. Add the half-and-half.

4. Slice the ham into matchstick pieces about ¼ inch wide and ¾ inch long and add them to the soup. Bring to a simmer and cook for 5 minutes. Season with freshly ground black pepper and Tabasco and add salt to taste. (The soup may not need salt since canned chicken broth and smoked ham can be quite salty.)

5. Serve while hot in large soup bowls. Sprinkle a little chopped mint over the top of each serving.

YIELD: 6 SERVINGS.

NOTE: This vichyssoise can be stored in the refrigerator for 3 days or frozen.

Cream of Bacon, Lettuce, and Tomato Soup

Our friend Sue loves BLTs so much that she thinks the concept should be expanded beyond a mere sandwich. Throwing her hands up in frustration, she cried, "Why not a salad, why not a soup? You food people have no imagination. Invent one." We accepted the challenge and set out to capture the classic ingredients in a new form and are more than pleased with the tasty result. So for you, Sue, here is our BLT soup. Make it whenever you have a surplus of really ripe, meaty tomatoes.

Adding cooked chicken or turkey pieces with the lettuce will turn this into a club sandwich soup. End this nostalgic, yet light meal with Red, White, and Blueberry Short-cakes (see page 232) or Black Devil Cupcakes with Double Fudge Frosting (see page 240).

4½ pounds (about 12 large) ripe, meaty
   tomatoes such as beefsteak
12 slices bacon
1 large onion, coarsely chopped
1 large rib celery with leaves, coarsely chopped
1 large carrot, coarsely chopped
1 clove garlic, minced
½ cup dry unseasoned bread crumbs
6 cups good-quality canned or homemade (see
   page 2) chicken stock
1 large bay leaf, broken
6 sprigs parsley
1 tablespoon brown sugar
¼ teaspoon red pepper flakes

2 cups light cream
About ½ head romaine lettuce,
   thinly sliced (3 cups)
3 tablespoons minced fresh basil or
   1 tablespoon dried basil
1 teaspoon Worcestershire sauce
Salt and freshly ground black pepper
   to taste

TOAST:

12 pieces French bread, sliced ¼ inch thick
3 to 4 tablespoons mayonnaise
1 teaspoon coarsely ground black pepper

1. Core the tomatoes. Peel, seed, and dice one large tomato and reserve for the garnish. Coarsely chop the remaining tomatoes.

2. In a heavy 5-quart saucepan, fry the bacon until crisp. Remove with a slotted spoon, drain on paper towels, crumble, and reserve. Pour off all but 4 tablespoons of the drippings.

3. Add the onion, celery, and carrot to the

drippings and sauté over medium-low heat until softened, about 5 minutes. Add the garlic and sauté 1 minute. Add the bread crumbs, chicken stock, bay leaf, parsley, brown sugar, red pepper flakes, and tomatoes.

4. Simmer, uncovered, over low heat, stirring often for 30 minutes. Remove and discard the bay leaf. Purée the soup in batches in a food processor and then strain the mixture back into the saucepan. Push on the solids in the strainer with the back of a spoon to extract as much liquid as possible.

The soup may be made several days ahead up to this point and refrigerated or frozen up to 2 months.

5. Stir in the cream and bring to a simmer. Stir in the lettuce, basil, Worcestershire sauce, and reserved diced tomato. Simmer gently for 2 minutes. Season to taste with salt and pepper and keep warm while making the toast.

6. Preheat the broiler. To make the toast, brush one side of the bread lightly with mayonnaise and sprinkle with pepper. Broil about 4 inches from the heat until toasted (about 1 minute). Turn the bread, brush with more mayonnaise, sprinkle with more pepper, and broil until toasted.

7. To serve, stir the reserved bacon back into the soup, ladle into soup bowls and float 1 piece of toast in each bowl. Pass the remaining toast.

YIELD: 6 SERVINGS.

MAIN-COURSE SALADS

"*First he ate some lettuces and some French beans; and then he ate some radishes; and then, feeling rather sick, he went to look for some parsley. But round the end of a cucumber frame, whom should he meet but Mr. McGregor!*"

—*BEATRIX POTTER*

The Tales of Peter Rabbit (1900)

"*Ho! 'Tis the time of salads!*"

—*LAURENCE STERNE*

Tristram Shandy (1760–1767)

Greek Chicken and Fusilli Salad

Inspired by the classic Greek country salad, this summery combination is just right for a light supper on a warm evening. Since the main components can be made well in advance and the salad tossed together about an hour ahead of serving, this is a terrific party main course. The recipe can be doubled or even tripled and served from a large lettuce-lined platter for buffet entertaining.

A large basket with an assortment of breads including a peasant loaf, fat breadsticks, and Plain Muffins (see page 219) along with a tub of sweet butter rounds out the meal nicely. Purple Plum Crumble (see page 258) or Maggie Valley Buttermilk Pie (see page 244) (or both if it is a big party) would be a wonderful dessert.

½ cup walnut halves

2 cups water

¾ teaspoon salt

4 tablespoons lemon juice

1 pound boneless and skinless chicken thighs or breasts, or a combination.

½ teaspoon freshly ground black pepper

10 tablespoons olive oil

2 tablespoons walnut oil

1 tablespoon red wine vinegar

2 tablespoons minced fresh dill or 2 teaspoons dried dill

1 clove garlic, minced

8 ounces fusilli (short pasta twists), cooked al dente and drained

4 ounces feta cheese, crumbled into chunks (about 1 cup)

½ English seedless cucumber, unpeeled and sliced ⅛ inch thick (about ⅔ cup)

½ yellow bell pepper, seeded and cut into ½-inch squares (about ½ cup)

1 head (about 12 ounces) red leaf lettuce, washed, dried, and separated into leaves

2 medium tomatoes, peeled, seeded, and each cut into 6 wedges

⅔ cup Calamata olives

Fresh dill sprigs for garnish (optional)

1. Preheat the oven to 350 degrees.

2. Toast the walnuts in the oven for about 10 minutes, stirring occasionally, until lightly browned and fragrant. Reserve.

The nuts can be toasted a day ahead and kept, covered, at room temperature.

3. Bring the water, ½ teaspoon of the salt, and ½ tablespoon of the lemon juice to a simmer in a skillet or saucepan just large enough to hold the chicken comfortably. Add the chicken, cover the pan, and poach at a bare simmer, turning once, until the chicken is cooked through, about 8 to 12 minutes. Let the chicken cool and then cut

it into ¾-inch chunks. (You will have about 2 cups of chicken.) Sprinkle with salt and pepper.

The chicken can be poached a day ahead and refrigerated, covered.

4. To make the dressing, whisk together the olive oil, walnut oil, remaining 3 tablespoons of lemon juice, vinegar, dill, ½ teaspoon pepper, ¼ teaspoon salt, and garlic.

5. Pour ½ of the dressing over the pasta in a large mixing bowl and toss to coat thoroughly. Add the chicken, cheese, cucumber, bell pepper, and toasted nuts. Add the remaining dressing and toss again until all ingredients are coated.

6. To serve, make a bed of lettuce on a large platter or 6 serving plates. Spoon the pasta salad in the center of each plate and garnish with the tomatoes, olives, and dill sprigs.

YIELD: 6 SERVINGS.

NOTE: The salad may be tossed about 2 hours before serving. Refrigerate, but serve at cool room temperature.

Crispy Chicken and Radish Salad

This easy and colorful salad tastes as good as it looks. Boneless chicken breasts, dusted with aromatic spices and sesame seeds, are quickly sautéed to a golden crispness and then a heady vinaigrette is made from the pan drippings. When the chicken is set atop a bed of sliced romaine and shredded radishes and garnished with buttery avocado slices, the plate is a rainbow of bright hues. A squeeze of lime finishes this happy, light main course.

Accompany this salad with a napkin-lined wicker basket filled with The Absolute Best Buttermilk Biscuits (see page 220), Plain Muffins (see page 219), or Peppery Corn Bread (see page 228).

The light and whimsical salad main course is especially well complemented by a dessert splurge such as Cranberry Bread Pudding with Whiskey Sauce (see page 252) in winter or Red, White, and Blueberry Shortcakes (see page 232) in summer.

Crispy Chicken and Radish Salad (cont.)

10 large radishes
1 medium head (about 12 ounces) romaine
  lettuce
2 tablespoons sesame seeds
1½ teaspoons ground cumin
1½ teaspoons ground coriander
½ teaspoon salt
¼ teaspoon freshly ground black pepper
⅛ teaspoon cayenne pepper
1 to 1¼ pounds boneless, skinless chicken
  breasts, split
2 tablespoons peanut oil

DRESSING:

1 large clove garlic, minced
2 teaspoons grated fresh gingerroot
4 tablespoons rice wine vinegar
1 tablespoon soy sauce
2 tablespoons sesame oil

Salt and freshly ground black pepper to taste
⅓ cup thin, diagonally sliced scallions,
  including green tops
1 large ripe avocado, peeled and cut into
  8 slices
1 lime, cut into 8 wedges

1. Trim the radishes and shred them in a food processor. Core the lettuce and thinly slice the leaves crosswise.

The vegetables can be prepared a few hours ahead and refrigerated in plastic bags.

2. Combine the sesame seeds, cumin, coriander, salt, black pepper, and cayenne pepper in a small bowl. Sprinkle both sides of each piece of chicken with the spice mixture, rubbing it in with your fingers.

3. Heat the peanut oil in a large skillet and sauté the chicken over medium heat until crisp and browned on both sides and cooked through, about 7 to 10 minutes total cooking time. Remove the chicken from the pan and cut it crosswise into ¾-inch slices.

4. To make the dressing, add the 4 tablespoons peanut oil to the pan and heat. Add the garlic and gingerroot and sauté over medium-low heat for about 30 seconds. Pour in the vinegar and soy sauce and simmer, stirring, about 1 minute. Stir in the sesame oil.

5. To assemble the salad, make a bed of lettuce on a large serving platter or on each of the four plates. Scatter the radishes over the lettuce and sprinkle with salt and pepper to taste. Arrange the chicken over the radishes. Drizzle the dressing over the chicken and vegetables. Scatter the scallions over the chicken and garnish with avocado slices and lime wedges. Serve immediately.

YIELD: 4 SERVINGS.

Bacon and Deviled Egg–Stuffed Pasta Salad

Mustard-laced egg salad is one of our favorite sandwich fillings, and one day on a whim we decided to try it as a filling for giant pasta shells. The soothing egg salad, sprinkled with crumbled bacon and set on a frilly lettuce-lined plate garnished with ripe tomato, crunchy carrots, gherkins, and black olives turned out to be a terrific way to set out a warm-weather supper. Squares of Peppery Corn Bread (see page 228) or breadsticks and sweet butter would be nice go-alongs, and Georgia Peach-Pecan Skillet Cake (see page 234) or Double Lemon Loaf (see page 236) and a sauce of sweetened puréed raspberries would be an excellent ending.

12 ounces jumbo pasta shells
8 large eggs
½ cup mayonnaise
2 tablespoons sour cream
4 tablespoons coarse-grained mustard
½ teaspoon salt
¼ teaspoon freshly ground black pepper
2 tablespoons snipped fresh chives
1 tablespoon minced parsley

**1 large head (about 1 pound) frilly green-
    leaf lettuce**
6 slices bacon, cooked, drained, and crumbled
**2 ripe tomatoes, peeled, seeded, and cut in
    wedges**
**3 carrots, peeled and cut into about
    ¼-by-2-inch sticks**
12 small gherkins
12 good-quality black olives

1. Cook the pasta shells until al dente in a large amount of boiling, salted water. Drain well, rinse under cold water, drain again, and cool completely in a single layer. Choose 36 unbroken shells; use immediately or chill them, covered, for about 2 hours or up to 24 hours.

2. To hard-boil the eggs, place them in a saucepan and cover with cold water. Cover the pan and bring to a boil. Immediately remove the covered pan from the heat and let stand for 20 to 30 minutes. Drain and rinse the eggs under cold water.

The eggs may be cooked a day ahead and refrigerated.

3. Peel and finely chop the eggs. In a mix-ing bowl, combine the mayonnaise, sour cream, mustard, salt, pepper, chives, and parsley. Add the chopped eggs and stir gently until well combined.

4. Stuff each pasta shell with about 1 table-spoon egg salad.

The shells may be stuffed 2 hours ahead of serving and chilled, covered, in a single layer on a baking sheet.

5. When ready to serve, arrange the pasta shells on a large platter or 6 individual plates lined with the lettuce. Sprinkle the shells with the bacon. Garnish the platter or plates with the tomatoes, carrots, gher-kins, and olives.

YIELD: 6 SERVINGS.

Couscous and Beef Salad with Horseradish-Herb Dressing

Couscous is a tiny form of dried semolina pasta from Morocco. Now packaged in a slightly precooked form, all it needs is a quick five-minute soak in hot water to soften it. Couscous is becoming even more widely distributed, but if you can't find it in your store, substitute pastina or other tiny pasta, cooked according to package directions.

This lovely warm-weather salad would be wonderful with Plain Muffins (see page 219) or toasted pita breads, and a piece of store-bought baklava or Baked Amaretti Nectarines (see page 261) for dessert.

1½ cups packaged couscous
2¼ cups boiling water
1 teaspoon salt
1 large green or yellow bell pepper, chopped
    (1½ cups)
½ cup chopped red onion

HORSERADISH-HERB DRESSING:

¼ cup packed parsley sprigs
¼ cup packed mint sprigs or 2 teaspoons
    dried mint
1 clove garlic, peeled

2 tablespoons lemon juice
1 tablespoon red wine vinegar
1½ tablespoons grated fresh or drained
    prepared horseradish
1 teaspoon Dijon mustard
½ cup olive oil
½ teaspoon salt
¼ teaspoon freshly ground black pepper

18 leaves romaine lettuce
12 ounces cooked rare roast beef,
    cut in 1-inch strips
2 ripe tomatoes, seeded and cut in wedges

1. Place the couscous grains in a large bowl. Pour the boiling water over the couscous, sprinkle on the salt, and stir once with a fork. Cover with a sheet of foil and let stand for 5 minutes. Uncover, stir again to fluff the grains, and set aside for 5 minutes before adding the other ingredients.
2. Add the pepper and onion and stir gently to combine.

3. To make the dressing, place the parsley, mint, garlic, lemon juice, vinegar, horseradish, and mustard in the workbowl of a food processor or blender. Pulse several times to make a purée. With the motor running, slowly pour the oil through the feed tube. Season with the salt and pepper.
4. Pour all but 2 tablespoons of the dressing over the couscous and toss well. Taste

and correct the seasoning if necessary.

5. Arrange the romaine leaves on a large platter with tips pointing outward and heap the salad onto the lettuce.

6. Scatter the roast beef over the couscous, and arrange the tomato wedges over the salad. Serve at room temperature or refrigerate for up to 2 hours. Spoon the remaining 2 tablespoons of dressing over the beef and tomatoes before serving.

YIELD: 6 SERVINGS.

NOTE: The salad may be eaten with a fork or in the traditional Moroccan manner by wrapping the couscous in the romaine leaves and eating it in your hand.

Tuscan Bread Salad

It is hard to get a bad meal in food-loving Italy, as Melanie and her family found out when they traveled the countryside one lovely April. In the hills of Tuscany, a house specialty in many of the trattorias was bread salad, a dish conceived as a thrifty way to use up yesterday's unsalted, crusty peasant bread. The bread was mixed with seasonal, sunny vegetables, which always included luscious ripe tomatoes, and doused in a vinaigrette made of sublime olive oil and vinegar so fresh that it smelled like good wine. Fresh basil leaves were usually added. The salad was served as a first course, along with other assorted antipasti.

This is a re-creation of both the delicious dish and the delectable memory. Instead of an antipasto, we serve this as a light main course garnished with Italian cold meats and cheeses (we have suggested some of our favorites, but you may improvise, as Italians always do). Baked Amaretti Nectarines (see page 261) or Giant Anise Sugar Cookies (see page 267) and sliced peaches would be a perfect dessert choice.

Tuscan Bread Salad (cont.)

10 tablespoons excellent-quality extra-virgin
   olive oil
5 tablespoons red wine or balsamic vinegar
½ teaspoon salt
⅛ teaspoon freshly ground black pepper
About 10 ounces (2 medium) ripe tomatoes,
   peeled, seeded, and diced (about 1 cup)
About ½ seedless cucumber, unpeeled and
   sliced thin (1 cup)
About 1 small yellow bell pepper, diced
   (½ cup)
About 1 to 2 ounces thinly sliced mushrooms
   (½ cup)
1½ tablespoons drained capers
2 tablespoons minced fresh basil leaves or
   2 teaspoons dried basil
About 10 ounces (¾ of a loaf) day-old, good-
   quality Italian or French bread

About 1 small head (1½ cups) romaine lettuce,
   sliced thin
Salt and freshly ground black pepper to taste

GARNISH (use as many as you wish):

Radicchio and/or romaine lettuce leaves to
   make a bed for the salad
12 thin slices prosciutto
12 thin slices mortadella
6 ounces smoked or fresh mozzarella cheese,
   sliced thin
6 ounces Gorgonzola cheese
⅓ cup thinly sliced roasted red peppers or
   pimientos
12 oil-cured olives
12 brine-cured olives
3 hard-boiled eggs, quartered

1. In a large bowl, whisk together the oil, vinegar, salt, and pepper. Add the tomatoes, cucumber, onion, bell pepper, mushrooms, capers, and basil; toss to combine. Let stand about 20 minutes.

2. Tear the bread into approximately ½- to ¾-inch cubes and add to the vegetables; toss to combine. Cover and let stand 30 minutes to 1 hour, to allow the bread to soak up the juices. Add the radicchio and romaine and toss again.

3. Spoon the salad onto a large serving platter or bowl or individual plates lined with radicchio or romaine leaves. Garnish the salad by decoratively arranging the meats, cheeses, red peppers, olives, and eggs around the bread salad, or place them on a separate platter.

YIELD: 4 TO 6 SERVINGS.

Jambalaya Salad

If you love the taste of jambalaya as much as we do but consider it to be a little too much cooking for the warm-weather months, this recipe is for you. We've taken the basic jambalaya ingredients and turned them into a simple and refreshing rice salad. Served with a basket of The Absolute Best Buttermilk Biscuits (see page 220) and Georgia Peach-Pecan Skillet Cake (see page 234), it makes a very lovely southern supper.

2 cups good-quality canned or homemade
   (see page 2) chicken stock
1 cup raw long-grain rice
1 tablespoon olive oil
1 teaspoon dried thyme
1 bay leaf, broken in half
½ teaspoon salt (omit if using canned stock)
½ pound medium or large shrimp, shelled and
   deveined
6 ounces smoked ham, cut in ½-inch cubes
3 large (about 8 ounces) plum tomatoes, seeded
   and diced (1 cup)
1 medium green pepper, coarsely chopped
   (1 cup)
¾ cup thinly sliced celery

½ cup chopped red onion
About 3½ tablespoons minced parsley

JAMBALAYA DRESSING:

3 tablespoons red wine vinegar
1 teaspoon coarse-grained mustard
⅓ cup olive oil
1 clove garlic, minced
¼ teaspoon dried oregano
½ teaspoon salt
½ teaspoon Tabasco
¼ teaspoon filé powder (optional)
¼ teaspoon freshly ground black pepper
⅛ teaspoon cayenne pepper

1. Bring the chicken stock to a boil in a medium saucepan. Add the rice, olive oil, thyme, bay leaf, and salt (if needed), and stir once. Reduce heat, cover, and cook on the lowest heat for 15 minutes. Place the shelled shrimp on top of the rice, cover again, and cook until the shrimp have turned pink and the rice is just tender, about another 3 to 4 minutes. Transfer the rice and shrimp to a large mixing bowl and cool for 5 minutes. Discard the bay leaf.
2. Add the ham, tomatoes, pepper, celery, red onion, and 3 tablespoons of the parsley to the rice and toss to combine.

3. To make the jambalaya dressing, whisk the vinegar and mustard together in a small bowl. Whisk in the oil and add the garlic, oregano, salt, Tabasco, filé powder, black pepper, and cayenne pepper.
4. Pour the dressing over the salad and toss gently until thoroughly mixed. Taste and season with additional salt if necessary. Serve tepid, or cover and refrigerate for up to 4 hours. To serve, transfer the salad to a pretty glass bowl and garnish with the remaining chopped parsley if desired.

YIELD: 4 to 6 servings.

Hot Ham and Potato Salad

This recipe is a takeoff on hot German-style potato salad. It makes a delicious supper served with buttered rye or pumpernickel bread and some sour pickles or pickled mixed vegetables. Warm applesauce or Baked Ginger–Bay Leaf Apples (see page 262) would be nice to serve for dessert.

2 pounds red-skinned potatoes
8 ounces smoked ham, such as a ham steak or
    Canadian bacon, cut into ½-inch cubes
½ cup thinly sliced celery
½ cup chopped red onion
3 tablespoons cider vinegar
1 tablespoon honey
2 teaspoons coarse-grained mustard
⅓ cup vegetable oil

2 tablespoons mayonnaise
¼ teaspoon freshly ground black pepper or
    more to taste
¼ teaspoon salt or more to taste
¼ teaspoon Tabasco
¼ cup chopped parsley
3 hard-boiled eggs, peeled and halved
3 plum tomatoes, cored and quartered

1. Scrub the potatoes and cut them into 2-inch chunks. Place the potatoes in a saucepan, cover with water, and lightly salt the water. Bring to a boil, lower the heat, and simmer until the potatoes are just tender, about 15 minutes.

2. Meanwhile, cook the ham in a skillet over medium-low heat, stirring now and then, until lightly browned, about 5 minutes. The ham should have enough fat so that it doesn't scorch; if it doesn't, add a couple of teaspoons of oil to the pan. Using a slotted spoon, remove the diced ham to a large bowl. Add the celery and onion to the bowl.

3. Pour vinegar into the warm skillet, stirring to dissolve browned bits in the bottom of the pan. Stir in the honey and mustard. Slowly whisk in the oil and the mayonnaise and season with pepper, salt, and Tabasco.

4. When the potatoes are cooked, drain them, and while still warm, cut into ¼-inch-thick slices. Add them to the mixing bowl, and pour the dressing in the skillet over the potatoes. Toss gently to combine and set aside for 5 minutes so that the dressing can be absorbed. Sprinkle on the chopped parsley and stir it in gently. Season the salad with additional salt and pepper to taste.

5. Present the salad in a shallow bowl or on a platter encircled by the eggs and tomatoes. Sprinkle them with salt and pepper. Serve the salad while still warm.

YIELD: 4 SERVINGS.

NOTE: You may hard-boil the eggs along with the potatoes if you like. Rinse the eggs, place them in the water along with the potatoes, and cook for about 12 minutes. Rinse the eggs under cold water to cool them.

Warm Lentil and Sausage Salad

This salad is an adaptation of one that Richard Sax offered in a *COOK'S* magazine article a couple of years ago. It's absolutely beautiful to look at—and makes a lovely presentation as a room-temperature buffet salad—as well as wonderful to eat. The recipe works well using any kind of lentils, but if you find the small green French lentils, they make this salad even more special.

Serve with squares of Peppery Corn Bread (see page 228) or, for a real treat, Parmesan Polenta (see page 215). Try either Pear Strudel (see page 250) or Cranberry Bread Pudding with Whiskey Sauce (see page 252) for dessert.

2 cups lentils

2 cups good-quality canned or homemade (see page 2) chicken stock

2 cups water

½ teaspoon salt (omit if using canned stock)

1 carrot, peeled, and cut in 3-inch lengths

½ rib of celery

1 red bell pepper

1 yellow bell pepper

1 pound sausage in casing (either smoked sausage such as kielbasa, or hot spicy sausage such as andouille or chorizo), cut in ½-inch lengths

4 tablespoons balsamic vinegar

2 teaspoons lemon juice

½ cup olive oil

¼ teaspoon freshly ground black pepper

½ cup thinly sliced scallions, including green tops

½ cup large black olives such as Calamata

About 24 leaves (4 ounces) arugula, thoroughly washed and dried

Salt to taste

1. Place the lentils in a strainer, rinse them, and inspect them carefully to make sure they are free of any small stones or dirt. Combine in a saucepan with the chicken stock, water, salt, carrot, and celery. Bring to a simmer, lower the heat, cover, and cook over low heat for 25 to 30 minutes, or until just tender. Do not overcook the lentils or they will get mushy. Remove and discard the carrot and celery and drain off any remaining liquid.

2. Meanwhile, roast the peppers. Place the whole peppers directly over a gas flame, turning until they are evenly blackened. (Or cut the peppers in half, place them skin side up on a baking sheet, and broil until the skins are blackened.) Place the roasted peppers in a plastic or paper bag, seal the bag, and set aside for 10 minutes to allow the skins to steam, which makes them easier to peel. Using a small, sharp knife, scrape the charred skin off the peppers,

seed them, and cut them into thin strips.

3. In a large skillet, cook the sausage over low heat until well browned and cooked through, about 10 to 12 minutes. Remove the sausage to a plate, and cover it with foil to keep it warm.

4. To make the dressing, stir the vinegar and lemon juice into the drippings in the pan, and gradually whisk in the oil. Season with the pepper. Pour a spoonful of dressing over the pepper strips. Pour the remaining dressing over the warm lentils, tossing gently to combine, and let the mixture rest for 5 minutes so the dressing can be absorbed.

5. Spoon the lentils onto a large serving platter and arrange the warm sausage over the lentils. Sprinkle with the sliced scallions, pepper strips, and black olives. Arrange the arugula around the edge of the platter. Pass the salt shaker, though the salad may not need it since the sausage and olives can be quite salty.

YIELD: 6 SERVINGS.

Caesar's Chicken Salad

One of America's classics, Caesar salad is generally thought to be the creation of Tijuana restaurateur Caesar Cardini, who invented it one day with ingredients on hand, including the then-considered-exotic romaine lettuce.

Although there is some dispute about the rest of the original ingredients, particularly whether or not anchovies were included, the salad seems to have changed little over the years. It has, however, often become the subject of ritual tableside preparation in some glitzy restaurants. We think that the choice of top ingredients, such as freshly grated cheeses and fine quality olive oil and French bread for the croutons, is far more important than a showy presentation. Thus, our "whole meal" Caesar salad is traditional, uncomplicated, and adorned only with slices of broiled chicken. The warm chicken on the cool greens is a positively delicious addition.

Our favorite accompaniments to this salad are more good French bread and lots of sweet butter. Potato Pan Rolls (see page 224) or Peppery Corn Bread (see page 228) would be a lovely option, too. Choose a splashy dessert such as Miss Hulling's Banana-Coconut Cream Pie (see page 246) or a warm sweet such as Pear Strudel (see page 250).

Caesar's Chicken Salad (cont.)

2 medium heads (about 1½ pounds total)
    romaine lettuce
2 tablespoons butter, softened
½ large clove garlic, minced
4 slices French bread, cut ½-inch thick
1½ to 1¾ pounds boneless chicken breasts,
    with skin left intact (about 2 to 2½ pounds
    in weight before boning)
1 tablespoon olive oil
Salt and freshly ground black pepper to taste

DRESSING:

1 egg

2 tablespoons lemon juice
2 tablespoons balsamic or red wine vinegar
1½ teaspoons Worcestershire sauce
½ teaspoon Dijon mustard
½ teaspoon freshly ground black pepper
½ large clove garlic, minced
8 tablespoons extra-virgin olive oil
1 (2-ounce) can flat anchovies, drained and
    chopped
¼ cup freshly grated Romano cheese
¼ cup freshly grated Parmesan cheese

1. Wash and dry the romaine leaves, discarding any particularly tough outer leaves. Tear the leaves into large pieces.

The lettuce may be prepared early in the day and refrigerated in a plastic bag.

2. Preheat the broiler.

3. Blend the minced garlic into the butter. Spread the butter on both sides of the bread, then cut the bread into ½-inch cubes. Place the bread on a baking sheet in a single layer and broil, about 4 inches from the heat source; turn frequently until the cubes are golden brown and evenly toasted, about 1 to 2 minutes. Reserve.

The croutons can be made early in the day and held at room temperature.

4. Brush all sides of the chicken with a total of about 1 tablespoon olive oil and sprinkle generously with salt and pepper. Broil the chicken, skin side up, about 4 inches from the heat source until the skin is nicely browned, about 4 minutes. Turn over and broil about 4 minutes more until

the chicken is cooked through.

5. To prepare the dressing, coddle the egg by lowering it into boiling water for exactly 45 seconds and then removing it. Break the egg into a wooden salad bowl and use a spoon to scrape out the thickened white that may cling to the shell. Whisk in the lemon juice, vinegar, Worcestershire sauce, mustard, pepper, and minced garlic. Whisk in olive oil until well blended. Stir in the anchovies. Remove about 3 tablespoons of the dressing and reserve.

6. Place the lettuce in the salad bowl and toss to coat all leaves with dressing. Sprinkle with both cheeses and toss again. Add croutons and toss once more.

7. To assemble the salad, arrange the salad greens on each of 4 to 6 serving plates. Cut the warm chicken into ½-inch-thick crosswise slices and arrange in the center of each plate. Drizzle the chicken with the reserved dressing. Serve immediately.

YIELD: 4 TO 6 SERVINGS.

Southern Fried Chicken Salad

We never met anyone who didn't like fried chicken. But that is where the consensus ends. All over the South (and in parts of the North, too) a discussion about the best ways to fry chicken is sure to raise eyebrows in polite company and cause downright feuds among fried chicken aficionados. Opening ourselves up to a lot of controversy, we put in our bid for chicken coated in a mixture of equal parts of seasoned flour and yellow cornmeal, which gives a crispy, corn pone–tasting crust.

Even more heretical, we fry up boneless bite-size pieces and use them in one of the most delicious salads we have ever eaten.

1 small head (8 ounces) romaine lettuce
1 small head (about 6 ounces) radicchio or
   ½ small head (about 6 ounces) red cabbage
1 pound boneless, skinless chicken pieces
   (breasts, thighs, or a combination)
⅓ cup all-purpose flour
⅓ cup yellow cornmeal
½ teaspoon salt
¼ teaspoon freshly ground black pepper

½ cup buttermilk
⅔ cup cooking oil, such as safflower oil

Dressing:

1 tablespoon minced shallots
2 teaspoons Dijon mustard
2 tablespoons balsamic vinegar or red wine
   vinegar
Salt and freshly ground black pepper to taste

1. Wash, dry, and tear the lettuce and radicchio into bite-size pieces. (If using red cabbage, slice thinly.) Place in a large salad or mixing bowl.
2. Cut the chicken into approximately 1½-inch chunks.
3. In a shallow dish, combine the flour, cornmeal, salt, and pepper. Pour the buttermilk into another shallow dish. Begin heating the oil in a large skillet.
4. Dip the chicken first into the buttermilk and then into the flour mixture, coating lightly and shaking off any excess. Without crowding the pan, cook the chicken in the oil over medium heat for 5 to 7 minutes, turning often, until it is crisp, golden brown, and cooked through. Remove the chicken with a slotted spoon and drain on paper towels. (If your skillet is not large enough to cook all the chicken without crowding, cook in two or three batches.)
5. To make the dressing, add the shallots to the drippings in the skillet and sauté about 1 minute. Add the mustard and vinegar and stir or scrape up the browned bits clinging to the bottom of the pan. Remove the pan from the heat, and add salt and pepper to taste.
6. Toss the warm dressing with the lettuce and radicchio or cabbage. Divide the mixture among 4 serving plates and arrange the chicken on top. Serve immediately.

YIELD: 4 servings.

Barbecued Spring Lamb Salad

Serve this on a warm spring or summer night with Peppery Corn Bread (see page 228) made into corn sticks if you have the pans. Angel Food Cake with Summer Fruit Ambrosia (see page 238) or Green Tomato Cobbler (see page 260) would be a stunning finish.

MARINADE/DRESSING:

¼ cup red wine vinegar

1 teaspoon whole-grain mustard

¼ cup extra-virgin olive oil

¾ cup vegetable oil

2 tablespoons chopped fresh mint or
    2 teaspoons dried mint

2 teaspoons chopped fresh thyme or
    ¾ teaspoon dried thyme

1 teaspoon salt

¼ teaspoon freshly ground black pepper

1½ pounds lean lamb (leg or shoulder),
    trimmed and cut into 1½-inch cubes

12 firm cherry tomatoes

1 large yellow bell pepper, cut into 18 1-inch
    cubes

4 cups chilled salad greens, torn into bite-size
    pieces (use a combination of Boston or Bibb
    lettuce and chicory or arugula)

4 ounces soft, fresh goat cheese such as
    Montrachet, crumbled or cut in ½-inch
    cubes (about 1 cup)

½ cup thinly sliced red onion

2 tablespoons chopped fresh mint or 1 teaspoon
    dried mint

Mint sprigs for garnish

1. To make the marinade/dressing, whisk together the vinegar and mustard in a small bowl. Gradually whisk in the oils and season with the mint, thyme, salt, and pepper. Set aside.

2. In another bowl, toss the lamb cubes with ½ cup of the marinade/dressing. Set aside to marinate at room temperature for 1 hour or in the refrigerator for 3 to 4 hours.

3. Build a barbecue fire, preheat a gas grill, or preheat the oven broiler. On each of 6 12- or 14-inch metal or bamboo skewers (see note) thread 2 cherry tomatoes, then alternate the lamb and pepper cubes. Brush the vegetables and meat with some of the marinade/dressing and cook over a moderately hot grill or under the oven broiler for about 3 minutes on each side, or until the lamb is charred on the outside and still rosy on the inside.

4. Spread the greens on a large platter. Place the skewers of lamb atop the greens and sprinkle the crumbled goat cheese over the hot meat so that the cheese melts slightly. Scatter the red onion slices over the top and sprinkle on the chopped mint.

5. Remove the skewers from the meat, spoon about ¼ cup of dressing over the salad, garnish with mint sprigs, and serve. Pass any remaining dressing at the table.

YIELD: 6 SERVINGS.

NOTE: If you use bamboo skewers, soak them in cold water for 30 minutes before using them so they will be less likely to burn.

Succotash Supper Salad

Tossed with a tangy sour cream dressing, the salad is lovely served in lettuce cups and, because it can be made entirely in advance, is a marvelous buffet salad as well. Serve it with warm Plain Muffins (see page 219) or Potato Pan Rolls (see page 224) and thickly sliced beefsteak tomatoes sprinkled with crumbled blue cheese. End this updated old-fashioned meal with Georgia Peach-Pecan Skillet Cake (see page 234) or Candied Ginger-bread with Vanilla Cream (see page 256).

2 cups fresh baby lima beans or 1 10-ounce package frozen baby lima beans
About 6 ounces fresh green beans, diagonally sliced in 1-inch pieces
2 cups corn kernels, cut fresh from the cob or 1 10-ounce package frozen corn kernels
About 6 ounces smoked ham, diced (1½ cups)
About 4 ounces Swiss cheese, julienned (1 cup)
½ cup thinly sliced celery
½ cup diced red bell pepper

DRESSING:

1 cup sour cream
¼ cup thinly sliced scallions, including most of the green part

5 teaspoons white wine vinegar
2 teaspoons lemon juice
1½ teaspoons honey
1½ teaspoons Dijon mustard
⅛ teaspoon paprika
½ teaspoon salt
¼ teaspoon freshly ground black pepper
Large leaves from green-leaf lettuce or romaine to make lettuce "cups" or bed
¼ cup thinly sliced scallions, including most of the green part
1 or 2 ripe tomatoes, peeled, seeded, and cut into 8 to 12 wedges

1. To make the salad, cook the fresh lima beans in a large pot of boiling, salted water for 15 to 20 minutes; cook frozen lima beans for about 8 minutes. When the lima beans have about 5 minutes of cooking time remaining, add the green beans to the boiling water. Cook 3 minutes, then add the corn. Cook 2 minutes, then turn the vegetables into a strainer and rinse under cold water to stop the cooking and set the color. Drain well and place the vegetables in a large mixing bowl. Add the ham,

cheese, celery, and bell pepper. Toss to combine. Cover and chill 1 to 4 hours.

2. To make the dressing, whisk together the sour cream, scallions, vinegar, lemon juice, honey, mustard, paprika, salt, and pepper. Pour dressing over the salad in the bowl and toss gently but thoroughly to combine.

3. Spoon the salad into lettuce cups; garnish each serving with a sprinkling of the scallions and some tomato wedges. Serve immediately.

YIELD: 4 TO 6 SERVINGS.

NOTE: The salad may be chilled, covered, up to 3 hours before being garnished and served. If you plan to prepare salad and dressing ahead of time and chill it, don't add scallions until right before serving time.

Grilled Tuna Salad Niçoise

The classic *salade Niçoise* from the south of France is one of the sunniest, freshest, and most beautiful supper salads that we have ever tasted. In this, our version, we have used marinated and grilled fresh tuna steaks along with the traditional vegetables. Fresh herbs are absolutely sublime in this summery salad, but good dried herbs are fine, too, if, before using, you rub them a bit between your fingertips to help release their fragrant oils. Do not be put off by the lengthy ingredient list here since virtually all the preparation can be done in advance and the salad merely assembled at serving time.

This main-course salad really needs nothing more than a loaf of crusty French bread and some butter, but a basket of Great Garlic Bread (see page 225) would be terrific. We would especially recommend Maggie Valley Buttermilk Pie (see page 244) or Double Lemon Loaf (see page 236) with a bowl of fresh fruit for dessert.

Grilled Tuna Salad Niçoise (cont.)

VINAIGRETTE:

3 tablespoons red wine vinegar
8 tablespoons extra-virgin olive oil
4 tablespoons safflower oil
1½ teaspoons minced fresh thyme or
  ½ teaspoon dried thyme
1½ teaspoons minced fresh rosemary or
  ½ teaspoon dried rosemary
¾ teaspoon minced fresh savory or ¼ teaspoon
  dried savory
½ teaspoon salt
¼ teaspoon red pepper flakes
⅛ teaspoon freshly ground black pepper

3 tablespoons red wine vinegar
3 tablespoons olive oil
1 clove garlic, minced
1 pound fresh tuna steaks, cut about
  ¾ inch thick
1 pound small red-skinned new potatoes
½ pound slim fresh green beans, trimmed
1 medium head romaine lettuce, separated
  into leaves
12 small cherry tomatoes
½ cup Niçoise olives
½ cup thinly sliced red onion
1 2-ounce can anchovy fillets
3 hard-boiled eggs, quartered
3 tablespoons minced parsley
1½ tablespoons drained capers

1. To make the vinaigrette, whisk together the vinegar, both oils, thyme, rosemary, savory, salt, red pepper flakes, and black pepper. Let stand about 1 hour before using.

2. To prepare the tuna, combine the vinegar, oil, and garlic in a shallow dish just large enough to hold the fish. Add the tuna, and turn to coat both sides. Cover and marinate 30 minutes at room temperature or 1 hour in the refrigerator.

3. Grill the tuna over medium–hot coals or in an indoor broiler for about 3 minutes on each side until the centers are barely pink. Cool the tuna, then break it into chunks with a fork.

The tuna can be prepared early in the day and refrigerated.

4. Cook the potatoes in a large pot of boiling, salted water until just fork tender,

about 8 to 10 minutes. Remove the potatoes with a slotted spoon and toss with 3 tablespoons of the vinaigrette. Let cool.

5. Add the beans to the boiling water. Cook for 2 minutes, or until crisp-tender. Drain and rinse under cold water to stop their cooking and set the color.

The potatoes and beans can be prepared early in the day and refrigerated.

6. To assemble the salad, line a large platter or 6 serving plates with the lettuce leaves. Decoratively arrange the tuna, potatoes, beans, tomatoes, and olives in individual sections. Sprinkle the tuna with the onion and drape the anchovies over the beans. Dip the egg quarters in the parsley and arrange on the salad.

7. Whisk the capers into the remaining vinaigrette and drizzle over the salads.

YIELD: 4 TO 6 SERVINGS.

Tortellini and Shrimp Pesto Salad

Many people probably have a favorite recipe for traditional pesto. This one is nonstandard in that it calls for dry-roasted peanuts to replace the more usual pine nuts and Parmesan cheese. We happen to like it on all kinds of pastas but think it goes particularly well on this cheese tortellini and shrimp salad.

This salad is great for a buffet and could be multiplied easily to serve a crowd. If you do make a large quantity, try to use both spinach and egg tortellini for a nice touch of extra color.

For a smaller group, serve this with thickly sliced ripe tomatoes and some Italian bread. Lemon-Blueberry Mousse (see page 259) or Wine-Washed Strawberries (see page 257) and cookies would round out the meal beautifully.

1 cup packed parsley sprigs
½ cup packed fresh basil
1 clove garlic, peeled
¼ cup dry-roasted peanuts
3 tablespoons red wine vinegar
¾ cup olive oil
1 teaspoon Dijon mustard

About 2½ teaspoons salt
¼ teaspoon freshly ground black pepper
½ pound medium shrimp, shelled, and
**   deveined if necessary**
1 pound good quality frozen cheese tortellini
Basil leaves for garnish

1. To make the pesto, combine the parsley, basil, garlic, peanuts, and vinegar in the workbowl of a food processor or blender. Pulse until a coarse paste is formed. With the motor running, slowly pour the oil through the feed tube. Scrape down the sides of the bowl, season with the mustard, ½ teaspoon of the salt or more to taste, and the pepper, and pulse again to combine.

The pesto can be made up to one day ahead.

2. Bring a large pot of water to a boil. Add about 1 teaspoon of the remaining salt and the shrimp, and cook for 2 minutes. Remove the shrimp with a slotted spoon, refresh under cold running water to stop their cooking, and drain. Add 1 more teaspoon of the salt to the water and return it to a boil. Cook the tortellini in the rapidly boiling water until al dente, about 5 minutes. Drain in a colander and refresh under cold water to stop the cooking.

3. Transfer the pasta and shrimp to a large bowl. Pour the pesto sauce over the pasta and shrimp and toss gently to coat. Serve at room temperature or cold; garnish with basil leaves if desired.

YIELD: 4 TO 6 SERVINGS.

Spicy Sesame Noodle Salad

Brooke was all grown up before she had her first taste of cold sesame noodles, and that experience was so memorable she can remember precisely where and when it happened. What is it about this dish that people find so addictive? There's something about the combination of fiery-hot seasoning and cold noodles and the garlicky-smoky taste of the sesame dressing that does seem to grab people!

Here is our favorite version. Since the salad has both vegetables and meat in it, it really needs very little in the way of accompaniments, though a plate of ripe sliced tomatoes and some Sky-High Popovers (see page 222) would be a lovely addition to the meal. Serve fruit and ice cream for dessert.

8 ounces smoked ham, such as a ham steak or
    Canadian bacon
8 ounces boneless chicken breast
6 tablespoons peanut oil
1 clove garlic, minced
4 tablespoons red wine vinegar
3 tablespoons soy sauce
3 teaspoons granulated sugar
½ teaspoon red pepper flakes
¼ teaspoon freshly ground black pepper

3 tablespoons sesame oil
1 pound fresh oriental noodles or 10 ounces
    dried pasta such as vermicelli (see note)
3 carrots, peeled and sliced very thin
4 ounces snow peas (about 30), strings
    removed, left whole if small, sliced in half
    diagonally if large
1 cup sliced scallions, including green tops
Salt and freshly ground black pepper to taste
2 tablespoons sesame seeds

1. Slice the ham and chicken into strips about ¼ inch thick and 1½ inches long. (The chicken is easier to slice if it is partially frozen.) Heat 2 tablespoons of the peanut oil in a large nonreactive skillet. Cook the ham and chicken over medium-high heat until nicely browned and the chicken is cooked through, about 3 min-

utes. Remove with a slotted spoon to a large bowl. Remove the skillet from the heat, add the garlic, and cook in the residual heat for 30 seconds. Stir in the vinegar, soy sauce, sugar, red pepper flakes, and black pepper, scraping up any browned bits from the bottom of the skillet. If the sugar does not dissolve, return the pan to low heat and stir for a minute. Add the remaining 4 tablespoons of peanut oil and the sesame oil and set aside.

2. Meanwhile, bring a large pot of water to a boil. Cut or break the noodles so that the strands will be no more than 4 inches long. (Otherwise the salad tends to clump together and is hard to serve and eat.) Salt the water and cook the noodles at a rapid boil until al dente—about 2 minutes for fresh noodles, about 7 minutes for dried pasta. Add the carrots and snow peas during the last 30 seconds of cooking time.

Drain in a colander. Run cold water over the noodles and vegetables to stop their cooking and transfer to the bowl with the chicken and ham.

3. Pour the dressing over the noodles, tossing with two forks to combine. Sprinkle on the scallions and toss again. Add salt and black pepper to taste. Cover and refrigerate for at least 30 minutes or for as long as 8 hours.

4. Place the sesame seeds in a heavy skillet and cook, stirring over medium heat for about 3 minutes, until fragrant and lightly toasted.

5. Toss the salad again before serving since the dressing and heavier ingredients tend to fall to the bottom of the bowl. Present the salad in a large shallow bowl or on a rimmed serving platter, sprinkle with the toasted sesame seeds, and serve.

YIELD: 6 SERVINGS.

NOTE: If your supermarket carries fresh oriental noodles in the refrigerator case, use them. If not, use 1 pound fresh, thin-strand pasta, 1 10-ounce package of dried oriental noodles (any kind except the translucent rice noodles), or 10 ounces of Italian pasta such as vermicelli.

SANDWICHES

"Think I'll just mosey on down and get a little something to eat."

—DAGWOOD

"Too few people understand a really good sandwich."

—JAMES BEARD

"Little Tommy Tucker
Sings for his supper
What shall we give him?
White bread and butter."

—ANONYMOUS

Contemporary Kentucky Hot Brown

Kentucky "Hot Brown" is named after the Brown Hotel in Louisville, where that open-faced hot sandwich of sliced turkey on white toast covered in a mild cheese sauce and topped with a couple of bacon slices was created. We like whole wheat toast for its nuttiness, cheddar cheese for its zip, and a dash of sherry for its depth of flavor. Stir a few sautéed mushrooms into the sauce for another delicious departure.

A large green salad with slices of red pepper and chopped scallions goes well with this sandwich. Finish with Georgia Peach-Pecan Skillet Cake (see page 234) or Purple Plum Crumble (see page 258).

8 slices bacon
2 tablespoons minced shallots
2 tablespoons all-purpose flour
1 cup plus 2 tablespoons milk
1 teaspoon Worcestershire sauce
⅛ teaspoon cayenne pepper
4 ounces sharp cheddar cheese, grated
  (about 1 cup)

1 tablespoon sherry
4 slices whole wheat bread, toasted
Butter for toast
12 ounces cooked white meat of turkey or
  chicken, cut in slices about ¼ inch thick
2 tablespoons grated Parmesan cheese

1. Preheat the broiler.
2. Fry the bacon in a medium skillet until crisp. Drain the bacon on paper towels. Discard all but 2 tablespoons of the bacon drippings.
3. Add the shallot to the bacon drippings in the skillet and sauté over medium heat for about 1 minute. Stir in the flour and cook, stirring constantly, over medium-low heat for about 3 minutes. Slowly whisk in the milk and cook, stirring over medium-low heat until thickened, smooth, and bubbly, about 2 minutes. Add the Worcestershire sauce and cayenne pepper. Take the pan off the heat and stir in the grated cheese until melted and smooth. Stir in the sherry.

The sauce may be held for up to 2 hours before serving with a sheet of plastic wrap placed directly on the surface to prevent a skin from forming.
4. Lightly spread one side of each piece of toast with butter. Place the toast, buttered side up, in four individual gratin dishes or a single shallow baking dish just large enough to hold them. Lay the turkey in equal portions atop the toast and then spoon the cheese sauce over the turkey. Lay two bacon strips atop each sandwich and then sprinkle evenly with the Parmesan cheese.
5. Heat the sandwiches under the broiler for 30 to 45 seconds until bubbly and flecked with brown. Serve while hot.

YIELD: 4 SERVINGS.

Chicken Cutlet and Wilted Arugula Sandwich

One of the better food-marketing ideas of recent years is the increased availability of boned and skinned chicken breasts and thighs. The breasts are also sold thinly sliced as cutlets, fillets, or paillards and are extremely versatile and quick to prepare. In fact, overcooking is the only caveat for these chicken cutlets. Since they are so lean and thin, they quickly toughen and dry out if sautéed longer than a minute or two.

This recipe is perfect for people who have to put together a supper on very short notice since all of the preparation takes less than 30 minutes. Add a salad of sliced tomatoes if you are in a real hurry or a bowl of Cream of Bacon, Lettuce, and Tomato Soup (see page 24) if you are not pressed for time. Finish the meal with a quick dessert like Baked Amaretti Nectarines (see page 261) or an equally fast bowl of ice cream with sliced, sweetened peaches or berries.

1 pound boneless chicken breast cutlets
1 teaspoon dried tarragon
Salt and pepper to taste
2 tablespoons olive oil
1 tablespoon butter
1 tablespoon minced shallots

3 tablespoons balsamic vinegar
1 large bunch arugula, cleaned and tough stems
 discarded
½ cup mayonnaise
4 long French rolls, split

1. Sprinkle the chicken on both sides with the tarragon and generous amounts of salt and pepper. Heat 1 tablespoon of the olive oil and the butter in a large skillet and sauté the chicken breasts over medium-high heat, in batches if necessary, until lightly golden and just cooked through, about 1 to 2 minutes on each side. Remove to a warm platter. Do not wash the skillet.
2. Add the remaining 1 tablespoon oil to the skillet and sauté the shallots for about 1 minute. Add the vinegar and cook about 30 seconds, scraping up the browned bits that cling to the bottom of the skillet. Add the arugula and toss until the leaves are coated, about 5 seconds. Remove the arugula with tongs or a slotted spoon.
3. Over very low heat, stir the mayonnaise into the drippings in the skillet until just blended.
4. Assemble the sandwiches by spreading a generous layer of mayonnaise over the cut sides of the rolls. Place the chicken and then the arugula on the roll bottoms, and cover with the roll tops. Cut each sandwich in half on the diagonal. Serve immediately.

YIELD: 4 SERVINGS.

Fried Fish Po'boy

"Po'boy" is New Orleans jargon for what is known variously as a grinder, hoagie, sub, or hero, depending upon its region or origin. It is often filled with the usual meats, cheeses, and trimmings. In a flight of fancy one day, we decided to build a po'boy from some of the things we love best about Cajun food. First there is catfish, an ugly specimen with perfectly beautiful little fillets that panfry to a terrific crunch when coated with highly seasoned cornmeal. We piled it on really good French rolls or big diagonal slices of French bread and added some shredded lettuce and a liberal slathering of garlic-and-lemon mayonnaise sauce.

We like the fried fish po'boy so much that in moments of writing frustration, we have toyed with the idea of chucking it all for the vagabond life of hawking these po'boys on a street corner in the French Quarter. But when common sense returns, we just cook up the po'boys, some of Marianne's Macaroni Salad (see page 208) and a few Luscious Pecan Pie Bars (see page 266) and we feel much better.

3 tablespoons all-purpose flour
3 tablespoons yellow cornmeal
½ teaspoon paprika
¼ teaspoon salt
¼ teaspoon dried thyme
¼ teaspoon dried oregano
¼ teaspoon cayenne pepper
⅛ teaspoon freshly ground white pepper
⅛ teaspoon freshly ground black pepper
4 skinned catfish or other firm fish fillets, such
    as perch or snapper, each about 4 ounces

¼ cup milk
4 tablespoons vegetable oil
1 clove garlic, minced
2 teaspoons lemon juice
½ cup mayonnaise
½ teaspoon grated lemon zest
4 French rolls or 1 16-inch baguette, cut
    diagonally into 4 pieces
1½ cups shredded iceberg lettuce

1. In a shallow dish combine the flour, cornmeal, paprika, salt, thyme, oregano, cayenne, white, and black peppers. Dip the fish first into the milk and then into the seasoned flour and cornmeal to coat. Heat the oil in a large skillet and panfry the fish over medium heat until golden brown, crusty, and just cooked through, about 4 to 5 minutes on each side. Remove to a warm platter.

2. Add the garlic to the drippings in the pan and sauté about 30 seconds. Add the

lemon juice and stir to scrape up browned bits clinging to the bottom of the pan. Take the pan off the heat and stir in the mayonnaise and lemon zest until well blended.

3. Split the rolls or bread and pull out and discard a small portion of the doughy insides to make more room for the sandwich filling. Spread the bottoms with a small amount of mayonnaise and top each with a fish fillet and some lettuce. Spread the cut side of each roll top liberally with the remaining mayonnaise, place one on each sandwich, and serve.

YIELD: 4 SERVINGS.

Our Favorite Turkey Sandwich

We unashamedly admit that our favorite part about Thanksgiving is this turkey sandwich made late at night by the light of the open refrigerator door and eaten in solitude after the dishes are washed and the relatives have gone home.

Most everyone likes turkey sandwiches, but Brooke (never one to miss the good stuff) cuts off a piece of cold stuffing and layers it between the cranberry sauce and the lettuce for the most wonderful and flavorful bread-on-bread sandwich you can imagine. To Brooke's mind, the sign of a really good stuffing is that, when cold, it is rich and moist enough to slice. If it crumbles, it wasn't the real thing in the beginning. To get the right texture for the stuffing, be sure to use a healthy amount of butter. (For our stuffing recipe, see The Perfect Roast Chicken [and Stuffing], page 114.) Thanksgiving is no time to skimp. The cranberry sauce should be the chunky, whole-berry kind and not too sweet. You can, of course, use your favorite recipe, but we offer you our standard cranberry sauce. Double the quantity to use as a dinner condiment.

Since you just might want to try this when you don't happen to have a filled refrigerator to raid alone late at night, you can use any cooked white meat of turkey or chicken, an excellent-quality, canned whole-cranberry sauce, and skip the stuffing. Try Pumpkin Custard (see page 255) for dessert unless you have some leftover pie.

Our Favorite Turkey Sandwich (cont.)

WHOLE-BERRY CRANBERRY SAUCE:

1½ cups raw cranberries
6 tablespoons orange juice
6 tablespoons granulated sugar
½ teaspoon grated orange zest
1 teaspoon prepared horseradish
9 tablespoons mayonnaise

12 thin slices good-quality white bread
12 slices cooked white meat of turkey
Salt and freshly ground black pepper to taste
¾ cup whole-berry cranberry sauce (see left) or
    good-quality canned cranberry sauce
¾ cup leftover cooked turkey stuffing
6 leaves romaine lettuce

1. To make the cranberry sauce, combine the cranberries and orange juice in a heavy, nonreactive saucepan. Bring to a boil, stirring. Add the sugar and orange zest. Lower the heat and simmer until the cranberries have popped, and softened, and the mixture is thickened, about 10 minutes. Stir in the horseradish.

2. To assemble the sandwiches, spread the mayonnaise evenly on one side of each of the 12 bread slices. Top 6 of the slices with the turkey and sprinkle with salt and pepper. Spread the turkey with 2 tablespoons cranberry sauce, then 2 tablespoons stuffing. Add the lettuce and then top with the remaining 6 slices of bread, mayonnaise side down.

YIELD: 6 SERVINGS.

Renaissance Philly Cheese Steak

The quintessential Philadelphia cheese steak as served up in luncheonettes all over that city is made with chip steaks, those superthin sandwich steaks, piled onto a roll with browned onions and (usually) processed American cheese.

We call ours a "renaissance" version because we suggest using rare roast beef, some thyme and brandy with the sautéed onions, and a nice, mellow Muenster cheese for melting on top.

Classic Creamy Coleslaw (see page 223) is good on the side, and Classic Rice Pudding (see page 243) studded with raisins would make a marvelous dessert.

6 tablespoons butter

1 large (about 8 ounces) sweet onion, thinly sliced

½ teaspoon dried thyme leaves

Salt and freshly ground black pepper to taste

2 tablespoons brandy

2 teaspoons Dijon mustard

1 teaspoon prepared horseradish

4 Italian "hero" rolls, each 6 or 7 inches long

1 pound rare roast beef, thinly sliced, at room temperature

4 ounces Muenster cheese, thinly sliced, at room temperature

1. Preheat the broiler.

2. Heat 2 tablespoons of the butter in a medium skillet. Add the sliced onion and sauté over low heat, stirring occasionally, for 10 minutes or until the onion is very soft, but not browned. Sprinkle on the thyme, salt, and pepper, turn up the heat to medium, and cook, stirring often, until the onion is just golden, about 3 to 5 minutes. Stir in the brandy and cook about 45 seconds to burn off the alcohol.

3. Melt the remaining 4 tablespoons butter and stir in the mustard and horseradish. Slice the rolls in half lengthwise and brush the cut sides liberally with the flavored butter. Broil the roll about 45 seconds until lightly browned.

4. Divide the onions and pan juices equally over the bottom halves of the rolls. Top with equally divided portions of the roast beef, and season the meat with salt and pepper to taste. Lay the cheese slices over the meat. Place the sandwiches, without the tops, under the broiler until the cheese is melted, but not browned, about 30 to 45 seconds.

5. To serve, replace the tops of each sandwich and cut each in half on the diagonal.

YIELD: 4 SERVINGS.

Incendiary Sloppy Joes

Sloppy Joes, the stuff of some of our fondest childhood memories, have been disappointingly downgraded in recent years. You can buy the standardized seasonings in packages and just "add your own meat." You can even buy the entire filling in a can and just "add your own bun." Both taste predictably bland, stale, and unappetizing. The idea is ridiculous anyway since homemade sloppy Joes, using your own good shelf spices, take only a few minutes to prepare. A word about dried herbs and spices: they don't last forever. After about six months, they lose their potency and fresh taste, so, unless you use vast quantities, buy them in the smallest available sizes from a store that does a large volume of business.

Our sloppy Joes use both herbs and spices for a savory bite with an incendiary aftereffect that makes a tall mug of cold beer or iced tea nice to have handy. We like to serve this hearty, eat-it-with-a-fork sandwich with Classic Creamy Coleslaw (see page 223) or Old-Fashioned Picnic Potato Salad (see page 207) and Hot Brownies with Brandy–Ice Cream Sauce (see page 265) or Tin Roof Sundaes (see page 270) for a nostalgic finish.

2 pounds lean ground chuck
1 large onion, chopped
1 large green bell pepper, seeded and chopped
2 cloves garlic
4 tablespoons chili powder
1 teaspoon salt
¾ teaspoon dried oregano
¾ teaspoon ground cumin
½ teaspoon cayenne pepper
¼ teaspoon cinnamon

⅛ teaspoon allspice
Pinch of ground cloves
1½ teaspoons Worcestershire sauce
½ teaspoon Tabasco
1 bay leaf, broken
1 28-ounce can (3 cups) crushed tomatoes in purée
⅔ cup red wine
6 large seeded sandwich buns

1. In a large skillet, break up the ground beef with a fork and cook for 3 to 5 minutes over medium heat until it begins to lose its red color. Add the onion and green pepper and cook for 3 minutes until the vegetables are just softened. Add the garlic and chili powder. Cook, stirring, for 1 minute.
2. Add the salt, oregano, cumin, pepper, cinnamon, allspice, cloves, Worcestershire sauce, Tabasco, and bay leaf and stir well. Stir in the tomatoes and wine and bring just to a boil. Lower the heat and simmer, partially covered, for 25 minutes. Discard the bay leaf.
3. Taste and correct seasoning. Serve spooned into the buns.

YIELD: 6 SERVINGS.

NOTE: The sloppy Joe filling may be made a day ahead and refrigerated; reheat before serving.

The Reubenesque

These ingredients were made for each other. Of course, every authority you consult has his or her own recipe for the "definitive" Reuben, but we tried lots of combinations and will now stand behind this one as The Reubenesque.

RUSSIAN DRESSING:

⅔ cup good-quality mayonnaise
3 tablespoons chili sauce or ketchup
3 tablespoons minced green pepper
3 tablespoons minced celery
½ teaspoon Worcestershire sauce
¼ teaspoon freshly ground black pepper
8 large slices seeded rye bread

Butter for the bread
1 pound lean corned beef, sliced medium thin, not paper thin
1 to 2 tablespoons butter
½ pound thinly sliced Swiss cheese
1½ cups shredded iceberg lettuce
Sour dill pickles, as an accompaniment

1. To make the Russian Dressing, combine all the ingredients in a small bowl and refrigerate until ready to use.
2. Toast the rye bread very lightly—just to give it a slight crunchiness, not until it's browned and crisp. Lightly butter 4 of the pieces of toast.
3. While the bread is toasting, sauté the corned beef a few pieces at a time in a large skillet in 1 tablespoon of butter until the meat is heated through and just beginning to frizzle at the edges. Add the remaining butter to the pan as needed for succeeding batches.
4. Heap the hot corned beef on the buttered sides of 4 pieces of the toasted bread. Lay the slices of cheese over the meat. Add a layer of shredded lettuce over the cheese. Spread the remaining slices of bread with 2 to 3 tablespoons Russian Dressing and place on top of the sandwiches. Slice in half diagonally and serve with sour dill pickles.

YIELD: 4 SERVINGS.

Skirt Steak Fajitas

Many years ago, when Melanie lived in San Antonio, fajitas were common street food, sold by vendors who grilled up the quickly cooked marinated skirt steaks, wrapped them in a fresh flour tortilla, and sold them as is. Guacamole, raw salsas, and other condiments were in containers at the back of the cart and one spooned them on as desired—sort of like the hot dogs, ketchup, mustard, and relish that are a New York street classic.

Since then, fajitas have become high-tech Americana, but to Melanie's mind some of the real thing has often been lost in the upgrade. Skirt steak, common in the Southwest, is an oddity in other parts of the country. Nevertheless, since every cow has one, it is possible to request it from a butcher. And it is well worth becoming acquainted with this marvelously juicy and flavorful cut of beef. Shaped a little like a flank steak, it is thinner, needs far less marinating time, and when cut across the grain, is as tender as the finest fillet. And it is the real thing for fajitas. If you absolutely cannot convince your butcher to stock it, buy boneless sirloin that is no more than ½ inch thick, but we warn you not to serve it to a San Antonian.

This hearty sandwich is excellent with a salad of alternating slices of red onion and oranges on a bed of romaine lettuce and drizzled with a red wine vinaigrette. End the meal with Tin Roof Sundaes (see page 270) or Pumpkin Custard (see page 255).

SALSA:

1 clove garlic, minced
1 small onion, chopped
1 large tomato, peeled, seeded, and chopped
1 freshly roasted and peeled (or canned) mild
  green chili, seeded and chopped
1 fresh (or canned) jalapeño pepper, seeded
  and minced (note: wash your hands
  carefully after working with hot
  peppers)
Salt and freshly ground black pepper
  to taste

GUACAMOLE:

1 large ripe avocado, peeled
1 tablespoon lemon or lime juice
2 tablespoons sour cream
Salt and freshly ground black pepper to taste

4 large flour tortillas
1 pound skirt steak
Salt and freshly ground black pepper
1½ tablespoons lime juice
1½ tablespoons vegetable oil
4 ounces Monterey Jack, shredded (about 1 cup)

1. Combine all salsa ingredients and let the mixture stand for 15 to 30 minutes at room temperature to allow the flavors to blend.

The salsa may be made up to 8 hours in advance but may lose a bit of its "fire" after a couple of hours.

2. To make the guacamole sauce, purée the avocado, lemon juice, and sour cream in a food processor until smooth. Add salt and pepper to taste. Cover and set aside until ready to use.

The guacamole sauce can be made 1 or 2 hours ahead and refrigerated.

3. To make the fajitas, build a medium-hot barbecue fire (see note). Wrap the tortillas together in aluminum foil.

4. Cut the skirt steak into pieces 4 or 5 inches long. Sprinkle both sides of each piece with salt and pepper. Combine the lime juice and vegetable oil in a shallow glass or ceramic dish. Add the steaks and turn to coat them completely. Let the steaks stand for 15 minutes at room temperature, turning once.

5. Place the wrapped tortillas at the edge of the grill to warm. Place the steaks in the center of the grill directly over the coals. Grill about 2 minutes on each side until medium-rare.

6. To assemble, cut the steaks across the grain into thin strips. Spread one side of each of the warmed tortillas with some of the guacamole. Divide the meat among the tortillas, being sure to pour any pan juices over the meat. Then top with the salsa and cheese. Roll or fold up the tortillas and eat in your hand or with a fork.

YIELD: 4 SERVINGS.

NOTE: The skirt steaks may also be cooked in 1 tablespoon oil in a large skillet over medium-high heat for 2 minutes on each side.

Italian Sausage and Pepper Grinder

It's a grinder in New England, a submarine in the Midwest, a hoagie in Philadelphia, a po'boy in New Orleans, and a hero to New Yorkers. And it's always a split long roll, generously filled with various and sundry combinations of meats, cheeses, vegetables, and so on. Our recipe evokes the New England pizza parlor sausage grinders of Brooke's fond recollection—but ours is a little bit better; in those grinders the pepper strips were always bitterly overcooked from too many reheatings in their sauce.

An Italian grinder is hearty supper fare, especially when accompanied by a green salad or antipasto.

Italian Sausage and Pepper Grinder (cont.)

1 to 1½ pounds hot or sweet Italian sausage
1 cup red wine
3 tablespoons olive oil
1 onion, thinly sliced
1 large or 2 medium green peppers, cut into
   ½-inch-wide strips
1 clove garlic, chopped
1 28-ounce can (3 cups) crushed plum tomatoes

1 8-ounce can (1 cup) tomato sauce
½ teaspoon dried basil
¼ teaspoon dried oregano
⅛ teaspoon dried red pepper flakes
Salt
4 crusty grinder rolls, each 6 or 7 inches long
Parmesan cheese for passing at the table

1. Cut the sausages into 3-inch lengths if they are not already in links. Prick them in several places. Place in a nonreactive skillet just large enough to hold them in a single layer and pour the red wine over them. Simmer, uncovered, over medium heat, turning occasionally, until the wine has evaporated and the sausages are no longer pink inside, about 15 minutes. Lower the heat slightly and brown the sausages on all sides.

2. Preheat the oven to 400 degrees.

3. In a large, nonreactive skillet, heat the olive oil. Add the onion and cook over medium heat until softened and beginning to brown slightly, about 5 minutes. Add the green pepper strips and garlic and toss with the onion for 30 seconds. Add the crushed tomatoes and tomato sauce, season with the basil, oregano, and red pepper flakes, and simmer, uncovered, over medium heat, until the sauce is somewhat reduced and thickened, about 10 minutes.

4. Wrap the rolls in foil and place in the oven to warm for 10 minutes.

5. When the sausages are cooked, cut each one in half lengthwise and add to the tomato sauce.

6. Split the rolls in half lengthwise and pull out some of the soft interiors with your fingertips. (This allows for a greater proportion of crusty exterior per bite.) Place the roll bottoms on plates and evenly divide the sausage and peppers and sauce among the rolls. Replace the roll tops and cut each grinder into two or three portions with a sharp knife. Pass Parmesan cheese at the table to sprinkle on the sandwiches.

YIELD: 4 SERVINGS.

NOTE: The sauce can be made ahead and reheated. If you're worried about the peppers getting overcooked, remove them with tongs and replace them at the last minute.

Mediterranean Grilled Cheese Sandwich

There seem to be as many styles of grilled cheese sandwiches as there are devotees of the same. Basic yellow cheese and white bread aficionados like them flattened with cheese oozing out, almost as if they had been ironed or run over by a steam roller. (We confess to this leftover childhood addiction.) More educated (adult) folks discovered the French *croque monsieur,* which is a cross between a grilled sandwich and French toast. (We think these are pretty good, too.)

Then there is the condiment issue. Purists insist on only cheese, white bread, and butter. But we have become enamored of our own invention, born out of a love for the basic ingredients, and offer it to you as a wonderful, summery supper sandwich that needs little to accompany it except perhaps some cucumbers dressed with a little vinaigrette and Lemon-Blueberry Mousse (see page 259) or Baked Amaretti Nectarines (see page 261) for dessert.

8 slices good-quality, firm, white sandwich bread
¼ cup mayonnaise
6 ounces thinly sliced Fontina cheese at room temperature
4 ounces thinly sliced smoked ham at room temperature

1 large tomato, thinly sliced
8 large or 16 small fresh basil leaves
½ sweet red onion, thinly sliced
4 tablespoons unsalted butter, melted

1. Thinly spread one side of the bread slices with mayonnaise. On 4 slices of the bread, mayonnaise side up, evenly layer half of the cheese, all of the ham, the tomato slices, basil, onion, and, finally, the remaining cheese. Top with the remaining bread, mayonnaise side down.
2. Heat a griddle or skillet large enough to hold the four sandwiches. Brush the top of the sandwiches with half of the melted butter and then invert onto the hot griddle. Grill about 5 minutes over medium-low heat until a rich golden brown, brush the uncooked side with the remaining butter, flip, and grill about 5 minutes more.
3. Serve immediately.

YIELD: 4 SERVINGS.

Sage Sausage and Cornmeal Biscuits

Melanie ate many different versions of sausage and biscuit sandwiches when she visited North Carolina. In this variation of a country classic, a small amount of cornmeal added to the biscuit gives it a pleasant texture.

Don't be deterred from trying this homemade sausage recipe. It's really not hard. No special equipment is needed and you don't have to stuff anything into anything! Follow our system for grinding the partially frozen pork cubes in a food processor or ask your butcher to do it for you. Serve with Creamy Classic Colelsaw (see page 223) and Tin Roof Sundaes (see page 270).

1½ pounds boneless pork with about 30 percent
    fat content (such as pork shoulder or butt),
    gristle removed
1 small clove garlic
1 teaspoon salt
2 teaspoons minced fresh sage or 1 teaspoon
    dried sage
1½ teaspoons cracked or coarsely ground black
    peppercorns
⅛ teaspoon cayenne pepper
⅛ teaspoon nutmeg
1 to 2 tablespoons butter for frying sausage
    patties
8 to 10 cornmeal biscuits (see right)

3 tablespoons butter, softened
2 teaspoons coarse-grained mustard

CORNMEAL BISCUITS:

1½ cups all-purpose flour
½ cup yellow cornmeal
4 teaspoons double-acting baking powder
2 teaspoons granulated sugar
1 teaspoon salt
3 tablespoons cold butter
3 tablespoons cold vegetable shortening
⅔ cup whole milk

1. Cut the pork into 1½-inch chunks, arrange in a single layer on a baking sheet, and freeze until partially frozen, about 45 minutes.
2. Place about ¼ of the meat at a time in the workbowl of a food processor. Pulse the machine on and off until the meat is ground to a crumbly, coarse, but even texture. Transfer the ground pork to a mixing bowl and repeat the process with the rest of the meat.
3. Using a large knife, mince the garlic and

the salt together to a fine paste. Add this to the meat, along with the sage, black pepper, cayenne pepper, and nutmeg. Mix the meat and seasonings together with your fingertips, making sure all the seasonings are evenly distributed, but don't work the meat into a too-smooth paste. Chill the sausage mixture for at least 1 hour or up to 8 hours to allow the seasonings to mellow.

4. To make the biscuits, preheat the oven to 425 degrees. Sift the flour, cornmeal, baking powder, sugar, and salt together into a large bowl. Cut the cold butter and shortening into small cubes and distribute it over the flour mixture. Work it in with your fingertips until the mixture resembles coarse meal with a few pieces of shortening the size of corn kernels remaining. Make a well in the center, pour in the milk, and mix with a few strokes of a wooden spoon until the dough clumps together. Turn out onto a floured board and knead about six times to finish combining the dough. Roll out to a thickness of $\frac{1}{4}$ to $\frac{1}{2}$ inch and cut biscuits with a $2\frac{3}{4}$- or 3-inch cutter. Reroll the scraps and cut the remaining biscuits. (You should get a total of 8 to 10 biscuits.) Place on a baking sheet and bake in the center of the preheated oven for 15 to 18 minutes or until a pale golden brown.

5. To cook the sausage patties, heat a large skillet over medium heat. (Black cast iron produces the best crusty sausages.) Shape the pork mixture into 8 to 10 flat patties about $3\frac{1}{4}$ inches in diameter. Fry in a small amount of butter over medium-low heat until the sausages are a rich, crusty brown on the outside and no longer pink within, about 4 to 5 minutes on each side.

6. Combine the softened butter and the mustard in a small bowl. Split the warmed biscuits, spread the tops with some of the mustard butter, place a sausage patty on the bottom halves, and replace the tops. Serve while still warm.

YIELD: 4 SERVINGS.

NOTE: Unbaked biscuits may be stored on the baking sheet in the refrigerator, lightly covered with plastic wrap, for up to 4 hours before baking. Baked biscuits may be reheated for a few minutes in a 350-degree oven.

Barbecued Pork and Coleslaw Sandwich

This very unconventional barbecued pork is based on a preparation method taught to Melanie by a dear friend who was raised in East St. Louis, Illinois, which is directly across the river from its Missouri namesake. It was originally made with pork shoulder steaks and store-bought barbecue sauce available only locally. When Melanie moved away from St. Louis and her sauce source, she was forced to develop a recipe to approximate the sweet-sharp bite that is an integral part of the dish. She has recently started to use the now widely available boneless pork steaks instead of pork shoulder and urges you to look for ones that have an ample amount of marbling for best flavor.

Unchanged, though, is the ritual of sloshing the meat in a moppin' mixture while grilling, then brushing with sauce and giving it a final tenderizing simmer in more sauce. The recipe sounds a lot more complicated than it is. The sauce and Classic Creamy Coleslaw (see page 223) can be made a day ahead. The pork gets better and better the longer it sits in the sauce, so it should be made early in the day of serving or even the day before. Serve this very hearty sandwich with lots of napkins, a simple salad, some corn on the cob in summer, and finish with Miss Hulling's Banana-Coconut Cream Pie (see page 246) for an authentic East St. Louis meal.

1 recipe Classic Creamy Coleslaw (see
    page 223)

BARBECUE SAUCE:

1 large onion, finely chopped
2 tablespoons vegetable oil
1 large clove garlic, minced
1 teaspoon dry mustard
1 cup bottled chili sauce
1 8-ounce can (1 cup) tomato sauce
1 12-ounce can beer
⅓ cup molasses
¼ cup Worcestershire sauce
3 tablespoons cider vinegar

1 teaspoon paprika
½ teaspoon dried oregano
½ teaspoon coarsely ground black pepper
¼ teaspoon cayenne pepper

PORK:

1 quart water
2 tablespoons cider vinegar
1 bay leaf, broken
1 clove garlic, thinly sliced
3 pounds thin-cut boneless pork chops, each
    about ¼ inch thick
½ to 1 teaspoon Tabasco
6 to 8 Portuguese or kaiser rolls

1. Make the Classic Creamy Coleslaw and refrigerate, but remove it from the refrigerator about ½ hour before serving.

2. To make the sauce, sauté the onion in the oil in a large, heavy saucepan over medium-low heat for about 3 minutes. Add the garlic and sauté 1 minute more. Stir in the mustard and then the remaining sauce ingredients. Simmer, uncovered, over low heat for 15 minutes, stirring often.

The sauce can be made a day ahead up to this point. Cover and refrigerate. Reheat before using.

3. To prepare the pork, build a barbecue fire and let the coals burn down slightly. Bring the water, vinegar, bay leaf, and sliced garlic to a simmer and then keep warm at the side of the grill.

4. Grill the chops 1 minute on each side to sear. Use tongs to remove the chops one at a time from the grill and dunk in the simmering water mixture. Grill the chops on one side for 2 to 3 minutes more, dunk again, and then grill the other sides. Repeat the grilling, dunking, and turning twice more and then brush with some of the barbecue sauce. Grill the chops for 2 to 3 minutes, brush again, and then turn and grill the other sides for 2 to 3 minutes more. Remove the chops from the grill and place in the saucepan with the sauce. Simmer indoors, covered, over low heat for about one hour or until the pork is fork tender. Add the Tabasco during the last 10 minutes of cooking. If the sauce seems thin, uncover the pan and continue to simmer for 10 to 15 minutes more. Spoon off any excess fat that accumulates on the top.

The recipe can be completed a day ahead up to this point, refrigerated, and then gently reheated just before serving.

5. To assemble the sandwiches, spoon a generous amount of hot pork and sauce on the bottoms of the split rolls, top with a generous spoonful of the coleslaw, and replace the tops. Cut the sandwiches in half and serve immediately with additional coleslaw on the side.

YIELD: 6 TO 8 SERVINGS.

Lobster Roll Bagaduce Lunch

When Brooke's family goes to coastal Maine every summer, one of their very first excursions is always to a pristine little white and red "clam shack" on Bagaduce Bay called Bagaduce Lunch. There they feast on the best lobster rolls in the state. When you're in Maine you always want to eat as much lobster as possible. Heaping a simple lobster salad into butter-grilled soft rolls is such a succulent and also wonderfully convenient way to eat this delicious crustacean for lunch. And then you get to have it again at dinner, boiled, with all the trimmings!

We think a lobster roll also makes a lovely treat back at home as a supper, served with potato chips and perhaps a cup of chowder. Purchase precooked and picked lobster meat if you have a good source. If you cook your own, buy four 1-pound live lobsters. Bring a very large pot of water to a rolling boil. Add salt liberally. Place the lobsters headfirst in the rapidly boiling water, cover, bring the water back to a boil, and cook for 10 to 12 minutes. Drain the lobsters and run under cold water to stop their cooking. When cool enough to handle, crack the shells and extract all the meat.

2 cups (about 12 ounces) cooked lobster meat, chopped into chunks no smaller than ½ to ¾ inch
1 tablespoon lemon juice
½ cup finely chopped celery
½ cup good-quality mayonnaise or enough to bind the salad

Pinch of cayenne pepper
Salt
1 tablespoon butter
4 New England–style frankfurter rolls (see note)
4 leaves green-leaf lettuce (optional)

1. Toss the lobster meat with the lemon juice and celery, add enough mayonnaise to bind the salad and season with cayenne pepper and salt to taste. (You may not need salt since lobster meat can be salty.)
2. Melt the butter in a heavy skillet or griddle. Toast the rolls in the skillet over medium heat on both of their crustless sides until golden.
3. Gently pull open the rolls. Lay a lettuce leaf in each cavity if desired and divide the salad among the rolls, heaping it high.

YIELD: 4 SERVINGS.

NOTE: New England–style frankfurter rolls are slightly taller than conventional rolls and are split down the center through the top crust rather than the side. Since they are baked side by side in a pan, their main virtue is that their crustless sides can be easily grilled. However, if they are unavailable, just use conventional hot dog rolls and grill the crusty top and the bottom, not the interior.

Cornmeal Waffles with Red-Eye Cream

Red-eye gravy is a southern invention. You fry up some nice country ham until the fat begins to brown and then pour some black coffee into the skillet. We've added a bit of cream to help smooth out its rough edges, but the basic taste is still there.

Serve these waffles with a salad of light lettuces mixed with a bitter green such as chicory, and Baked Ginger–Bay Leaf Apples (see page 262)for dessert.

1 cup all-purpose flour
1 cup yellow cornmeal
1 tablespoon granulated sugar
1 tablespoon double-acting baking powder
¾ teaspoon salt
2 eggs
3 tablespoons vegetable oil
1¼ cup milk
2 tablespoons butter

12 ounces baked ham, sliced ¼ inch thick
2 tablespoons brewed coffee (or use ½ teaspoon instant coffee powder and 2 tablespoons boiling water)
1 cup heavy cream
Freshly ground black pepper
Salt to taste
1 tablespoon chopped parsley

1. Following the manufacturer's directions, grease (if necessary) and preheat a waffle iron.

2. To make the waffles, sift the flour, cornmeal, sugar, baking powder, and salt into a mixing bowl. Beat the eggs with the oil and milk in a small bowl. Make a well in the center of the dry ingredients, pour in the milk mixture, and stir until just blended. Do not overmix or waffles will be tough.

3. Using ¾ cup to 1 cup of batter for each 8-inch waffle, make 4 waffles, following manufacturer's directions for your iron. Cook until the steaming stops and the waffles are crisp and golden brown. Remove to a baking sheet, cover loosely with foil, and keep warm in a 225 degree oven until all the waffles are made.

4. While the waffles are cooking, heat the butter in a large, nonreactive skillet and cook the ham over medium-high heat until the edges are tinged with brown. Remove the meat and add the coffee to the skillet, stirring over medium heat for 30 seconds to dissolve the browned bits in the bottom of the pan. Add the cream and cook, uncovered, over medium heat until the sauce is slightly thickened, about 2 minutes. Taste and season with black pepper and a tiny bit of salt if necessary.

5. Place the waffles on individual plates, cutting them into segments and overlapping two to four pieces on each plate. Arrange the ham over the waffles, top with the red-eyed cream, and sprinkle each serving with chopped parsley.

YIELD: 4 SERVINGS.

Western Omelet Burrito

This recipe is a result of experimenting with some favorite Tex-Mex ingredients (flour tortillas, pinto beans, taco sauce) and that delicious old standard, a western omelet. A "western" is traditionally not a bit like any French omelet ever made. It's supposed to be firm on the outside and soft but not at all runny on the inside so that it can be neatly tucked into bread (or in this case, a tortilla) to be picked up and eaten.

This makes a wonderful supper accompanied by a salad of greens, thinly sliced oranges, and slivered red onion, dressed with a vinaigrette flavored with cumin. Molasses-Ginger Crinkles (see page 268) and butter-pecan ice cream would be a nice dessert.

MEXICAN BEAN PURÉE:

1 15-ounce can cooked pinto beans or other
    pink beans
½ teaspoon ground cumin
½ teaspoon chili powder
¼ teaspoon dried oregano

4 large (10-inch) or 8 small (7-inch) flour
    tortillas
3 tablespoons butter

1 large or 2 medium onions, chopped (1 cup)
1 large or 2 medium red bell peppers, diced
    (1 cup)
6 ounces cooked ham, diced (1½ cups)
1 to 2 jalapeño peppers, seeded and minced or
    ¼ teaspoon dried red pepper flakes (note:
    wash your hands carefully after working
    with hot peppers)
6 eggs
1 tablespoon water
Bottled taco sauce as a condiment (see note)

1. To make the Mexican Bean Purée, drain the beans and place in the workbowl of a food processor along with the cumin, chili powder, and oregano. Pulse on and off to make a somewhat coarse purée. Transfer to the saucepan and cook, stirring now and then, until heated through and bubbly. The purée should be thick enough to be spread but not stiff. Add a little water if necessary to achieve the right consistency.
2. Preheat the oven to 350 degrees. Wrap the tortillas in a large sheet of foil. Place directly on an oven rack and bake until softened and heated through, about 10 minutes.
3. Melt the butter in a 12-inch skillet. Add the onions and cook over medium heat for 3 to 4 minutes. Add the red pepper and ham and cook for about 5 minutes more, or until the vegetables are softened and the ham is just slightly browned. Stir in the minced jalapeños or pepper flakes.

4. Break the eggs into a mixing bowl, add the water, and whisk until thoroughly combined but not frothy. Pour the beaten eggs over the vegetable-ham mixture in the skillet and cook over low heat, stirring almost constantly. When the omelet has reached the consistency of scrambled eggs, flatten with a spatula and cook until the bottom is firm and just tinged with golden brown. Cut the omelet into 4 or 5 sections with the side of your spatula. Turn each section and cook for 1 minute more or until just firm on the bottom but still slightly soft in the center.

5. To construct the burrito, spread a warm tortilla with bean purée, fill with a portion of the omelet, tuck in the ends of the tortilla, and roll up. Repeat with the remaining tortillas. Pass taco sauce at the table for those diners who would like to add a little to their burritos.

YIELD: 4 SERVINGS.

NOTE: Bottled taco sauce is available in specialty stores or in supermarkets that carry a line of Mexican foods. Its degree of hotness varies, so taste it before using.

Country "Club"

Melanie cut her culinary eye teeth on club sandwiches. By the age of eleven she was a connoisseur, having honed her talent for determining tactfully from the waiter whether the chicken in the kitchen was real breast meat or "chicken loaf." Early on, she had discerned that a heap of crinkle-cut potato chips in the center of the plate did not bode well for the quality of the sandwich. The better places always have *plain* potato chips and sweet bread-and-butter pickles on the side. *Thinly* sliced white bread is required because then a three-decker sandwich can be constructed and eaten without having to take it apart first.

Herewith is our idea of the perfect club sandwich. We think it makes a lovely light supper, along with a tall glass of iced tea and the above-mentioned pickles and chips. A sundae made with vanilla ice cream, hot fudge sauce, whipped cream, and a cherry on top would be a most fitting finish to the meal.

Country "Club" (cont.)

1½ pounds split chicken breasts
2 cups water
½ cup white wine
1 bay leaf
½ teaspoon salt
4 peppercorns
1 cup good-quality mayonnaise

¼ cup snipped chives or scallion greens
12 slices bacon
2 tomatoes, thinly sliced
Soft lettuce leaves
12 thin slices white sandwich bread
Freshly ground black pepper to taste

1. Place the chicken in a saucepan with the water, wine, bay leaf, salt, and peppercorns. Simmer for about 20 minutes, or until the chicken is no longer pink inside. Remove to a plate with tongs and set aside. When the chicken pieces are cool enough to handle, strip off the meat, discarding the skin and bones. Slice the meat into thin pieces and use right away or refrigerate until ready to use and then slice.

2. In a small bowl, combine the mayonnaise and the chives. Refrigerate until ready to use.

3. Cook the bacon until crisp. Drain on paper towels.

4. When all of the elements are prepared, begin making the sandwiches. Spread one side of each of eight slices of bread with the chive mayonnaise. Layer equal amounts of the chicken and tomatoes on four slices of the bread and sprinkle them with black pepper. Spread the remaining four slices of bread with the mayonnaise (on both sides if you like) and stack one slice on each of the chicken-tomato layers and top each with three strips of bacon, a lettuce leaf, and a slice of the remaining bread. Carefully cut each sandwich diagonally into quarters and stick a frilled sandwich pick into each quarter to help it from toppling. For each serving, arrange the sandwich quarters on a large plate with potato chips in the center and pickles on the side.

YIELD: 4 SERVINGS.

Smoked Salmon Waffles with Poached Eggs and Chive Butter

A small amount of smoked salmon adds a pleasantly salty-smoky taste to these waffles. A salad of watercress and endive with a light vinaigrette makes a nice accompaniment and our suave Mocha Pudding with Coffee Cream (see page 254), a pleasant finish.

1¾ cups all-purpose flour

2 teaspoons granulated sugar

2 teaspoons double-acting baking powder

¼ teaspoon salt

4 ounces smoked salmon, chopped (about ¾ cup) (see note)

6 to 10 eggs

2 tablespoons vegetable oil

½ cup sour cream

1¼ cups milk

6 tablespoons butter, softened

2 tablespoons minced chives or scallion tops

1 teaspoon vinegar

Salt

Freshly ground black pepper

Chive spears for garnish (optional)

1. Following manufacturer's directions, grease (if necessary) and preheat a waffle iron.

2. To make the waffles, sift the flour, sugar, baking powder, and salt into a mixing bowl. Add the chopped salmon and toss to mix. In a small bowl, beat together 2 eggs, the oil, sour cream, and milk. Make a well in the center of the dry ingredients, pour in the milk mixture, and stir to combine. Do not overmix.

3. Using ¾ cup to 1 cup batter, make 4 8-inch waffles. Cook until the steaming stops and the waffles are crisp and golden brown. Remove to a baking sheet, cover loosely with foil, and keep warm in a 225 degree oven while you make the chive butter and cook the eggs.

4. Bring water to a boil in a large, nonreactive skillet for poaching the eggs.

5. Meanwhile, make the chive butter. Combine the softened butter and the chives in the workbowl of a food processor and pulse to mix, or beat them together in a small bowl.

6. Lightly salt the egg-poaching water and add the vinegar. Using one or two eggs per serving, depending on the occasion and the rest of the menu, break each egg into a custard cup and clip it into the simmering water. Cook the eggs at a gentle simmer, spooning the water over the yolks, until softly set, about 2 minutes. Remove with a slotted spoon, dip in a bowl of hot water to rinse off any remaining vinegar taste, and drain briefly on paper towels.

7. To serve, spread each smoked salmon waffle with about 1½ tablespoons chive butter. Divide the waffles into segments if desired. Top each serving with one or two poached eggs, sprinkle lightly with salt and freshly ground black pepper, and garnish with chive spears if available.

YIELD: 4 SERVINGS.

NOTE: Use smoked salmon ends if your delicatessen has them. They are considerably cheaper than buying slices, and since the salmon is chopped in this recipe, the ends are fine.

Nick's Pizza Parlor Calzone

We are quite fond of calzone, the pizzalike giant turnover from southern Italy, and we are particularly enamored of Nick's filling of three cheeses. The combination of three cheeses, chopped prosciutto, lots of cooked Swiss chard, and a touch of herbs is enclosed and baked in an egg-enriched pizza dough. The calzone is terrific served hot from the oven, but is also great cold, which makes it fine picnic fare. We like it with sliced ripe tomatoes dressed with a bit of olive oil and wine vinegar and a dessert of Giant Anise Sugar Cookies (see page 267) or Luscious Pecan Pie Bars (see page 266) and a bowl of fresh fruit.

CALZONE DOUGH:

3¼ cups all-purpose flour

1 package quick-rise or regular active dry yeast

1 teaspoon salt

1 egg

1 tablespoon olive oil

1 cup warm water (120 to 130 degrees)

2 tablespoons yellow cornmeal for the baking
    sheets

1 pound Swiss chard, cleaned, and stems and
    leaves separated

2 leeks, cleaned and chopped

3 tablespoons olive oil

1 large clove garlic, minced

1 15-ounce container (2 cups) ricotta cheese

4 ounces mozzarella cheese, cut in ¼-inch
    cubes

¼ cup grated Romano cheese

4 ounces prosciutto, minced

1 teaspoon dried marjoram

½ teaspoon freshly ground black pepper

1 egg beaten with 1 tablespoon water, for glaze

1. To make the dough, place the flour, yeast, and salt in a food processor. Pulse 2 or 3 times to mix. Add the egg and oil and then, with the machine running, pour the water through the feed tube. When the dough forms a ball, process for about 45 seconds to knead. (If you are making the dough by hand, stir the dry ingredients to-

gether in a bowl. Add the liquid ingredients and beat to form a soft dough. Turn the dough out onto a lightly floured surface and knead for 10 minutes.) Place the dough in an oiled bowl, turning to oil the top. Cover lightly with a towel and let rise in a warm place until doubled in bulk, about 1 hour for quick-rise yeast and about 1½ to 2 hours for regular yeast. (This dough takes longer to rise than ordinary pizza dough since it is enriched with egg.)

2. While the dough is rising, prepare the filling. Bring a pot of salted water to a boil. Cut the Swiss chard stems into 2-inch pieces and boil for 5 minutes; add the leaves and cook for 3 minutes more. Drain well and run under cold water to cool, then squeeze all excess moisture from the chard. Chop the chard by hand or in a food processor.

3. Sauté the chard and leeks in the oil over medium-low heat until softened, about 4 minutes. Add the garlic and sauté 1 minute. Let cool.

4. In a large mixing bowl, combine the ricotta, mozzarella, Romano, prosciutto, marjoram, pepper, and the chard mixture.

The filling may be made a day ahead and refrigerated, covered.

5. Preheat the oven to 475 degrees. Sprinkle 1 tablespoon cornmeal on each of 2 uninsulated baking sheets.

6. Punch down the risen dough and divide it into 6 pieces. Shape each into a ball. On a lightly floured surface, flatten each ball and roll into an 8-inch circle. Spread about ⅔ cup filling on the lower half of each circle, leaving a 1-inch border all around. Brush the border with the egg wash, then fold the dough over to make a half-moon. Seal the edges with the tines of a fork, then use a spatula to transfer each calzone to a baking sheet.

7. Prick the tops of the calzones in 5 or 6 places with a fork and then brush the tops with the remaining egg wash. Bake on the lower and center racks of the oven for about 15 minutes, switching the positions of the baking sheets after 7 minutes for even cooking, until the calzones are crisp and golden brown.

8. Serve warm at room temperature.

YIELD: 6 SERVINGS.

PASTA

"*I never get tired of pasta, any more than I get tired of bread. I eat it when I'm exhausted and want a quick meal that will give me a lift. I eat it when I'm in an ambitious mood, looking for something pleasant and different to compliment a guest.*"

—*JAMES BEARD*
Beard on Pasta (1983)

"*However you eat them, noodles are not only amusing, but delicious.*"

—*JULIA CHILD*
Julia Child and Company (1979)

"*Everything you see I owe to spaghetti.*"

—*SOPHIA LOREN*

Green and White Lasagna

Lasagna has always been a good idea as an economical, make-ahead dinner for a crowd. However, since by now everyone has a favorite recipe for the standard tomato sauce variety, we offer this rather elegant (though still thrifty) alternative. Spinach or egg lasagna noodles are layered with a creamy bechamel, three cheeses, and a savory ground meat–spinach filling. Many supermarkets carry ground turkey, so if it's available to you, do use it in this recipe—it contributes a wonderful flavor. Ground veal is a fine alternative.

Serve with a green-leaf lettuce and bell pepper salad, garlic bread, and Peanut Butter–Chocolate Chip Brownies (see page 263) or Double Lemon Loaf (see page 236) and fresh fruit for dessert.

12 ounces spinach or egg lasagna noodles
    (about 12 standard-size noodles)
1 tablespoon vegetable oil
5 tablespoons butter
1 pound ground turkey or veal
½ cup chopped onion
1 clove garlic, minced
½ cup white wine
1 10-ounce box frozen chopped spinach,
    thawed and drained
2 teaspoons dried basil

1 teaspoon salt
¼ teaspoon freshly ground black pepper
4 tablespoons all-purpose flour
1½ cups good-quality canned or homemade
    (see page 2) chicken stock
1½ cups milk
¼ teaspoon freshly grated nutmeg
8 ounces (1 cup) ricotta cheese
About 12 ounces fontina cheese, grated (3 cups)
    (see note)
3 tablespoons Parmesan cheese

1. Cook the lasagna noodles in a large pot of rapidly boiling, generously salted water until al dente, about 8 minutes. Drain into a colander, refresh under cold water, and drain again.

2. Meanwhile, heat the oil and 1 tablespoon of the butter in a large skillet over medium heat. Add the ground meat and onions and stir, breaking up the meat with the side of a spoon, until the meat loses its

pink color. Add the garlic and continue to cook until the meat is cooked through and the onions are softened. Spoon off any excess fat. Add the wine to the skillet and cook over high heat until almost all of the liquid has evaporated. Add the drained spinach and season with the basil, ½ teaspoon of the salt, and ⅛ teaspoon of the pepper. Mix well and set aside.

This meat mixture may be made up to 1 day ahead.

3. To make the bechamel, melt the remaining 4 tablespoons of butter in a medium saucepan. Stir in the flour and cook, stirring with a whisk or wooden spoon, over medium heat for 2 minutes. Stir in the chicken stock and milk and bring to a boil over medium-high heat, whisking almost constantly. Cook and stir for 1 minute after the sauce boils. Remove the sauce from the heat and season with the nutmeg and the remaining salt and pepper.

4. Lightly butter a 9-by-13-inch lasagna pan. Spoon a little sauce into the pan, tilting it to coat the bottom. Begin the layering, first with 3 or 4 of the lasagna noodles, then with half the meat-spinach mixture, then dotting with half the ricotta and about ⅓ of the grated fontina. Spoon about ⅓ the sauce over the cheese layer. Repeat with a second layer. The top should be a layer of noodles, the last of the sauce, and a sprinkling of the last of the fontina and the Parmesan cheese.

The recipe may be made ahead up to this point. Cover well and refrigerate or freeze. If frozen, thaw in the refrigerator overnight before baking.

5. Preheat oven to 375 degrees. Bake the casserole, uncovered, in the center of the preheated oven until heated all the way through and the top is light brown, about 30 to 45 minutes. Remove lasagna from the oven and let it cool for 5 minutes before serving.

YIELD: 8 SERVINGS.

NOTE: Fontina is a flavorful, semisoft cheese. It is easiest to grate when chilled.

Southwest Stuffed Shells

This dish is a happy intermingling of pasta and the fresh and lively flavors of the American Southwest. The filling for the cooked jumbo pasta shells is a simple mixture of three very different, but complementary cheeses sparked with the green flecks and characteristic lemony bitterness of fresh cilantro. The sauce is nothing more than a lightly cooked blend of chopped onion, fresh plum tomatoes, and chopped green chilies.

As with many pasta dishes, the meal is rounded out with a green salad. Here we would serve a red wine and oil vinaigrette seasoned with a pinch of chili powder. Hester's Citrus Pudding Cake (see page 242) or Angel Food Cake with Summer Fruit Ambrosia (see page 238) would be a fitting finale.

1 pound jumbo pasta shells

FILLING:

1½ pounds (about 3 cups) ricotta cheese
1 egg
6 ounces Monterey Jack, cut in ¼-inch cubes
¼ cup grated Parmesan cheese
¼ cup chopped fresh cilantro
¼ teaspoon black pepper

TOMATO-CHILI SAUCE:

1 large onion, chopped
6 tablespoons olive oil

3 pounds fresh plum tomatoes, cored and coarsely chopped or 2 28-ounce cans plum tomatoes, drained, with liquid reserved
6 tablespoons red or white wine
½ to 1 teaspoon salt (add the greater amount if using fresh tomatoes)
½ teaspoon freshly ground black pepper
1 4-ounce can green chilies, drained and coarsely chopped
1 fresh or canned jalapeño pepper, seeds and ribs discarded, finely minced (note: wash your hands carefully after working with hot peppers)

1. Bring a large pot of water to a boil for the pasta.
2. Meanwhile, make the filling. Whisk together the ricotta cheese and egg. Stir in the Monterey Jack and Parmesan cheeses, the cilantro, and the pepper.

The filling can be made a day ahead and refrigerated. Bring back to room temperature before using.

3. Cook the shells in boiling, salted water just until al dente, about 10 to 12 minutes. Do not overcook the shells. Drain well. (Some of the shells will probably be broken. You will need only 36 to 40 perfect shells for the recipe, however.)

4. While the pasta is cooking, make the tomato-chili sauce by sautéeing the onion in the olive oil in a large skillet over medium-low heat until the onion is softened, about 5 minutes. Add the tomatoes, wine, salt, and pepper. (If using canned tomatoes, add about 1 cup of the liquid.) Simmer, uncovered, about 5 minutes. Add the green chilies and jalapeño pepper and simmer until slightly reduced, about 5 minutes more.

The sauce can be made a day ahead and refrigerated.

5. Spread about ½ cup of the sauce over the bottoms of each of two shallow 2-quart (about 7 by 11 inches) baking dishes.

6. Preheat the oven to 350 degrees.

7. Stuff the shells by spooning about 1 tablespoon of filling into each. Place the shells, filled side up and close together but not touching, in the sauce-coated baking dishes.

The recipe may be prepared to this point up to 4 hours before serving. Cover and refrigerate. Bring back to room temperature before baking.

8. Cover the dishes with foil and bake in the preheated oven until hot, about 15 to 20 minutes. Meanwhile, reheat the reserved sauce over low heat.

9. Serve the shells by spooning a liberal coating of tomato-chili sauce onto six serving plates or a large platter. Arrange about 6 shells on the sauce for each person. Pass the remaining sauce separately.

YIELD: 6 SERVINGS.

Cincinnati-Style Five-Way Chili

Cincinnati chili is an American food phenomenon that defies categorization. This midwestern river city has a dominant German heritage and an almost negligible Mexican population. No matter: the chili parlors that dot nearly every corner are predominantly owned and operated by Greek families.

Though the spicy, meaty chili sauce is often served over frankfurters in a bun, it is best known in a "five-way" presentation that begins with a plate of spaghetti, a liberal ladle of the chili sauce, a thin layer of cooked kidney beans, a handful of chopped raw onion, and a sprinkling of grated Wisconsin cheddar cheese. There are those few who choose to omit one or more of these ingredients, but the taste of all five is indeed remarkably delicious!

Though the original formulas for the herbs, spices, and the touch of bitter chocolate in the sauce are still well-kept secrets, we think our version of Cincinnati chili tastes remarkably like the real thing. It is best made with top-quality dried herbs and spices and allowed to rest for a day or two before serving so that the flavors can mature. It is a marvelous informal supper for a crowd. Just heat up the sauce and beans, cook the pasta, and set the condiments out in separate bowls to allow each guest to build his own chili combo. Add a simple salad, a bowl of fruit, and trays of Giant Anise Sugar Cookies (see page 267) and Luscious Pecan Pie Bars (see page 266) for an almost totally made-ahead meal.

2 pounds ground chuck
2 onions, finely chopped (1½ cups)
3 cloves garlic, minced
2 cups beef stock
1 cup water
1 16-ounce can (2 cups) tomato sauce
2 tablespoons red wine vinegar
2 teaspoons Worcestershire sauce
3 tablespoons chili powder
1 tablespoon paprika
1 teaspoon ground cumin
1 teaspoon dried oregano
½ teaspoon cayenne pepper
¼ teaspoon salt or to taste
½ ounce (½ square) unsweetened chocolate

5 whole allspice berries
5 whole black peppercorns
4 whole cloves
1 small stick cinnamon, broken in half
1 large bay leaf, broken
1 pound spaghetti, cooked according to
    package directions
1 16-ounce can cooked kidney beans, drained
    and heated (optional)
1 cup chopped onion, for garnish
About 6 ounces cheddar cheese, preferably
    yellow cheddar from Wisconsin, grated
    (1½ cups)
Oyster crackers

1. In a heavy 5-quart pot, cook the meat, onions, and garlic over low heat until the meat has lost its red color but is not browned and the vegetables have softened, about 15 minutes. Stir often and mash the meat with the back of a spoon to break up any clumps and soften the texture. Spoon off the excess fat.

2. Add the beef stock, water, tomato sauce, vinegar, Worcestershire sauce, chili powder, paprika, cumin, oregano, cayenne pepper, salt, and chocolate to the pot and stir well. Tie the allspice, peppercorns, cloves, cinnamon, and bay leaf in a cheese-cloth bag and add to the pot.

3. Partially cover and simmer very gently until thickened to a sauce consistency, about 1½ to 2 hours. Watch carefully for the last 30 minutes and completely cover the pan if the sauce seems too thick. Discard the spice bag and add salt to taste.

The sauce can be made to this point up to 3 days ahead or frozen for up to 1 month.

4. Serve the sauce over the spaghetti. Pass the beans, onion, cheese, and oyster crackers separately.

YIELD: 6 SERVINGS.

Veal Pasta Gremolata

Whenever we see it on a good Italian restaurant menu, we order osso buco. The classic long-simmered casserole of veal knuckles in good stock is hearty and rich with flavor, but one of the inspirations brought to this dish is the last-minute addition of gremolata—a mixture of minced parsley, lemon zest, and garlic. Making osso buco at home is time consuming, but we felt the wonderfully flavorful ingredients would lend themselves well to a quick pasta preparation.

Many markets sell veal cut from the shoulder as budget-priced "scallops." This pasta makes excellent use of these tasty cutlets since they are nicely tenderized by just a short simmering in the sauce.

We particularly serve this dish in cool weather to brighten wintry meals with its spark of citrus and the freshness of its abundant parsley. It is well complemented by Roasted Vegetables (see page 218), especially broccoli or red peppers and Baked Ginger–Bay Leaf Apples (see page 262) or Pear Strudel (see page 250).

Veal Pasta Gremolata (cont.)

12 ounces fusilli (short pasta twists)
**1 pound veal scallops, cut from the shoulder or
  leg**
Salt and freshly ground black pepper to taste
2 tablespoons butter
2 tablespoons olive oil
½ cup chopped onion
2 carrots, peeled and sliced thin
2 ribs celery, sliced thin
1 clove garlic, minced
1 bay leaf, broken in half

½ cup white wine
**1 cup good-quality canned or homemade (see
  page 2) chicken stock**
½ cup heavy cream
1 teaspoon lemon juice

GREMOLATA:

¼ cup minced flat-leaf parsley
1½ teaspoons grated lemon zest
1 large clove garlic, minced

1. Cook the pasta in a large pot of boiling, salted water until al dente, about 8 minutes. Drain well. Return the pasta to the cooking pot to keep warm.

2. While the pasta is cooking, season both sides of the veal with salt and pepper. In a large skillet, sauté the veal in 1 tablespoon of the butter and 1 tablespoon of the oil over high heat until lightly browned, about 30 to 45 seconds. (You may need to do this in two batches. Add more butter and oil if needed.) Cut the veal into strips about ½ by 1½ inches.

3. Add the remaining butter and oil to the skillet and sauté the onion, carrot, and celery over medium-low heat until just softened, about 4 minutes. Add the garlic and sauté for 30 seconds. Add the bay leaf, wine, and stock and simmer until slightly reduced, about 3 minutes. Add the cream, veal, and any juices that have accumulated from the veal. Simmer, uncovered, until the meat is tender and the sauce is slightly reduced, about 5 minutes. Stir in the lemon juice. Discard the bay leaf. Taste and season generously with pepper and, if needed, with salt. (The amount of salt needed depends on the saltiness of the chicken stock.)

4. To make the gremolata, mix the parsley, lemon zest, and garlic.

5. Pour the veal mixture over the pasta in the pot. Toss gently, but thoroughly. Add the gremolata to the pasta, and toss again. Serve immediately.

YIELD: 4 SERVINGS.

Vermicelli with Scallops, Lemon, and Tarragon

The greatest disservice done to a scallop is overcooking—and that can be done in a matter of seconds. We once knew a sage fishmonger who maintained that scallops should be "cooked" by holding a handful under very hot tap water. Finding this to be an effective but rather tedious (not to mention flavorless) method, we have applied the principle to "cooking" scallops with hot pasta. In this recipe, we combine the delicate shellfish with an equally delicate, yet refreshingly simple sauce, place it in the pan used to cook the pasta, and then add the pasta as a heat blanket. A minute or so of tossing results in perfectly cooked scallops and a fabulous, light, pasta main course.

The no-cook feature has the greatest appeal in the summer when any additional kitchen heat is to be avoided in our unair-conditioned houses. The season also makes serving a salad of light lettuces, sliced tomatoes, and a dessert of sliced peaches and chocolate wafers most appealing and equally easy.

1½ teaspoons grated lemon zest
¼ teaspoon coarsely ground black
    pepper
¼ teaspoon salt
1 tablespoon Pernod
3 tablespoons lemon juice
6 tablespoons olive oil

1 pound small bay scallops or sea scallops,
    halved
2 tablespoons minced fresh tarragon or
    2 teaspoons dried tarragon
4 scallions
12 ounces vermicelli
Fresh tarragon sprigs for garnish (optional)

1. Bring a large pot of water to a boil for the pasta.
2. In a large mixing bowl, whisk together the lemon zest, pepper, salt, Pernod, lemon juice, and olive oil. Add the scallops and minced tarragon and toss gently. Thinly slice the scallions, using most of the green parts, and toss lightly with the scallops.
3. Cook the vermicelli in the rapidly boil-ing water to which about 2 teaspoons salt have been added until al dente, about 5 to 7 minutes. Drain well. Immediately pour the scallop mixture into the pasta pot and add the drained hot pasta. Toss gently but thoroughly until the scallops are opaque, about 1 minute.
4. Serve sprinkled with tarragon sprigs if desired.

YIELD: 4 SERVINGS.

American Chop Suey à la Mamie

Brooke's husband adores tomato sauce. He likes it flavored with ground meat, with sausage, with meatballs . . . with anything. On anything. Or on nothing, eaten straight out of the pot.

One of his favorite dishes is the tomato sauce–meat-pasta casserole that is known by various names around the country but that he calls "American Chop Suey." Richard has fond memories of American Chop Suey made with "cars and bikes" macaroni, a pasta shape that Brooke has searched out for twenty years to no avail. But she did get this recipe from her mother-in-law, Mamie, who says she usually made it with elbow macaroni anyway.

This is good with a green vegetable, a salad, and Candied Gingerbread with Vanilla Cream (see page 256) for dessert.

12 ounces elbow macaroni
1 tablespoon olive oil
¾ pound good-quality breakfast sausage (not links)
1 onion, chopped
2 cloves garlic, minced
¼ cup red wine
28-ounce can crushed plum tomatoes in purée
8-ounce can tomato sauce

½ teaspoon crumbled dried sage
¼ teaspoon cayenne pepper
3 tablespoons chopped parsley, preferably flat leaf
Salt to taste
About 3 ounces mozzarella cheese, grated (¾ cup)
¼ cup grated Parmesan cheese

1. Cook the macaroni in a large pot of rapidly boiling water to which 2 teaspoons of salt have been added until al dente, about 8 to 10 minutes. Drain.
2. While the macaroni is cooking, heat the olive oil in a large skillet. Add the sausage and cook over medium-high heat, stirring and breaking it up with the side of the spoon, until it has lost its pink color. Spoon off the excess fat. Add the onion and garlic and cook, stirring, until softened, about 3 to 4 minutes. Add the wine to the skillet and cook over high heat for 2 minutes or until most of the liquid has evaporated. Stir in the tomatoes, tomato sauce, sage, and cayenne pepper. Simmer the sauce, uncovered, for about 5 minutes. Stir in 2 tablespoons of the parsley.
3. Preheat oven to 400 degrees.
4. Toss the macaroni with the sauce. Taste for seasoning, adding salt if necessary, and transfer to a lightly oiled 2-quart baking dish. Toss the two cheeses together with the remaining tablespoon of parsley and sprinkle over the top of the casserole.

The recipe may be made ahead up to this point. Cover and refrigerate for up to 8 hours.

5. Bake in the center of the preheated oven until the casserole is bubbly around the edges and the cheese is melted and lightly browned, about 15 to 20 minutes.

YIELD: 4 TO 6 SERVINGS.

Rigatoni with Diablo Clam Sauce

The intense and lusty flavors in this sauce will make lovers of hot and spicy food literally weep with joy! If absolutely necessary, its fire can be tamed by cutting down on the chili powder and cayenne pepper. Serve with roasted peppers and black olives dressed with olive oil and red wine vinegar. Hester's Citrus Pudding Cake (see page 242) would be a refreshing dessert.

2 tablespoons olive oil

2 tablespoons butter

4 cloves garlic, peeled and chopped

1 tablespoon chili powder

1 16-ounce can (2 cups) crushed plum tomatoes
    with purée

2 teaspoons brown sugar

½ teaspoon freshly ground black pepper

½ teaspoon paprika

¼ teaspoon cayenne pepper or to taste

10 ounces chopped fresh clams with juices or
    1 10-ounce can baby clams with their liquid

2 teaspoons lemon juice

Salt to taste

12 ounces rigatoni or other large, sturdy pasta

4 ounces (½ cup) ricotta cheese

1. Heat a large pot of water for the pasta.

2. Heat the oil and butter in a large, nonreactive skillet. Add the garlic and cook it over medium heat with the chili powder, stirring constantly, for 1 minute. Add the tomatoes, brown sugar, black pepper, paprika and cayenne pepper. Bring to a boil, turn the heat to low, and simmer, uncovered, for 10 minutes. Add the clams, clam liquid, and lemon juice and cook for another 5 minutes. Add salt to taste and correct the other seasonings if necessary.

3. Meanwhile cook the rigatoni in the rapidly boiling, salted water until al dente, about 8 minutes.

4. Drain the pasta and pour it onto a rimmed platter or pasta bowl or onto individual plates. Spoon the sauce over the pasta, top with dollops of ricotta cheese, and toss to combine at the table.

YIELD: 4 SERVINGS.

Egg Noodles Choucroute

This dish came into existence one winter day when we were hankering for *choucroute garnie,* the famous Alsatian dish of smoked meats and sauerkraut. Rather than spending the hours necessary to make the real thing, a recently purchased bag of fresh, wide egg noodles provided the inspiration to create a quick facsimile made with readily available, high-quality smoked meats. We like to use a couple of kinds of sausages such as bratwurst and weisswurst along with smoked pork chops, but you shouldn't feel limited. Use whatever you like. The natural accompaniments are good dark bread, lots of mustard and sweet butter, finishing with Baked Ginger–Bay Leaf apples (see page 262).

12 ounces good-quality German or Polish sausage links, such as bratwurst or weisswurst or fine-quality kielbasa or a combination
4 thin smoked pork chops (about 5 ounces each)
2 tablespoons vegetable oil
1 medium onion, chopped
8 ounces savoy cabbage, sliced thin (3½ cups)

⅓ cup white wine
½ teaspoon dried thyme
¼ teaspoon caraway seeds
3 crushed juniper berries
1 bay leaf, broken
12 ounces wide egg noodles
¾ cup heavy cream
1 tablespoon Calvados or applejack
Salt and freshly ground black pepper to taste

1. Bring a large pot of water to a boil for the pasta.
2. In a large skillet, sauté the sausage and pork chops in the oil over medium-high heat until golden brown, about 10 minutes. (You may have to do this in two batches.) Remove from the skillet.
3. Add the onion to the drippings in the skillet and sauté over medium-low heat until just softened, about 4 minutes. Add the cabbage and cook, stirring, for 1 minute. Add the wine, thyme, caraway seeds, juniper berries, and bay leaf. Bring to a simmer, stirring constantly. Arrange the meats atop the cabbage, cover the skillet, and simmer over low heat until the sausage is cooked through, about 8 to 10 minutes.
4. Meanwhile, cook the pasta in the boiling water to which about 1 teaspoon salt has been added until al dente, about 6 to 8 minutes. Drain and return to the cooking pot.
5. Remove the cooked meats from the skillet. Stir the cream and Calvados into the cabbage mixture and simmer, uncovered, for 1 minute. Discard the bay leaf. Add salt to taste and season quite generously with pepper.
6. Pour the cabbage sauce over the pasta and toss gently but thoroughly. Serve the pasta on individual plates or on a large platter. Arrange the meats atop the pasta.

YIELD: 4 SERVINGS.

Springtime Pasta with Salmon and Peas

Salmon is not only a wonderfully flavorful fish with a delicate, yet sturdy texture but it is also the undisputed pastel beauty of the sea. Its beautiful pale pink color is rare in nature and when combined with the emerald green of tiny garden peas and the whimsy of bow-tie pastas, salmon is the essence of springtime.

Since we think that one of the many virtues of pasta is its fast and effortless cooking, we often like to capitalize on that trait. This sauce is put together in minutes while the pasta boils, and then tossed with the hot bow ties.

Serve this with breadsticks or Sky-High Popovers (see page 222), a salad of light springtime lettuces, and ice cream with sliced strawberries and a splash of Cointreau for an equally fast, light, and lovely dessert.

12 ounces boneless, skinless, salmon fillets
12 ounces bow-tie pasta or other pasta shapes
1 cup heavy cream
½ cup white wine
1 cup frozen tiny green peas, thawed
¼ cup thinly sliced scallions, including about
**   2 inches of the green tops**

¼ cup chopped fresh dill
1 teaspoon Dijon mustard
¼ teaspoon freshly ground black pepper
¼ teaspoon salt or to taste
Fresh dill sprigs for garnish

1. Bring a large kettle of water to a boil for the pasta.
2. Meanwhile, slice the salmon with the grain into ¼-by-2-inch strips and reserve.
3. Cook the pasta in the rapidly boiling water to which about 1½ teaspoons salt have been added until al dente, about 8 to 10 minutes.
4. While the pasta is cooking, combine the cream and wine in a saucepan; simmer 3 minutes, uncovered. Add the peas, scallions, dill, mustard, pepper, salt, and salmon. Simmer for 1 minute.
5. Drain the cooked pasta and immediately put back into the hot cooking kettle. Add the sauce and toss gently but thoroughly to combine. Add salt and pepper to taste.
6. Serve immediately, garnished with dill sprigs.

Yield: 4 servings.

Tossed Angel Hair Primavera

We like to make this simple but elegant tossed springtime pasta dish with very thin spaghetti such as capellini or fedelini. Serve as weekday or company fare with a salad of dressed arugula or other bitter greens and lemon sherbet with strawberries for dessert.

16 slender asparagus spears
1 medium yellow crookneck squash
1 medium zucchini
1 red bell pepper
6 ounces prosciutto, sliced about ⅛ inch thick
2 tablespoons butter
2 tablespoons olive oil
12 ounces capellini or thin spaghetti

1¼ cups heavy cream
1 cup frozen peas, thawed
½ cup grated Parmesan cheese
1 cup thinly sliced scallions, including green tops
¼ cup chopped fresh basil or 1 tablespoon dried basil
Salt and freshly ground black pepper to taste

1. Begin heating a large pot of water for the pasta.

2. Cut the tips off the asparagus about 2 inches down the stem and slice the stalks crosswise into ¼-inch pieces. Cut lengthwise strips about ½ inch thick from the two squashes. Discard the cores containing the seeds. Slice the squash into thin, crosswise strips. Cut the pepper into thin slices about 1½ inches long. Slice the prosciutto into strips about ¼ inch wide.

3. Heat the butter and oil in a large skillet. Add the asparagus tips and stems and cook, stirring frequently, over medium-high heat for 2 minutes. Add the squash, and continue to cook for 1 minute. Then add the red pepper strips and the prosciutto, and cook 1 minute more.

4. Cook the pasta in the rapidly boiling water to which about 2 teaspoons salt have been added until al dente, about 4 to 5 minutes.

5. Meanwhile, add the cream and peas to the pan with the vegetables and simmer for 2 minutes.

6. Drain the pasta, return it to its cooking pot, and add the vegetables and cream. Sprinkle on the cheese, scallions, and basil and toss together using two large forks until the pasta is well coated with the sauce. Add a generous grinding of black pepper and salt to taste. (Since both prosciutto and Parmesan cheese can be quite salty, additional salt may not be needed.) Serve immediately on warm plates.

YIELD: 4 SERVINGS.

Mussels and Garlic Linguine

We think it a shame that the mussel doesn't enjoy the same high status here as in Italy. This mollusk is plentiful, inexpensive, deliciously sweet, and clothed in a magnificent shiny black shell. Its distinctive taste is most admirably suited to lusty sauces such as this one, gutsy with garlic, olives, lots of parsley, and a mashed anchovy. Tossed with the wonderfully bland counterpoint of the linguine, this is a fabulous, fast dish that could instantly turn you into a mussel lover. Serve it with a big basket of good Italian bread and a simple salad, and try Hester's Citrus Pudding Cake (see page 242) or Lemon-Blueberry Mousse (see page 259) for a light and refreshing dessert.

5 dozen mussels
¾ cup white wine
1 pound fresh linguine or 12 ounces dried
    linguine
6 tablespooons good-quality olive oil
1 onion, chopped

4 cloves garlic, minced
¼ teaspoon red pepper flakes
1 anchovy or 1 teaspoon anchovy paste
¼ cup thinly sliced, good-quality black olives
½ cup chopped flat-leaf parsley

1. Bring a large pot of water to a boil for the linguine.
2. Scrub and debeard the mussels. Place the wine in a large kettle, add the mussels, cover the kettle, and steam over medium heat until the mussels open, about 5 to 8 minutes. Use tongs to remove the mussels, allowing any liquid to drip back into the pot, and discard any mussels that failed to open. Wrap 12 mussels in their shells in aluminum foil to keep warm, and reserve for the garnish. Remove the remaining mussels from their shells, discard the shells, and reserve the mussels to add to the sauce. Strain the cooking liquid through several layers of cheesecloth and reserve to add to the sauce.
3. Cook the pasta in the rapidly boiling water to which about 1 teaspoon salt has

been added until al dente. (Fresh pasta takes about 3 minutes; dried pasta takes about 8 to 10 minutes.) Drain and return to the cooking pot; cover and keep warm.
4. While the linguine is cooking, heat the oil in a large skillet and sauté the onion over medium-low heat until softened, about 5 minutes. Add the garlic and red pepper flakes and sauté over low heat for about 2 minutes. Add the reserved cooking liquid from the mussels and simmer about 1 minute. Add the anchovy and mash into the sauce with the back of a spoon. Add the olives and reserved mussels and stir for about 30 seconds. Pour the sauce over the linguine. Add the parsley and toss thoroughly but gently.
5. Serve the linguine garnished with the reserved mussels in their shells.

YIELD: 4 SERVINGS.

Martha's Calamari Pasta

This recipe came to us from Brooke's sister Martha in Portland, Maine. Portland is of course a great seafood town, and Martha always takes willing visitors with her to shop for their dinner at Harbor Fish, a wonderful old-fashioned fish market down on the docks. It's a sprawling, noisy, friendly establishment, with never a whiff of "fishiness"—just the clean, sea-breeze smell of the very freshest daily catch. Dozens of varieties of Atlantic seafood are displayed, glistening, on heaps of crushed ice.

For ever-increasing numbers of calamari lovers, Martha buys fresh squid. She asks the fishmonger to remove the heads and tentacles but prefers to finish the cleaning process at home to make sure it's done right. The calamari then simmers in this simple, Italian-style sauce until it is very tender and has contributed its flavor to the sauce. Ladle over long fusilli and pass the Parmesan cheese. Giant Anise Sugar Cookies (see page 267) and fruit for dessert would be a great finishing touch. Delicious!

1½ pounds calamari
1 35-ounce can Italian plum tomatoes in purée
3 tablespoons olive oil
2 cloves garlic, chopped
½ teaspoon dried oregano
¼ teaspoon dried red pepper flakes
2 tablespoons chopped parsley

1 tablespoon lemon juice
Salt and freshly ground black pepper to taste
Pinch of granulated sugar
12 ounces fusilli (corkscrew-shaped spaghetti strands) or linguine cooked al dente
Grated Parmesan cheese

1. Discard the heads and tentacles of the calamari. Pull out the long, rigid spines. Turn the calamari inside out as you would the fingers of a rubber glove and clean the insides under cool running water, pulling off any purplish or soft white material. Turn right side out and pull or rub off the thin purplish membrane on the outside. (Some fishmongers will do some or all of this cleaning for you.) Place the calamari on a cutting board and slice crosswise into ¼-inch-thick "rings."

2. Remove the tomatoes from the can with a slotted spoon, reserving the purée. Split the tomatoes in half and scoop out and discard some of the seeds with your fingertips. Coarsely chop the tomatoes.

3. Heat the olive oil in a large, heavy saucepan. Add the garlic and stir for 30 seconds. Add the tomatoes and the tomato purée. Add the calamari rings, bring to a simmer, and cook, uncovered, over low heat for 30 minutes, stirring occasionally. Add the oregano and red pepper flakes and continue to simmer for another 20 to 30 minutes or until the calamari is tender. The sauce should be fairly thick. If it's too thin, raise the heat to medium and cook for a few minutes to reduce it; if too thick, add a little water. Stir in the chopped parsley

and season with the lemon juice, salt and pepper to taste, and a pinch of sugar.

4. Serve over the cooked pasta, passing the Parmesan cheese at the table to sprinkle on top.

YIELD: 4 SERVINGS.

Baked Spaghetti Carbonara

We love the taste of spaghetti carbonara but have always thought it was just too soft and *too white*. In this recipe we use pretty much the classic carbonara ingredients but have sprinkled the dish with some tasty buttered crumbs and cheese and briefly baked it in a hot oven to give it a nice, crusty topping. It's a lovely, simple, and very quick dish that depends very heavily on excellent-quality, freshly grated Parmesan and good smoky bacon for its flavor.

Serve with a salad of thickly sliced tomatoes, sesame breadsticks, and Baked Amaretti Nectarines (see page 261) for dessert.

½ pound bacon, preferably thickly sliced

12 ounces spaghetti, preferably thick

3 eggs

1 cup heavy cream

½ cup plus 2 tablespoons freshly grated Parmesan cheese

½ teaspoon freshly ground black pepper

2 slices firm white bread, crusts removed

2 tablespoons butter, melted

1. Cook the bacon in a skillet until almost but not quite crisp. Drain on paper towels and coarsely chop.

This step may be done up to 4 hours ahead.

2. Preheat the oven to 450 degrees.

3. Break the strands of pasta in half and cook in a large pot of rapidly boiling, salted water until al dente. Drain into a colander.

4. In a large mixing bowl, whisk together the eggs, cream, ½ cup of the cheese, and the pepper. Add the pasta and the bacon, and toss to combine. Turn into a buttered 8-by-12-inch baking dish.

5. Tear the bread into 2-inch pieces and pulse in a food processor to make crumbs. Toss with the remaining 2 tablespoons cheese and sprinkle evenly over the top of the casserole. Drizzle with the melted butter.

6. Bake in the preheated oven until the top is golden brown and crusty, about 12 to 15 minutes.

YIELD: 4 TO 6 SERVINGS.

Hot Penne with Cold Tomato Sauce

The mixture of salty ham, melting cheese, fresh tomatoes, and herbs is both colorful and delicious. Just to be sure that you use the best of each, which to our minds means that this is a summer dish unless you grow basil indoors (which is amazingly easy to do). You can, of course, use dried basil as long as you haven't kept the opened jar around for longer than a few weeks. Dried herbs lose their potency quickly.

Another hot-weather selling point for this recipe is the fact that the sauce needs absolutely no cooking at all. The residual heat from the pasta warms the tomatoes, brings out the fragrance of the basil, and barely melts the cheese—a wonderful combination! Serve it with French bread, lots of butter, and Georgia Peach-Pecan Skillet Cake (see page 234) or Giant Anise Sugar Cookies (see page 267) and fruit for dessert.

1 tablespoon red wine vinegar
6 tablespoons olive oil
¼ teaspoon dried red pepper flakes
⅛ teaspoon coarsely ground black pepper
1 clove garlic, minced
1 pound ripe plum tomatoes (see note)
8 ounces mozzarella cheese

3 ounces very thinly sliced Smithfield ham
¼ cup lightly packed fresh basil leaves or
    1 tablespoon dried basil and 3 tablespoons
    chopped parsley.
12 ounces penne or other small pasta shapes
Salt to taste
Small fresh basil leaves for garnish (optional)

1. Bring a large pot of water to a boil for the pasta.
2. In a large mixing bowl, whisk together the vinegar, oil, pepper flakes, black pepper, and garlic.
3. Core the tomatoes and cut in half crosswise. Gently squeeze each half to remove the seeds. Cut the tomatoes and cheese into roughly ½-inch cubes. Add to the mixing bowl and toss. Cut the ham and fresh basil into slivers. Add to the mixing bowl and toss.

4. Cook the pasta in the rapidly boiling water to which about 2 teaspoons salt have been added until al dente, about 8 to 10 minutes. Drain well. Immediately pour the tomato mixture into the pasta pot and add the drained hot pasta. Toss lightly, but thoroughly, until the cheese begins to melt, about 45 seconds. Add salt to taste. (The ham and cheese can be quite salty.)
5. Serve garnished with basil leaves if desired.

YIELD: 4 SERVINGS.

NOTE: If good plum tomatoes are not available, substitute 1 16-ounce can plum tomatoes drained.

Hot and Sour Oriental Chicken Noodles

This recipe is the delicious result of experimenting with some of the now-very-readily-available oriental ingredients like sesame oil and fresh ginger to make a hot and sour sauce for vermicelli tossed with stir-fried chicken and vegetables. Like all dishes that involve stir-frying, it's quick to cook, but you have to be sure to have the chicken and all the vegetables sliced before you begin.

Serve with Sky-High Popovers (see page 222) and some sugared sliced fruit for dessert.

HOT AND SOUR SAUCE:

¼ cup rice wine vinegar
8 tablespoons peanut oil
2 tablespoons sesame oil
2 tablespoons soy sauce
2 teaspoons minced fresh ginger
1 clove garlic, minced

1 teaspoon granulated sugar
¾ teaspoon red pepper flakes
10 ounces vermicelli or other thin pasta, broken in half

3 tablespoons vegetable oil
12 ounces chicken breast cutlets, cut into thin strips
2½ cups small broccoli florets (the florets from about half a bunch of broccoli)
2 carrots, peeled and cut into thin diagonal slices
1 red bell pepper, seeded and cut into thin strips
2 tablespoons chopped fresh cilantro or parsley
⅓ cup lightly toasted cashews (optional)

1. To make the hot and sour sauce, combine in a small bowl the vinegar, oils, soy sauce, ginger, garlic, sugar, and red pepper flakes. Set aside at room temperature.
2. Bring a large pot of water to a boil for the pasta. Cook the pasta in the rapidly boiling water to which about 2 teaspoons of salt have been added until al dente, about 5 minutes. Meanwhile, prepare and assemble the rest of the ingredients.
3. Heat the vegetable oil in a large skillet. Pat the chicken strips dry with paper towels. When the oil is hot, add the chicken to the skillet and stir-fry over high heat for 1 minute. Add the broccoli and carrots and stir-fry for 2 minutes. Add the pepper slices and stir-fry for 1 minute more until the chicken is cooked through and the vegetables are crisp-tender.
4. Pour the reserved sauce over the chicken-vegetable mixture in the skillet, add the pasta, and toss gently but thoroughly until well combined. Sprinkle with chopped cilantro and transfer to a platter or serve on individual plates. Sprinkle with the cashews.

YIELD: 4 SERVINGS.

Better-Than-Old-Fashioned Tuna-Noodle Casserole

Tuna-noodle casserole is a perennial favorite (with very good reason), but we think our modern-day version, with its extra color and its zesty-tasting green chilies, minced scallions, and liquid hot-pepper sauce, is an improvement over the original.

Carrots tossed with butter and dill would be nice with this, and maybe Purple Plum Crumble (see page 258) for dessert.

10 ounces flat egg noodles
3 tablespoons butter
2 tablespoons all-purpose flour
2 cups milk
¾ teaspoon salt or to taste
⅛ teaspoon white pepper
¼ to ½ teaspoon Tabasco or other liquid hot-pepper sauce

1 7-ounce can tuna, drained and broken up into chunks
1 4-ounce can green chilies, drained and chopped
1 teaspoon lemon juice
¼ cup thinly sliced scallions, including some green tops
½ cup fresh bread crumbs

1. Cook the noodles in a large pot of rapidly boiling water to which about 2 teaspoons of salt have been added until al dente, about 8 minutes. Drain.

2. Meanwhile, melt 2 tablespoons of the butter in a medium saucepan. Sprinkle on the flour and cook over medium heat, stirring with a whisk or a wooden spoon, for 2 minutes. Stir in the milk, raise the heat to medium-high, and bring to a simmer, whisking almost constantly. Simmer for 1 minute. Season with salt, pepper, and Tabasco.

3. Combine the drained noodles, the sauce, the tuna, and the green chilies. Stir in the lemon juice and 3 tablespoons of the scallions and toss gently but thoroughly to combine. Transfer to a lightly buttered 1½-quart baking dish.

4. Preheat the oven to 375 degrees.

5. Melt the remaining tablespoon of butter in a small skillet. Add the bread crumbs and the remaining tablespoon of scallions and toss to combine. Sprinkle this mixture evenly over the top of the casserole.

The recipe may be made ahead up to this point and held for up to 8 hours.

6. Bake, uncovered, in the center of the preheated oven until lightly browned on top and heated through, about 20 to 25 minutes.

YIELD: 4 SERVINGS.

CHICKEN AND OTHER BIRDS

"I want there to be no peasant in my realm so poor that he will not have a chicken in his pot every Sunday."

—*WILLIAM SHAKESPEARE*

Henry IV

"Cut up fryer, clean with lemon only. Dredge in a mixture of flour, salt, pepper, and allspice. Put in ½ inch of hot lard. Fry one side then the other until well done. Eat directly out of the skillet. This is very good with a cold beer. If you're a strict Baptist, have a lemonade or a cold drink, and may God bless your home."

—*"MARGIE'S FRIED CHICKEN"*

White Trash Cooking (1986)

Matt's Favorite Bacon-and-Cheddar Chicken

This simple dish could easily become one of your most requested recipes. At Melanie's house, her youngest son, Matt, asks for it regularly, maintaining that it is in the same revered category as charcoal-grilled hamburgers and homemade pizza.

It is the perfect dish for last-minute fixing since it takes only a short time and uses ingredients that are easily obtainable and may well be in your refrigerator already. If you don't have cheddar cheese, try Swiss or Muenster or even a flavorful Monterey Jack—in short, it works with whatever bits and pieces are in your cheese supply. The herbs, too, can be varied to suit the occasion or the chosen side dishes. Just be sure not to overcook the thin-sliced chicken cutlets or they will quickly dry out.

Accompaniment selections can also vary according to your whim and the availability of ingredients. We particularly like Scalloped Potatoes Our Way (see page 209) and buttered green beans. A real treat for dessert is Miss Hulling's Banana-Coconut Cream Pie (see page 246), but quick and easy Hot Brownies with Brandy–Ice Cream Sauce (see page 265) are equally appealing.

4 slices bacon
½ cup unseasoned dry bread crumbs
½ teaspoon dried basil
¼ teaspoon dried oregano
¼ teaspoon dried marjoram
¼ teaspoon salt
⅛ teaspoon freshly ground black pepper
1 egg
1 pound chicken thigh or breast cutlets, sliced thin
4 ounces cheddar cheese, grated (about 1 cup)

1. In a large skillet, fry the bacon until crisp. Drain and crumble the bacon and reserve for garnish. Discard all but 3 tablespoons drippings in the skillet.

2. In a shallow dish, combine the bread crumbs, basil, oregano, marjoram, salt, and pepper. In another shallow dish, lightly beat the egg.

3. Dip the chicken first into the egg, then into the crumbs to coat. Heat the bacon drippings and sauté the chicken over medium-high heat for about 2 minutes on each side, until the chicken is golden brown and just cooked through. About 1 minute before the chicken is done, sprinkle with the cheese and cover the skillet to allow it to melt.

4. Serve the chicken garnished with the crumbled bacon.

YIELD: 4 SERVINGS.

Chicken "Hunter's Style"

This savory braised chicken, based on the traditional *cacciatore* (meaning "hunter's style") chicken stew from the Italian countryside, is flavored with garlic and mushrooms and simmered in a light sauce of wine and chopped plum tomatoes. We suggest using pieces of chicken breast meat with the skin left on because they cook quickly but stay moist and juicy.

Serve with a thin-strand pasta such as capellini, simply tossed with butter or olive oil and a little Romano cheese. Crusty Italian bread to sop up the sauce and a green salad will round out the meal beautifully. Some fruit and cookies are all you need for dessert.

1¼ to 1½ pounds boneless chicken breast meat with the skin still intact

⅓ cup all-purpose flour

½ teaspoon salt

¼ teaspoon freshly ground black pepper

3 tablespoons olive oil

1 onion, chopped

2 cloves garlic, minced

6 ounces fresh domestic or wild mushrooms, thinly sliced

½ cup white wine

1 1-pound can Italian plum tomatoes, coarsely chopped, and their juice

1 bay leaf, broken in half

½ teaspoon dried rosemary

¼ teaspoon dried marjoram

½ teaspoon grated lemon zest

3 tablespoons chopped Italian parsley

1. Cut the chicken into 3-inch pieces. Combine the flour, salt, and pepper in a paper or plastic bag; shake the chicken in the seasoned flour, shaking off the excess coating.

2. Heat the oil in a large nonreactive skillet and sauté the chicken over medium-high heat until lightly browned, about 2 minutes on each side. While the chicken is browning on its second side, add the onion, garlic, and mushrooms. Reduce heat to medium and cook, stirring frequently, for about 4 minutes. Add the wine and the chopped tomatoes, stirring to dissolve any browned bits on the bottom of the pan. Add the bay leaf, rosemary, and marjoram.

3. Cook the stew, uncovered, at a gentle simmer until the chicken is cooked through and the sauce is slightly thickened, about 7 to 8 minutes. Discard the bay leaf. Stir in the grated lemon zest and the parsley and season with additional salt and pepper to taste.

YIELD: 4 SERVINGS.

Country Chicken Stew and Scallion Dumplings

Chicken and dumplings can sometimes be an all-day undertaking, but this shortened version that starts with good canned chicken stock can be completed in under an hour. The savory green-flecked scallion dumpling dough thickens the broth slightly as the stew simmers, and the result is heavenly—yet absolutely simple. Serve a salad of escarole with balsamic vinegar and mustard dressing, and Mocha Pudding with Coffee Cream (see page 254) or Pumpkin Custard (see page 255) for dessert.

4 cups good-quality canned or homemade (see
   page 2) chicken stock
1 2½- to 3-pound chicken, cut into 8 pieces
6 carrots, peeled and sliced into 1-inch lengths
1 small onion, thinly sliced
1 rib celery, thinly sliced
1 bay leaf, broken in two pieces
1 teaspoon dried thyme
Freshly ground black pepper and salt to taste

SCALLION DUMPLINGS:

1⅓ cups all-purpose flour
1½ teaspoons double-acting baking powder
½ teaspoon salt
2 scallions, including most of the green tops,
   finely chopped
3 tablespoons chilled vegetable shortening
½ cup milk

1. To make the stew, combine the chicken stock and the chicken pieces in a large soup pot or Dutch oven and bring to a boil over high heat. Reduce heat and simmer, uncovered, for 10 minutes, skimming off any scum as it rises to the surface. Add the carrots, onion, celery, and bay leaf and simmer, partially covered, for 15 minutes.

2. Meanwhile, make the dumpling dough. Sift together the flour, baking powder, and salt into a mixing bowl. Stir in the minced scallions. Cut the shortening into about 5 pieces, add it to the flour, and work the mixture together with your fingertips until it resembles coarse meal. Make a well in the center, pour in the milk, and stir with a few strokes of a wooden spoon until the dough comes together. It should be sticky.

3. When the chicken has simmered for 15 minutes, spoon off most of the fat that has risen to the surface. (It is not necessary to remove it all.) Add the thyme to the stew and season with a generous amount of black pepper and salt to taste. (Since canned chicken stock can be salty, taste carefully.)

4. For each dumpling, first dip a spoon into the simmering liquid, measure out 1 generous tablespoon of dough, and then drop the irregularly shaped pieces of dough onto the top of the stew. You should be able to make about 12 dumplings. Cover

the pot and let the stew simmer and the dumplings steam over low heat for 20 minutes. Discard the bay leaf.

5. Serve in shallow soup bowls or on rimmed plates. Pull off and discard the chicken skin before serving if desired.

YIELD: 4 SERVINGS.

Rosemary Marinated Chicken and Grilled Lemon

Serve this simple and delicious broiled chicken with a selection of red, green, and yellow pepper strips brushed with olive oil and grilled. Thickly sliced French bread, lightly toasted over the coals, would be nice, too. Offer either Green Tomato Cobbler (see page 260) or Lemon-Blueberry Mousse (see page 259) for a lovely seasonal dessert.

½ teaspoon grated lemon zest
3 tablespoons lemon juice
½ cup olive oil
2 teaspoons Dijon mustard
1 tablespoon minced fresh rosemary or
   1 teaspoon dried rosemary

½ teaspoon salt
⅛ teaspoon coarsely ground or cracked black
   pepper
4 pounds chicken parts
2 lemons
Sprigs of fresh rosemary, if available

1. Prepare a charcoal fire on the grill or preheat a gas grill or your oven broiler.
2. Combine the lemon zest, lemon juice, olive oil, mustard, rosemary, salt, and pepper in a small bowl. Pour the marinade over the chicken and turn so that the pieces are evenly coated. Set aside for at least 20 minutes, or for up to 2 hours. Cut the lemons into thin, crosswise slices.
3. Grill the chicken over a moderately hot fire, basting once or twice with the mari-

nade. Cook the breast pieces for about 20 minutes, and the thigh and leg pieces for 25 to 30 minutes, or until the skin is a crisp, golden brown and the chicken meat is firm and no longer pink. Grill the lemon slices until they are softened and browned, about 1 to 2 minutes.
4. Remove the chicken to a platter and garnish with the lemon slices and with fresh rosemary sprigs if available.

YIELD: 6 SERVINGS.

Basque Chicken-and-Rice Casserole

The Basque provinces of Guipúzcoa, Álava, and Vizcaya occupy the northernmost tip of Spain, separated from France by the Pyrenees. The fiercely independent people who live in this rugged and beautiful area have a language, customs, and culture quite distinct from the rest of Spain. They are passionate about food, and many believe that Basque cuisine is among the most dynamic in the world. Flavors are invariably assertive, and Basque dishes make use of the native abundance from land and sea.

This dish is our interpretation of an American one served to us in a restaurant in Nevada, where several strong Basque communities flourish. The quality of the olives makes a big difference in the finished dish.

Wonderful accompaniments would be a crusty, round peasant loaf of bread and an arugula or other bitter green salad dressed with fine olive oil and balsamic vinegar. Either Pumpkin Custard (see page 255) or Hester's Citrus Pudding Cake (see page 242) would be a marvelous dessert.

1 2½- to 3-pound frying chicken, cut into 8 pieces
¼ teaspoon coarsely ground black pepper
⅛ teaspoon cayenne pepper
3 tablespoons olive oil
6 ounces smoked ham, cut ½ inch thick
1 medium onion, chopped
1 medium red or yellow bell pepper, chopped
1 large clove garlic, minced
1 cup raw long-grain white rice

½ cup white wine
1½ cups good-quality canned or homemade (see page 2) chicken stock
½ cup frozen green peas, thawed
¼ cup pitted and sliced excellent-quality black olives
2 tablespoons minced flat-leaf parsley
2 or 3 dashes Tabasco
Salt

1. Sprinkle the chicken with the black and cayenne peppers. Heat the oil in a large skillet and sauté the chicken over medium heat until golden brown on all sides, about 8 minutes. Remove the chicken from the skillet.

2. Add the ham, onion, and bell pepper to the skillet and cook, stirring, over me-

dium-low heat until the vegetables begin to soften and the ham begins to brown, about 3 to 5 minutes.

3. Add the garlic and rice and cook about 1 minute until the rice is coated with the oil and begins to look translucent. Stir in the wine and stock. Replace the chicken in the pan and bring the liquid to a boil. Cover the pan, lower the heat, and simmer until most of the liquid is absorbed, about 20 minutes.

4. Add the peas and olives to the skillet. Stir gently to distribute. Cover the pan and simmer until the peas are cooked, about 2 minutes. Stir in the parsley, Tabasco, and salt to taste. (No salt may be needed since ham and chicken stock can be quite salty.)

5. Serve directly from the skillet.

YIELD: 4 TO 6 SERVINGS.

Chicken-and-Leek Fricassee

According to Julia Child, a fricassee is a French dish that is halfway between a sauté and a stew. It usually refers to a skillet dish using chicken parts that are first sautéed gently in butter until golden, but not browned. Then an aromatic liquid is added to the skillet and the chicken finishes cooking at a simmer. This is a rather complicated definition for all manner of simple and wonderfully savory chicken dishes, from classic coq au vin to homey chicken cacciatore.

We particularly like fricassees since they take well to advance preparation and gentle reheating, which make them terrific party food. This especially delicate version derives its flavor from a good white wine, such as Riesling; leeks, which are among the gentlest of onions; mushrooms, which add a woodsy dimension; and cream, which softens all the edges of this dish, one of the most sublime fricassees we know.

Serve it with buttered green noodles and Mixed Fruit–Chocolate Pan Soufflé (see page 264) or Lemon-Blueberry Mousse (see page 259) for a lovely, light supper any season of the year.

Chicken-and-Leek Fricassee (cont.)

5 slender leeks
1 2½- to 3-pound frying chicken, cut into 8
 pieces
Salt and freshly ground black pepper to taste
4 tablespoons butter
1 cup good white wine such as Riesling

½ cup good-quality canned or homemade (see
 page 2) chicken stock
8 ounces mushrooms, sliced (about 3½ cups)
1 cup heavy cream
3 tablespoons minced parsley

1. Wash and trim the leeks. If the leeks are larger than ¾ inch in diameter, halve or quarter them lengthwise. Using the white and pale green parts, cut the leeks into 1½-inch lengths.

2. Sprinkle the chicken all over with salt and pepper. Heat the butter in a large skillet and sauté the chicken on all sides over medium–low heat until pale golden but not browned, about 5 minutes.

3. Remove the breast and wing portions and move the leg and thigh portions to one side of the skillet. Add the leeks and turn them to coat with the butter. Cover the skillet and let the leeks and chicken parts simmer over low heat for about 5 minutes.

4. Return the breast and wing portions to the skillet and add the wine and chicken stock. Bring to a boil, then lower the heat and cover the pan. Simmer gently for about 20 minutes until the chicken is cooked through and the leeks are tender. Using a slotted spoon, remove the chicken and most of the leeks from the skillet and

keep warm on a platter loosely covered with foil.

5. Turn the heat to high and boil the sauce, stirring constantly to dislodge browned bits clinging to the bottom of the skillet, for about 3 to 4 mintues or until the sauce is reduced to about 1 cup.

6. Add the mushrooms and cream and return to a boil. Lower the heat and simmer until the mushrooms are softened and the sauce has reduced and is slightly thickened, about 5 minutes.

7. Return the chicken and leeks to the skillet along with any juices accumulated on the platter. Simmer until the chicken and leeks are heated through, about 2 minutes. Taste the sauce and add salt and pepper as needed.

The dish may be made a day ahead up to this point. Let cool and then refrigerate. Reheat gently to serve.

8. Stir in the parsley. Serve directly from the skillet or place on a deep, wide-rimmed platter.

YIELD: 4 TO 6 SERVINGS.

Molasses-Mustard Chicken

Unlike most chicken barbecues, this recipe first marinates the chicken pieces so that the savory flavors permeate the meat itself. Then the marinade is used as a basting sauce. Heat and charring change the character of the molasses so that the finished chicken has a caramelized skin and a subtle, sweet-and-sour interior, a combination that is most pleasing. The effect is almost as good when broiled indoors, but the recommended hickory chips on a charcoal fire add yet another dimension. Use any chicken parts that you favor. Brooke particularly likes wings and can make a whole meal on these.

All sorts of summery foods go well with this dish. Of course, Corn Grilled in the Husk (see page 227), Classic Creamy Coleslaw (see page 223), or Old-Fashioned Picnic Potato Salad (see page 207) are naturals. But you might want to try Confetti Rice Salad (see page 211) or New New-Potato Salad (see page 213) along with Roasted Vegetables (see page 218, zucchini) for a contemporary twist. Either way, we want Red, White, and Blueberry Shortcakes (see page 232) for dessert.

½ cup molasses
¼ cup cider or wine vinegar
2 tablespoons coarse-grained mustard
2 tablespoons vegetable oil
1 tablespoon Worcestershire sauce

¼ teaspoon salt
⅛ teaspoon freshly ground black pepper
4 pounds chicken parts of your choice
Dampened hickory chips, if available

1. In a shallow dish just large enough to hold the chicken, combine the molasses, vinegar, mustard, oil, Worcestershire sauce, salt, and pepper. Add the chicken and turn to coat completely with the mixture. Cover and marinate at least 1 and up to 3 hours in the refrigerator, turning the chicken 2 or 3 times.
2. Build a medium-hot barbecue fire, adding the hickory chips (if using) as the coals turn gray.
3. Remove the chicken from the marinade and reserve the remaining marinade. Grill the chicken pieces, skin side down, for about 5 minutes. Brush with some of the reserved marinade, turn, and grill another 5 minutes. Continue to brush and turn the chicken until the skin is lightly charred and the interior juices run clear when the flesh is pierced with the point of a knife, about 15 to 20 minutes more. (Light meat will cook faster than dark meat.)
4. Serve the chicken while still warm, or let it cool for up to an hour and then serve at room temperature.

YIELD: 6 SERVINGS.

Tarragon Chicken Hash

Chicken hash can sometimes be a rather bland, featureless dish. The soft, creamy quality is indeed part of the appeal of chicken hash, but we like our food to have an interesting texture and taste, so we have livened up this dish with tarragon and some bright green peas. A flavorful cheese and bread crumb mixture sprinkled over the casserole gives it a nice, crusty topping as it bakes.

This hash is good accompanied by a radicchio salad with a mustardy vinaigrette and some warm rolls or Sky-High Popovers (see page 222). Fresh pineapple and cookies or Baked Amaretti Nectarines (see page 261) would be a fine dessert.

3 tablespoons butter
½ cup chopped onion
¾ cup thinly sliced celery
1 pound boneless chicken breast meat
1 tablespoon all-purpose flour
½ teaspoon salt or to taste
⅛ teaspoon black or white pepper
1 cup heavy cream

1 tablespoon dry sherry
1 cup frozen peas
2 teaspoons chopped fresh tarragon or
   ¾ teaspoon dried tarragon
¼ teaspoon Tabasco
1 slice firm white bread for crumbs
3 tablespoons grated Parmesan cheese

1. Melt the butter in a large skillet. Add the onion and celery and sauté over medium heat until softened and very lightly browned, about 4 minutes.

2. Mince the chicken in a food processor or chop it by hand into ¼- to ½-inch pieces. (It is easier to do this if the chicken is slightly frozen first.) Add the chicken to the skillet, sprinkle it with the flour, salt, and pepper, and cook, stirring for 2 minutes. Pour in the cream and simmer, stirring frequently, until the sauce is smooth and thickened, about 3 minutes. Stir in the sherry. Remove from the heat and add the peas, tarragon, and Tabasco. Taste the sauce and add more salt and pepper if nec-

essary. Transfer the hash to a lightly buttered 1½-quart baking dish.

3. To make the Parmesan crumbs, tear the slice of bread into pieces and pulse it in a food processor with the Parmesan. Sprinkle the mixture evenly over the top of the hash in the baking dish.

The recipe may be made ahead up to this point and held, covered, in the refrigerator, for 1 day. Bring to room temperature before baking.

4. Preheat the oven to 375 degrees. Bake, uncovered, until the hash is bubbly around the edges and the top is golden brown, about 20 to 30 minutes.

YIELD: 4 SERVINGS.

Turkey Cutlets "à la King"

We invented this because we love to cook with the newly available turkey breast cutlets or paillards, and we thought they'd be good sautéed and topped with an updated "à la king"–style sauce that makes use of the pan drippings. They are, in fact, *very* good this way! Serve on toasted and buttered Italian bread with a beet or grated carrot salad, and Peanut Butter–Chocolate Chip Brownies (see page 263) for dessert.

1 pound thinly sliced turkey breast meat
    (oftened packaged as "cutlets")
½ teaspoon salt
⅛ teaspoon freshly ground black pepper
2 tablespoons vegetable oil
2 tablespoons butter or more if necessary
2 tablespoons chopped shallots
1 tablespoon all-purpose flour
1 cup milk

¼ cup white wine
½ teaspoon dried tarragon
3 ounces snow peas, trimmed and sliced into
    2 or 3 diagonal pieces
1 small red pepper, seeded and sliced very thin
Additional salt to taste
Freshly ground white pepper to taste
4 slices Italian bread, cut about ½ inch thick,
    toasted and buttered

1. Dry the turkey cutlets on paper towels and sprinkle with the salt and pepper.
2. You will need to sauté the meat in two batches. Heat 1 tablespoon each of the oil and butter in a large skillet. Sauté the turkey over high heat until golden brown, about 1 minute on each side. Remove with tongs to a warm plate, add the remaining tablespoon of oil and butter to the skillet, and sauté the second batch of meat. Remove it to the plate, cover loosely with foil, and keep warm in a low oven.
3. There should be about 1 tablespoon of butter in the skillet. If not, add more to make up the difference. If there is more than 1 tablespoon, pour some off. Add the shallots and cook for 1 minute, stirring. Sprinkle on the flour, and cook, stirring, for 1 minute. Gradually whisk in the milk and the wine and cook until smooth and thickened, about 2 minutes. Add the tarragon. Stir in the snow peas and the red pepper strips and simmer for 2 minutes. If any juices have accumulated on the turkey plate, add them to the sauce, and season with salt and white pepper to taste.
4. Place the turkey cutlets on the toasted Italian bread and spoon the sauce over the meat.

YIELD: 4 SERVINGS.

Fabulous Fried Chicken

The simple goodness of old-fashioned, homemade fried chicken is another one of those tastes that has been all but lost since the proliferation of fast-food fried chicken franchises.

We're here to campaign for its comeback in a starring role at informal feasts. Heaped high on a platter, center stage on a groaning board surrounded by a cast of supporting players such as deviled eggs, Old-Fashioned Picnic Potato Salad (see page 207), The Absolute Best Buttermilk Biscuits (see page 220), sliced tomatoes, pickled beets, and Spiced and Pickled Watermelon Rind (see page 226), it should receive a standing ovation. After the curtain call, lay out a spread of mile-high Angel Food Cake with Summer Fruit Ambrosia (see page 238).

The rules for creating perfect fried chicken are few and simple—but very strict. The chicken pieces should be soaked a minimum of 2 hours in buttermilk or clabbered milk (overnight is best) for the tenderest, most flavorful chicken you've ever tasted. The flour must be seasoned with *plenty* of salt and black pepper—enough so you can really taste it —and the coating needs just that little bit of cornmeal for a pleasant, crunchy texture. And the frying oil must be hot. That's all—except for the final cardinal rule: *never* refrigerate fried chicken. The crust absorbs every bit of humidity in the refrigerator and becomes miserably and irretrievably soggy. The chicken can be held at room temperature for up to about 2 hours, and an attempt can be made to recrisp it in a hot oven, but it's really best if it can be eaten within an hour or so of its being fried.

Just one more thing: never eat fried chicken with a knife and fork!

1 2½- to 3-pound frying chicken, cut into 8
    parts
2 cups buttermilk or clabbered milk (see note)
⅛ teaspoon Tabasco
Vegetable oil for frying

¾ cup all-purpose flour
¼ cup cornmeal (yellow or white)
1 teaspoon salt
¾ teaspoon freshly ground black pepper

1. Place the chicken pieces in a large bowl and pour the buttermilk or clabbered milk and the Tabasco over the chicken. Turn the pieces so they are evenly coated with milk. Cover the bowl and let the chicken soak in the refrigerator for at least 2 hours but no longer than overnight. Turn the pieces once or twice.

2. When ready to cook the chicken, pour off and discard the soaking milk. Heat about ½ inch of vegetable oil in 2 large frying pans (preferably cast-iron skillets) set over medium-high heat. Combine the flour, cornmeal, salt, and pepper in a paper or plastic bag and shake the damp chicken pieces in the seasoned flour. Shake off as much excess flour as possible so that the coating won't be too thick. When the oil is hot, arrange the chicken pieces in a single layer in the skillets and fry, uncovered, until they are a crusty, deep golden brown, and the meat is no longer pink near the bone when checked with the point of a sharp knife. Regulate the heat so that the chicken does not burn. Cook the breast and wing pieces about 18 minutes; the thighs and drumsticks about 22 minutes. Remove the chicken with tongs and drain on crumpled paper towels.

3. Serve hot, warm, or at room temperature. If the chicken has sat for more than about 2 hours at room temperature and has gotten soggy, it may be somewhat re-crisped in a 400-degree oven. Arrange in a single layer on a baking sheet and heat, uncovered, for 10 minutes.

YIELD: 4 SERVINGS.

NOTE: If buttermilk is unavailable, make clabbered milk by adding 2 teaspoons of lemon juice to 2 cups of whole milk. Let stand at room temperature for about 15 minutes.

Upper-Crust Chicken Potpie

When a couple of large food companies promoted chicken and beef potpies as a major part of their line of frozen-food products in the 1950s, homemade savory meat pies practically became extinct. People were just so enamored of the fact that you could simply pop them into the oven that in the beginning they chose to overlook the fact that they didn't taste half as good as mom's. By the time it finally began to dawn on some people that there is really nothing quite as good as a completely homemade chicken pie, a generation or two of cooks had been raised with absolutely no inkling of how to make the real thing.

It's time to remedy that. With this recipe we have tried hard to streamline the method by using boneless thighs and by cooking the meat and all the vegetables in the same pan in which you make the sauce, but do be aware that making a pie like this is never going to be super quick. However, the dish can be almost completely assembled ahead of time, and we can virtually guarantee ecstatic eaters—whatever their generation!

All this meal really needs is a salad of greens and sliced tomatoes with a red wine vinaigrette and maybe some crumbled bacon scattered over the top. For dessert, try Cranberry-Cointreau Sundaes (see page 269), Baked Ginger–Bay Leaf Apples (see page 262), or Pumpkin Custard (see page 255).

OLD-FASHIONED PASTRY:

1½ cups all-purpose flour

1 teaspoon salt

6 tablespoons lard or vegetable shortening, chilled

2 tablespoons butter, chilled

3 to 4 tablespoons ice water

1½ pounds boneless and skinless chicken thighs

8 ounces shiitake or other fresh wild mushrooms

4 tablespoons butter

2 tablespooons vegetable oil

1 onion, chopped

2 carrots, peeled and thinly sliced

Salt and freshly ground black pepper to taste

1 cup frozen peas, thawed

3 tablespoons all-purpose flour

1¾ cups good-quality canned or homemade (see page 2) chicken stock

½ cup heavy cream

2 tablespoons sliced scallions, including green tops

3 tablespoons minced parsley

1½ tablespoons minced fresh tarragon or 1½ teaspoons dried tarragon

1 egg yolk beaten with 2 teaspoons of water for glaze

1. To make the pastry, combine the flour and salt in a large bowl. Cut the lard or shortening into 8 pieces and butter into 4 pieces. Add them to the flour and toss with a fork or your fingertips to coat with flour. Work together with your fingertips until

most of the mixture is the texture of coarse meal, with some pieces of shortening the size of peas remaining. Sprinkle 3 tablespoons of the ice water over the flour mixture and stir with a fork or work with your fingers to form a dough. Gather the dough into a ball. If flour remains in the bottom of the bowl, moisten it with the remaining tablespoon of water. Shape dough into a flattened disk, wrap with plastic wrap, and refrigerate for at least 30 minutes or for up to 2 days. Dough will yield enough for a top crust for one pie.

2. Cut the chicken meat into 1-inch chunks and set aside.

3. Wipe the mushrooms carefully with a damp paper towel to remove all grit, and thinly slice them. If you are using shiitake mushrooms and their caps are very large, cut the slices in half to make pieces not more than 1½ inches long.

4. Heat 1 tablespoon each of the butter and oil in a large skillet. Add the mushrooms and sauté over medium high heat, stirring frequently, until lightly browned and tender and most of the liquid has evaporated, about 4 to 5 minutes. Remove with a slotted spoon to a large bowl.

5. Add another tablespoon of butter and the remaining tablespoon of oil to the same skillet. Add the onion and carrots, sprinkle lightly with salt and pepper, and cook over medium heat, stirring occasionally, for 10 minutes, or until softened. Remove with a slotted spoon to the bowl with the mushrooms, leaving behind as much of the butter and oil as possible. Add the peas to the bowl with the vegetables.

6. Raise the heat to medium-high. Add the remaining 2 tablespoons butter to the pan. Sprinkle the chicken pieces lightly with salt and pepper and sauté until nicely browned and almost cooked through, about 10 minutes. Remove to the bowl with the vegetables.

7. There should be about 2 tablespoons of fat remaining in the skillet. If not, add additional butter to make up the difference. Sprinkle the flour over the pan drippings, and stir over medium-high heat with a wooden spoon for 2 minutes. Gradually whisk in the chicken stock and cream, and continue to cook over medium heat until the sauce is smooth and quite thick, about 3 minutes. Be sure that all the flavorful browned bits have been stirred up from the bottom of the pan.

8. Combine the sauce with the chicken and vegetables and stir in the scallions, parsley, and tarragon. Season with salt and pepper to taste.

9. Pour the chicken mixture into a 2-quart baking dish. (The dish can measure 9 by 9 by 2 inches or 7 by 11 by 2 inches.)

The recipe may be made up to one day ahead up to this point.

10. Preheat the oven to 425 degrees.

11. Roll out the pastry on a lightly floured board to about ⅛-inch thickness, rolling to the approximate shape of the baking dish. Fit the crust on top of the pie and trim the edges so they extend only about ½ inch over the edges of the baking dish. Fold the edges of the crust under and pinch to crimp. The edge of the crust should be sitting on the rim of the dish. Make a deco-

Upper-Crust Chicken Potpie (cont.)

rative cut-out of a chicken with the pastry scraps if desired, and place on top of the pie. Cut several slashes in the top to allow steam to escape and paint the entire crust with the egg glaze.

The pie may be made ahead up to this point and held in the refrigerator for up to 3 hours, loosely covered with plastic wrap.

12. Place the pie in the preheated oven. Immediately reduce the heat to 375 degrees and bake until the crust is a rich, golden brown and the filling is bubbly, about 40 to 50 minutes. Serve hot.

YIELD: 6 SERVINGS.

Shepherd's Pie Carol Adrienne

This recipe is in honor of Brooke's dear friend who has the rare culinary ability to make everything she cooks taste very special. Shepherd's pie is one such example. Although traditionally made with lamb, our turkey version is "day after" Thanksgiving tradition at Brooke's house. She has also been known to cook up a roast turkey dinner any old time just so she will have the appropriate leftovers.

So that this savory dish is not seasonally limited at your house, you might want to roast a small unstuffed chicken following the method in The Perfect Roast Chicken (and Stuffing) (see page 114) recipe. It's a fairly effortless, make-ahead way to obtain the ingredients for the pie. Don't forget to make the gravy, though, since it is an integral part of the dish. If you happen to have any leftover creamed onions, use 1½ cups of them in place of the pearl onions, the cream, and the 1½ tablespoons flour called for in the recipe. Obviously, we are fans of Real Mashed Potatoes (see page 212) for the topping, but we are not opposed to substituting peas or asparagus for the cooked broccoli.

Though the dish seems like a bit of work, the actual assembly takes only a few minutes and can be done hours ahead of baking. In addition, it is almost a meal in itself with only a salad of light lettuces dressed with a fruity vinaigrette needed to round it out. Either Pumpkin Custard (see page 255) or Candied Gingerbread with Vanilla Cream (see page 256) is a nice dessert, but so is leftover mincemeat or pumpkin pie if the time is right.

4 cups cooked white and dark meat of turkey, cut in bite-size pieces

1½ tablespoons all-purpose flour

1 cup broccoli florets, blanched for 2 to 3 minutes

½ cup sliced carrots, blanched for 2 to 3 minutes

1½ cups pearl onions, cooked or frozen pearl onions, thawed

1¼ cups turkey gravy (see note)

¾ cup heavy cream

6 tablespoons white wine

¾ teaspoon dried sage

¾ teaspoon dried thyme

¾ teaspoon dried marjoram

Salt and freshly ground black pepper to taste

4 cups mashed potatoes

3 tablespoons melted butter

3 tablespoons grated Parmesan cheese

1. Preheat the oven to 400 degrees.

2. In a large mixing bowl, toss the turkey with the flour. Add the broccoli, carrots, onions, gravy, cream, wine, sage, thyme, and marjoram. Add salt and pepper to taste.

3. Spoon the mixture into a shallow 2- to 2½-quart casserole. Carefully spread the mashed potatoes over the top. Drizzle with the butter and sprinkle with the cheese.

The recipe may be prepared several hours ahead up to this point. Refrigerate, but set out at room temperature for at least 30 minutes before baking.

4. Bake until the casserole is hot and bubbly and the potatoes are flecked with a golden brown, about 25 to 30 minutes. (If the top of the casserole has not browned sufficiently, run it briefly under the broiler before serving.)

YIELD: 6 SERVINGS.

NOTE: If you don't have any gravy, you can make a reasonable facsimile by melting 1 tablespoon butter, stirring in 1 tablespoon all-purpose flour, and cooking about 2 minutes. Then stir or whisk in 1¼ cups good-quality canned or homemade (see page 2) chicken stock, bring to a boil, and simmer, stirring, for about 3 minutes.

The Perfect Roast Chicken (and Stuffing)

The standard by which many great chefs judge each other is the quality of their roast chicken. Classic sauces and fragile desserts require much skill and creativity, to be sure, but a simple roast chicken takes attention and a gut feeling for the food itself.

Purists roast chickens unstuffed, but neither of our families believes that an unstuffed chicken is a complete meal. All manner of elaborate stuffings are just right for the Thanksgiving turkey extravaganza, but a Sunday roaster, at least to our minds, should have a simple, herbal bread stuffing. Brooke, like many native Yankees, has always flavored her bread stuffings with Bell's seasoning, a wonderful product made since 1867 by the William G. Bell Company in East Weymouth, Massachusetts. We have tried to capture the flavor, but if you can find it use 2 teaspoons of Bell's in place of the dried herbs in our recipe. No matter how we season it, we agree that we want our stuffing "sliceable" when cold and thus perfect for use in Our Favorite Turkey Sandwich (see page 55), which is, incidentally, just as good made with chicken. This texture comes from a buttery beginning and also from being "packed" into the bird for cooking, a method we realize is at odds with a majority of recipes that say to "lightly spoon in the stuffing." The stuffing can be made early in the day, but the bird should not be stuffed until shortly before roasting.

We like our gravy simple, too: slightly thickened and flavored only with giblet stock and pan drippings. You can sauté the liver, chop it fine, and add it to either the gravy or the stuffing, but we prefer the latter, where its tasty presence is undetected by finicky children.

A roast chicken dinner is not a place for innovative, outrageous side dishes. Serve it traditionally with Real Mashed Potatoes (see page 212) and an unadorned green vegetable. Many desserts would fit, but Cranberry-Cointreau Sundaes (see page 269) or Double Crust Apple-Quince Pie (see page 248) would be our choice.

STUFFING:

6 tablespoons unsalted butter

1 large onion, chopped (about 1 cup)

1 large rib celery with leaves, chopped (about ¾ cup)

1 chicken liver, chopped finely

⅓ cup minced parsley

1 teaspoon dried thyme

1 teaspoon dried sage

1 teaspoon salt

¼ teaspoon freshly ground black pepper

¼ teaspoon dried oregano

¼ teaspoon dried marjoram

Pinch of ground ginger

About 8 slices day-old, firm white bread, cut into ½-inch cubes (5 cups)

2 or 3 tablespoons water or good-quality canned or homemade (see page 2) chicken stock

CHICKEN:

1 5- to 6-pound roasting chicken
Salt and freshly ground black pepper to taste
Stuffing
2 tablespoons unsalted butter, softened

GRAVY:

Chicken neck and gizzard
1 bay leaf, broken
4 whole peppercorns
2 tablespoons all-purpose flour
Salt and freshly ground black pepper to taste

1. To make the stuffing, heat the butter in a large skillet and sauté the onion and celery over medium-low heat until softened, about 5 minutes. If desired, add the liver and sauté, stirring, until it loses its red color, about 1 to 2 minutes. Stir in the parsley, thyme, sage, salt, pepper, oregano, marjoram, and ginger. Stir in the bread cubes and then enough of the water or chicken stock to lightly moisten them.

2. Preheat the oven to 425 degrees.

3. Pull off any excess fat from the chicken and set the neck and gizzard aside to use in making the gravy. (We discard the heart since it is bitter.) Use the liver in the stuffing, if desired. Rinse the chicken inside and out and pat dry. Sprinkle the neck and body cavities with salt and pepper and pack both cavities with the stuffing. (You should be able to get most of the stuffing into the bird, but any extra can be roasted in a covered dish along with the chicken for about 30 minutes.)

4. Tuck the neck skin flap under and skewer it if necessary to hold it closed. Place the chicken on a rack in a shallow roasting pan that is just large enough to comfortably hold the bird (too large a pan will allow the good pan juices to simmer away and too deep a pan will steam the chicken). Use kitchen string to tie the legs together. Rub the chicken all over with the softened butter and sprinkle the skin with salt and pepper. Roast in the lower part of the oven for 25 minutes, then lower the temperature to 350 degrees and roast the chicken until the thigh temperature registers 185 degrees, about 1 to 1½ hours more. Baste the chicken with the pan juices 2 or 3 times while it roasts.

5. While the chicken is roasting, begin to make the gravy. Place the neck, gizzard, bay leaf, and peppercorns in a saucepan and add 3 cups water. Bring to a boil, then lower the heat and simmer, partially covered, for 30 minutes. Strain and reserve the liquid, which should measure about 2 cups. If there is not enough, add water to make up the difference.

6. When the chicken reaches the proper temperature, remove it from the roasting rack to a warm platter, cover it loosely with foil, and allow it to rest for 10 minutes. Scrape any browned bits from the roasting rack back into the pan.

7. Pour all the pan drippings into a glass measuring cup. Leave the good browned bits and crusty morsels of stuffing in the pan. Let the drippings stand a few minutes to allow the fat to rise to the top. Spoon off 2 tablespoons of the fat and return it to the roasting pan. Spoon off and discard the

The Perfect Roast Chicken (and Stuffing) (cont.)

remaining fat from the pan juices in the measuring cup. Set the roasting pan over direct heat and stir in the flour. Cook, stirring, for about 2 minutes over medium heat until the flour just begins to color. Stir or whisk in the reserved giblet liquid and the pan juices and bring to a boil. Lower the heat and simmer about 3 minutes. Season to taste with salt and pepper.

8. Remove the stuffing from the chicken and place in a warm bowl. Carve the chicken and arrange on a warm platter. Pass the gravy separately.

YIELD: 4 TO 6 SERVINGS.

Basil-and-Chive Broiled Game Hens

This light, delicate dish is perfect for late spring or early summer when both fresh basil and chives are at their peak. The hens are easily prepared, delightful to the eye, and most pleasing to the palate.

The same cooking treatment can be applied to all manner of small game hens such as quail, guinea hen, or squab. Adjust the broiling time to suit the size of the bird. Although we especially favor this herb combination, you might try other fresh herbs such as tarragon or thyme. Sage is an excellent option for a cool-weather supper. In a pinch, dried herbs (use about 1 tablespoon) can be substituted.

Serve the hens with Special Rice (see page 216) and a seasonal buttered vegetable such as asparagus. Lemon-Blueberry Mousse (see page 259) would be a delightful ending.

2 1- to 1¼-pound Cornish game hens, split in
    half (ask the butcher to do this for you)
⅓ cup loosely packed fresh basil leaves
2 tablespoons snipped fresh chives plus 6 slim,
    whole chives for garnish

4 tablespoons softened butter
Salt and freshly ground black pepper to taste
⅓ cup white wine

1. Preheat the broiler. Use the palm of your hand to flatten the hens to as even a thickness as possible.
2. Reserve 4 attractive basil leaves for garnish. Finely sliver the remaining basil.

Blend the slivered basil with the snipped chives and butter.
3. Use your finger to loosen the skin from the breast meat portion of the hens. Place about 2 teaspoons herb butter under the

skin of each breast half. Season all sides of the birds with salt and pepper.

4. Place the hens, skin side up, on a rack and set on a broiler pan. Dot with the remaining butter. Broil 6 to 7 inches from the heat source for 7 to 10 minutes, turn, and brush with some of the drippings in the bottom of the broiling pan. Broil about 8 minutes, turn, and brush again. Continue to broil the hens until the juices run clear when the thighs are pierced with a knife tip and the skin is richly browned, about 2 minutes more.

5. Remove the hens to a warm platter. Place the broiler pan over direct heat. Add the wine and cook, stirring up browned bits, over medium heat until the sauce is slightly reduced, about 2 minutes.

6. To serve, spoon the pan juices over the hen halves and garnish each with a basil leaf and a length of chive.

YIELD: 4 SERVINGS.

Skewered Far Eastern Chicken

This delicious marinade for grilled chicken borrows elements both from the Indonesian-style peanut sauce and from the Indian method of using flavored yogurt as a tenderizer. We've used both chunky peanut butter and plain yogurt, plus some exotic sweet and spicy flavorings such as curry powder, sesame oil, and fresh ginger. The thick marinade forms a beautiful brown crust as it cooks, sealing in the meat juices. The skewers of charred chicken are then rolled in minced green scallions before serving for a texture and color contrast.

Boneless chicken thigh meat is called for here since it is a little juicier than breast meat and takes well to marinating and grilling. This kabob has no vegetables on the skewer. When grilling bite-size pieces of boneless and skinless chicken, we prefer to thread the meat onto the skewers so that it's quite closely packed, thus giving it less opportunity to dry out as it broils.

This skewered chicken is splendid cooked indoors under the broiler, as well as grilled. Offer Confetti Rice Salad (see page 211), grilled pita bread, and sliced cucumbers sprinkled with dill as accompaniments. Baked Amaretti Nectarines (see page 261) or fresh fruit and Giant Anise Sugar Cookies (see page 267) make a sweet ending.

Skewered Far Eastern Chicken (cont.)

1½ pounds boneless, skinless chicken thighs
½ cup plain yogurt
¼ cup chunky peanut butter
2 tablespoons sesame oil
1 tablespoon lemon juice
4 teaspoons soy sauce

1½ teaspoons minced fresh ginger
1 clove garlic, minced
¼ teaspoon curry powder
¼ teaspoon dried red pepper flakes
½ cup minced scallions, including green tops

1. Cut the chicken into 1½- to 2-inch pieces and set aside.
2. To make the marinade, whisk together in a mixing bowl the yogurt, peanut butter, sesame oil, lemon juice, soy sauce, ginger, garlic, curry powder, and dried red pepper flakes. Add the chicken pieces to the bowl and toss to coat evenly. Cover and set aside to marinate for 30 minutes at room temperature or for as long as 2 hours in the refrigerator.
3. Build a medium-hot barbecue fire or preheat the broiler.

4. Thread the chicken pieces onto six metal or bamboo skewers (see note). The chicken should still be coated with the marinade. Grill or broil 5 inches from the heat source for 7 to 10 minutes, turning the skewers 2 or 3 times, until all sides are golden brown and the meat is firm to the touch.
5. Place the minced scallions on a plate and roll the skewered meat in the scallions until coated on both sides. Arrange on a platter and serve.

YIELD: 6 SERVINGS.

NOTE: If you use bamboo skewers, soak them in cold water for 30 minutes before using them. This treatment will make them less likely to burn.

Hotter-Than-Hell Barbecued Chicken

Traditional American barbecue sauces are tomato-based. If we can judge from the dozens of bottled brands that line supermarket shelves all over the country, they are also well loved. We, too, are fans of these zingy sauces. They especially complement the assertive flavor of good-quality pork in such dishes as our Barbecued Ribs with Red Hot Mama Sauce (see page 150) or Barbecued Pork and Coleslaw Sandwich (see page 66). But for chicken, we have never thought them to be quite right: the sweet heaviness of a tomato sauce seems to mask instead of enhance the look and the more elusive natural flavor of chicken.

But we do like our barbecued chicken to be hot. This outrageously simple olive oil and lemon juice sauce is clear so that the finished chicken is nicely charred but not camouflaged. The liberal dousings of Tabasco and red pepper flakes are barely apparent to the eye but readily discernable to the palate. This type of sauce doesn't burn or scorch as do the sweetened tomato varieties and thus it takes particularly well to indoor broiling. The chicken is terrific hot off the grill. It is also good at room temperature, although its peppery "heat" tends to cool with the temperature.

Serve this uncomplicated dish with Classic Creamy Coleslaw (see page 223) or Old-Fashioned Picnic Potato Salad (see page 207) as soothing foils. If you like, add Corn Grilled in the Husk (see page 227) and The Absolute Best Buttermilk Biscuits (see page 220) for a real summery feast, and finish with Angel Food Cake with Summer Fruit Ambrosia (see page 238).

6 tablespoons olive oil
4½ tablespoons lemon juice
1 tablespoon Tabasco
1 clove garlic, minced
¾ teaspoon dried oregano

¾ teaspoon salt
½ teaspoon dried red pepper flakes
⅛ teaspoon cayenne pepper
4 pounds chicken parts of your choice

1. Build a medium-hot barbecue fire.
2. In a small saucepan, simmer the olive oil, lemon juice, Tabasco, garlic, oregano, salt, red pepper flakes, and cayenne pepper over low heat for about 5 minutes.

The sauce can be made a few hours ahead and kept at room temperature.

3. Grill the chicken, skin side down, for 5 minutes to sear. Brush with the sauce and turn. Grill for a total of 20 to 25 minutes more (the breast and wing meat will be done in less time than the thigh and leg meat), turning and brushing often with the sauce. If there is any sauce left after the chicken is done, brush it over the skin.

4. Serve hot or at room temperature.

Yield: 6 servings.

Cider-Braised Duck with Turnips and Apples

This method of braising a cut-up bird is very succulent. All the pieces are first browned, and then the breast meat is removed. The legs and thighs simmer in aromatic cider and red wine until they are tender. The breast pieces then finish cooking for the last few minutes with the apples and turnips, so that all of the flavors have a chance to mingle. Like most braised dishes, this is a perfect do-ahead meal for a party.

Serve a salad of watercress and endive dressing with a balsamic vinaigrette with this meal, along with hot French rolls and sweet butter. Cranberry Bread Pudding with Whiskey Sauce (see page 252) or Pumpkin Custard (see page 255) would make a grand dessert.

1 4½- to 5-pound duck, cut in pieces (see
    instructions below)
⅓ cup all-purpose flour
¾ teaspoon salt
¼ teaspoon freshly ground black pepper
1 tablespoon vegetable oil
1 large onion, chopped
1 carrot, peeled and chopped coarsely
1 rib celery, sliced thin
3 cloves garlic, chopped
1 teaspoon dried thyme

1 bay leaf, broken in half
1½ cups fresh apple cider
½ cup red wine
2 tablespoons butter
1 large turnip (8 to 10 ounces), peeled, cut in
    quarters, and sliced thin
1 large green apple (such as Granny Smith),
    cored and sliced
Additional salt and freshly ground black
    pepper to taste
2 to 3 tablespoons red wine vinegar

1. Ask the butcher to use his saw to cut the duck into 8 pieces: 4 pieces of breast, 2 thighs, and 2 drumsticks. Discard the wings since there is very little meat on them, or use them and the backs to make a simple duck stock. Leave the skin on the meat to protect it from drying out, but pull off as much fat as possible and trim off any excess flaps of skin.

2. Combine the flour, salt, and pepper in a

paper or plastic bag. Shake the duck pieces in the flour to coat, shaking off the excess.

3. Heat the oil in a large skillet. Cook the duck pieces over medium-high heat until crusty and golden brown on all sides, about 10 minutes. The duck breast pieces should be firm but the meat should still be slightly pink. Remove the meat to a plate with tongs and pour off all but 1 tablespoon of the fat from the skillet. Add the onion, carrot, and celery to the skillet and cook over medium heat until softened and lightly browned, about 5 minutes. Add the garlic, thyme, and bay leaf and cook for 1 minute. Stir in the cider and the wine and return the thighs and drumsticks to the skillet. Loosely cover the breast pieces on the plate and reserve. Bring the liquid to a simmer, cover the skillet, and cook over low heat until the duck is just tender, about 1 to 1¼ hours. Remove the meat from the skillet and spoon off as much fat from the surface of the sauce as possible. Return all the duck meat, including the breast pieces and any accumulated juices, to the skillet.

The recipe may be made ahead up to this point and kept refrigerated for 2 days, or frozen.

4. Meanwhile, melt the butter in another large skillet. Add the turnip and apple slices, sprinkle lightly with salt and pepper, and cook over medium heat for 10 minutes, stirring often, until slightly glazed and almost tender.

5. Add the turnips and apples to the skillet with the duck and stir in 2 tablespoons of the vinegar. Simmer, partially covered, until all the meat and vegetables are tender, about 15 minutes. Discard the bay leaf. Taste the sauce and add additional vinegar if you think it should be more tart. (This will depend on the sweetness of the cider you used.) Season with salt and pepper to taste and serve.

YIELD: 4 SERVINGS.

MEATS

Some hae meat, and canna eat,
   And some wad eat that want it;
But we hae meat, and we can eat,
   And sae the Lord be thankit.

—ROBERT BURNS
The Selkirk Grace

"You look a little shy; let me introduce you to that
leg of mutton," said the Red Queen. "Alice——
Mutton: Mutton——Alice." The leg of mutton got
up in the dish and made a little bow to Alice; and she
returned the bow, not knowing whether to be
frightened or amused.

—LEWIS CARROLL
Through the Looking Glass (1872)

Peppered Beef and Red Wine Vinegar Sauce

This recipe is for those occasions when we want to feel pampered. Tender fillet of beef remains, in our minds, a very special treat. This is a classic preparation, simple and absolutely delicious. It is also quick, taking less than 30 minutes from start to finish. Although it is wonderful served with the traditional accompaniments of baked potatoes and a steamed vegetable, we like to dress it up with Scalloped Potatoes Our Way (see page 209) and Roasted Vegetables (see page 218) if we have some extra time. Hot Brownies with Brandy–Ice Cream Sauce (see page 265) is a speedy and elegant dessert, but if you have some Pear Strudel (see page 250) in the freezer, it would be equally appealing.

1 teaspoon coarsely crushed black peppercorns
1 teaspoon coarsely crushed white peppercorns
¼ teaspoon salt
4 filet mignons (4 to 5 ounces each)
5 tablespoons butter

1 tablespoon vegetable oil
1 tablespoon minced shallots
1 tablespoon red wine vinegar
½ cup hearty red wine
Salt to taste

1. Combine the black and white peppercorns and the ¼ teaspoon salt in a small dish. For each filet mignon, press a total of about ½ teaspoon of the mixture evenly into both sides of the meat.

2. Heat 1 tablespoon of the butter with the oil in a skillet large enough to sauté the meat in one layer. Cook the meat over medium-high heat for 3 to 5 minutes on each side depending upon the desired degree of doneness. (Three minutes on each side will result in rare meat; 5 minutes on each side will result in medium meat.) Remove the meat from the pan and keep warm.

3. Pour off the excess drippings and add the shallots to the skillet. Sautée over medium-low heat until softened, about 1 minute. Add the vinegar and wine and cook over medium-high heat, stirring up browned bits with a wooden spoon, until the mixture is reduced to about 2 tablespoons, about 3 minutes.

4. Take the pan off the heat and whisk in the remaining 4 tablespoons butter, about ½ tablespoon at a time, adding each piece of butter just before the preceding piece is completely incorporated. In this way, a thickened emulsion will form. If the pan becomes too cool during the process, place it over very low heat, but do not allow the butter to melt on contact. Taste the finished sauce and add salt as desired. Stir any juices accumulated from the meat into the sauce.

5. Serve the beef with the sauce spooned over it.

YIELD: 4 SERVINGS.

Ginger Beef

With the ever-growing American interest in oriental cooking, creative cooks have taken to using some Western ingredients and techniques in conjunction with those of China, Thailand, Vietnam, and Japan. This is one of those East-West dishes: the predominance of fresh ginger is oriental and the skillet sauté is occidental. Chili paste is available in many supermarkets and most Chinese grocery stores. Try to find very fresh, firm garlic and ginger since their flavor will be much clearer. The orange juice and zest mellow the sharp ginger, giving this dish a wonderful contrast in flavors.

Serve it over plain white rice and add a side dish of steamed tiny carrots for color. An ideal dessert for this light and quickly prepared supper would be all-American Tin Roof Sundaes (see page 270) or vanilla ice cream and Luscious Pecan Pie Bars (see page 266).

1 pound boneless beef sirloin steak, partially frozen
¼ cup dry sherry
2 tablespoons soy sauce
2 tablespoons orange juice
¼ teaspoon chili paste or dried red pepper flakes

1 large clove garlic, minced
1 2- or 3-inch piece of fresh ginger
2 tablespoons vegetable oil
5 scallions, thinly sliced, including most of the green part
2 teaspoons grated orange zest
2 cups cooked white rice

1. Thinly slice the meat across the grain.
2. In a shallow dish large enough to accommodate the meat, stir together the sherry, soy sauce, orange juice, chili paste, and garlic. Add the meat and stir to combine. Let the meat marinate for 20 minutes.
3. Meanwhile, peel and slice the ginger paper-thin. You should have about ¼ cup.
4. Heat the oil in a large skillet. Drain the meat, reserving the marinade. Sauté the meat over high heat, stirring constantly, for 1 minute. Add the ginger and sauté until the ginger is softened and meat is barely rare, about 2 minutes. Add the scallions and sauté for 1 minute. Add the orange zest and reserved marinade and sauté about 30 seconds.
5. Serve the meat and juices spooned over the rice.

YIELD: 4 SERVINGS.

Deviled Short Ribs

Beef short ribs are a marvelous yet underused cut of meat. Their large proportions of bone and fat to meat put some people off, but when the ribs are skillfully cooked, these are the very qualities that make them so rich with flavor. We slowly brown them on all sides and then braise them in an aromatic liquid to a fork-tender turn. The accumulated fat is spooned off before the vegetables are added, and the sauce is completed with a generous amount of mustard and horseradish. We think the result is a piquant and robust main course that is perfect for wintry days when the temperature never sees the freezing mark. Another boon is that the meat is even better if cooked a day ahead since the flavors have a chance to blend and every bit of fat can be easily removed.

This complete meal-in-a-pot needs only a simple green salad and a warming winter dessert such as Cranberry Bread Pudding with Whiskey Sauce (see page 252) or Baked Ginger–Bay Leaf Apples (see page 262).

4 to 5 pounds beef short ribs, cut into 2- or 3-inch pieces (ask the butcher to do this for you)
Salt and freshly ground black pepper to taste
1 onion, chopped
2 cloves garlic, minced
1 teaspoon dried marjoram
½ teaspoon dried savory
½ teaspoon dry mustard
4 tablespoons Cognac or brandy

1 bay leaf
2 cups beef stock
20 to 25 baby peeled carrots, or 6 to 8 slim regular carrots, peeled and cut in 2-inch lengths
1 pound small red-skinned potatoes
2 tablespoons Dijon mustard
1 tablespoon prepared white horseradish
2 tablespoons minced parsley

1. Trim all excess fat from the short ribs. Lightly salt and pepper all sides of the meat. Heat a heavy 6-quart pot and brown the short ribs over medium heat in two batches. Begin browning with the fat side down and then use tongs to turn the pieces until all sides are browned. This will probably take about 30 minutes. Remove the meat to a platter.

2. There should be about 2 tablespoons

drippings in the pot. If there is more, pour off the excess. Add the onion and sauté over medium-low heat until softened, about 5 minutes. Add the garlic, marjoram, savory, and dry mustard, and sauté about 30 seconds. Add the Cognac and cook over medium-high heat until the sauce is reduced by half, about 1 minute. Stir constantly to loosen browned bits clinging to the bottom of the pan.

3. Stir in the bay leaf and beef stock. Return the meat and any accumulated juices to the pan. Bring just to a boil, then cover the pot, lower the heat, and simmer gently until the meat is nearly tender, about 1½ hours. Uncover and tip the pot so that the juices accumulate on one side. Spoon off all fat.

The recipe may be prepared a day ahead up to this point. Any excess fat will solidify and can be easily removed. Reheat before adding the vegetables.

4. Peel a ½-inch strip from around the center of the potatoes. Add the carrots and potatoes to the pot with the meat. Cover and simmer until the vegetables and meat are tender, about 30 to 35 minutes. Use tongs and a slotted spoon to remove the meat and vegetables to a warm platter. Discard the bay leaf.

5. Whisk the Dijon mustard and horseradish into the liquid in the pot and bring to a boil. Cook, stirring, until the sauce is slightly thickened, about 1 minute. Add salt and pepper to taste and then stir in the parsley. Spoon the sauce over the meat and vegetables.

YIELD: 6 SERVINGS.

Our Lady of the Lake Famous Swiss Steak

Melanie's in-laws have had a summer cottage on a small lake in rural Pennsylvania for three generations. It is idyllic, soothingly quiet, and the perfect tonic for weary and stressed East Coast urbanites. Aside from Friday night bingo at the fire hall and the Crawford County Fair, the summer social highlight is the annual Swiss Steak Supper at Our Lady of the Lake Church. It is the culmination of a day-long bazaar with white elephant sales, games for kids, and craft exhibitions. The ladies of the church begin making the Swiss steak early in the morning. The dinner is served family-style in the church hall where there are also bowls of mashed potatoes, hot homemade rolls, and a huge assortment of donated cakes and pies for dessert.

The recipe for the Swiss steak is handed down year to year, but each chairwoman manages to introduce just a little something of her own each time. The result is a dish that is embellished with a community's personality and the goodness of the farm women who know how to cook by flawless instinct.

The following is our version. Of course, we have added a little something of our own —the touch of wine vinegar.

2½ to 3 pounds lean boneless chuck steak, cut about 1½ inches thick
¼ cup all-purpose flour
½ teaspoon salt
¼ teaspoon freshly ground black pepper
1 tablespoon butter
1 tablespoon oil
3 large onions, sliced thin
1 large rib celery, sliced thin

1 large clove garlic, minced
1½ teaspoons dried thyme
¼ teaspoon granulated sugar
1 16-ounce can tomatoes with liquid
½ cup red wine
½ cup beef stock
1 tablespoon red wine vinegar
Salt and freshly ground black pepper to taste

1. Cut the steak into 6 serving pieces. Combine the flour, salt, and pepper and use a ridged mallet or the edge (rim) of a saucer to pound the flour mixture into the meat.

2. Heat the butter and oil in a large skillet and sauté the meat over medium-high heat until richly browned on both sides, about 10 to 12 minutes.

3. Remove the meat from the pan, add the onions and celery, and sauté over medium-low heat until the onions are pale golden, about 5 to 7 minutes. Add the garlic and sauté about 1 minute. Stir in the thyme, sugar, and tomatoes and their liquid, mashing the tomatoes against the side of the skillet to break them up.

4. Push the vegetables to the side of the skillet, replace the meat and any accumulated meat juices, and spoon the vegetables over the meat. Add the wine and beef stock and stir to combine.

5. Bring to a boil, cover the skillet, and lower the heat to a simmer. Simmer until the meat is tender, about 1 to 1½ hours. Spoon off the fat from the surface. Stir in the vinegar. Add salt and pepper to taste.
6. Serve the meat with the sauce spooned over it.

YIELD: 6 SERVINGS.

NOTE: This recipe may be prepared a day ahead. Reheat gently in the covered skillet or place in a 300-degree oven until hot, about 30 minutes.

Pork Chops with Caraway Cream

Here's a simple recipe for the boneless pork chops that have begun appearing in meat cases. Serve with steamed green cabbage, buttered black bread, and, for dessert, a plate of Molasses-Ginger Crinkles (see page 268) or Peanut Butter–Chocolate Chip Brownies (see page 263).

4 boneless loin pork chops, cut ¾ inch thick (about 6 ounces each)
¼ teaspoon salt or to taste
⅛ teaspoon freshly ground black pepper

2 tablespoons butter
1 teaspoon caraway seeds
⅓ cup dry white wine
¾ cup heavy cream

1. Lightly pound the pork chops to flatten them until about ½ inch thick. Season both sides of the meat with salt and pepper.
2. Heat the butter in a large skillet and sauté the pork over medium heat until both sides of the chops are browned and the meat is cooked through, about 10 minutes. Remove the meat from the pan and keep warm.
3. Add the caraway seeds to the skillet and cook for 30 seconds. Pour in the wine and cook over medium-high heat until the sauce is reduced by about half, about 2 to 3 minutes. Add the cream and simmer over medium heat until the sauce has thickened enough to coat the back of a spoon, about 5 minutes.
4. Return the meat to the pan to heat through. Spoon the sauce over the pork and serve.

YIELD: 4 SERVINGS.

Sicilian Braciole

The Sicily of Melanie's heritage is a poor country with an enormously rich culture. Having been occupied over the centuries by France, North Africa, Greece, and Italy, the inventive Sicilians took the best from the cuisines of their captors, and the result is a style of cooking that weaves the native ingredients of this sunny island into most wonderfully complex flavors.

This braciole, or meat roll, is filled with salty ham and cheese, sweet raisins, pungent spices, rich nuts, and heady wild mushrooms. The lean, thrifty cut of meat is deliciously tenderized by simmering in an aromatic liquid. Slice the rolls on the diagonal for the nicest presentation and serve with buttered pasta or rice, Roasted Vegetables (see page 218) and Classic Rice Pudding (see page 243) or Double Lemon Loaf (see page 236).

1 ounce dried porcini or cèpes
2 pounds round steak, sliced less than ¼ inch thick
2 tablespoons butter
2 tablespoons olive oil
1 onion, chopped
1 rib celery, chopped
2 tablespoons pine nuts or coarsely chopped almonds
1 clove garlic, chopped

2 cups fresh bread crumbs made from about 4 slices firm white or Italian bread
¼ cup grated Romano or Parmesan cheese
4 tablespoons minced flat-leaf parsley
2 tablespoons golden raisins
1 teaspoon dried oregano
½ teaspoon dried basil
¼ teaspoon freshly ground black pepper
6 very thin slices prosciutto
½ cup red or white wine

1. Soak the mushrooms in about 1½ cups hot water for 45 minutes. Drain well, straining the liquid through a coffee filter and reserving the liquid. Chop half of the mushrooms for the stuffing and slice the remainder for the sauce.
2. Cut the steak into 6 pieces and pound each until about ⅛ inch thick.
3. Heat 1 tablespoon of the butter and 1 tablespoon of the oil in a skillet and sauté

the onion, celery, and pine nuts until the vegetables begin to soften and the nuts begin to color, about 4 minutes. Add the garlic and sauté about 1 minute.
4. In a large bowl, mix the sautéed vegetables with the bread crumbs, cheeses, 2 tablespoons of the parsley, the raisins, oregano, basil, pepper, and the chopped mushrooms.
5. Lay a slice of prosciutto on each of the

pieces of meat. Dividing the stuffing equally, spread it on the lower third of each steak, leaving a ¼-inch margin all around. Roll each steak up, trying to fold in the ends to enclose the stuffing. Secure by tying with string or using toothpicks.

6. Heat the remaining butter and oil in a skillet large enough to comfortably hold all the meat rolls. Brown the rolls, turning carefully with tongs to brown all sides. This will take about 10 minutes. Add the sliced mushrooms to the skillet during the last 2 or 3 minutes and lightly sauté. Add the wine and the reserved mushroom stock, leaving any mushroom sediment behind. Bring just to a boil, then lower the heat, cover the pan, and simmer gently until the meat is tender, about 1 hour.

7. To serve, remove the string or toothpicks and carefully cut each roll diagonally into ½-inch-thick slices. Bring the pan juices to a boil and cook about 1 minute. Spoon over the meat.

YIELD: 6 SERVINGS.

Braised Sweet-and-Sour Brisket

Braised brisket is one of those dishes about which people hold fierce convictions—not, they will (occasionally) admit, based on anything reasonable, but on instinct. If Grandma never added carrots but always served it with horseradish, then that is the only way to do it. If Aunt Sarah made her brisket with a sweet-and-sour sauce but shuddered at the idea of horseradish, then hers is the definitive recipe.

Neither of us was blessed with an extra Jewish grandmother or aunt, so, after much pleasant and delicious research, we've been able to take one step back and decide this matter for ourselves. We like a sweet-and-sour sauce. Its tang is a wonderful counterpoint to the richness of the meat.

Serve the brisket with plain boiled potatoes or the traditional Lacy Potato Pancakes (see page 214) and a green vegetable or salad. Classic Rice Pudding (see page 243) or Pear Strudel (see page 250) would make a great dessert.

Braised Sweet-and-Sour Brisket (cont.)

1 3- to 3½-pound piece of brisket
   (first cut preferred)
Salt
Freshly ground black pepper
1 tablespoon vegetable oil
2 large onions, chopped (about 2 cups)
8 carrots, peeled

2 cloves garlic, chopped
1½ cups beef broth
¾ cup red wine
1 teaspoon paprika
1 bay leaf, broken in half
3 tablespoons brown sugar
4 tablespoons lemon juice

1. Rinse the brisket under cold water and dry it thoroughly with paper towels. Trim off any large pieces of fat, leaving a thin layer of fat on one side of the flat piece of meat if possible. Sprinkle lightly with salt and pepper.

2. Heat the oil in a large covered pot such as a Dutch oven and brown the brisket well on all sides over medium-high heat. Remove the meat, lower the heat to medium-low, and add the onions to the drippings in the pan. Cook, stirring frequently, until softened and lightly browned, about 10 minutes. Slice two of the carrots into 1-inch lengths. Add them to the pot along with the garlic. Return the meat to the pot and add the beef broth, wine, paprika, bay leaf, and 1 tablespoon each of the brown sugar and lemon juice. Cover closely and simmer over very low heat for about 3 hours or until the brisket is tender. Turn the meat two or three times during the braising process.

3. Remove the meat from the pot. Remove and discard the carrots. Skim as much fat off the surface of the juices as possible.

The recipe may be prepared a day ahead up to this point. Refrigerate the juices, and lift the fat off the top. Cover the meat well and refrigerate.

4. Bring the degreased juices to a simmer and whisk in the remaining brown sugar and lemon juice. Slice the remaining carrots into ¼-inch rounds and add them to the pot. Return the meat to the pot, cover, and simmer until the carrots are tender, about 20 minutes. Discard the bay leaf. Season with salt and pepper to taste. (Salt carefully since canned beef broth can be salty.)

5. Slice the meat thinly across the grain and serve it with the sauce and carrots spooned over the top.

YIELD: 4 SERVINGS.

NOTE: The completed dish will keep well in the refrigerator for up to 3 days.

Our Prize-Winning Meat Loaf

This is our adaptation of the "Prize-Winning Meat Loaf" recipe that appears on the back of the Quaker Oats box. From time to time we've made a few changes here and there, and this straightforward, delicious recipe has been winning us "prizes" in the form of praise from our families for years. Be sure to use excellent-quality ground meat for the best result.

We like this with baked potatoes or Scalloped Potatoes Our Way (see page 209) because either can cook in the same oven with the meat loaf. Serve with almost any vegetable and with Mocha Pudding with Coffee Cream (see page 254), perhaps, for dessert.

2 pounds ground meat, preferably a combination of beef, pork, and veal
1 cup milk
1 cup fresh bread crumbs or uncooked rolled oats (any kind except "instant")
½ cup chopped parsley

⅓ cup finely chopped onion
1 egg, lightly beaten
2 tablespoons chili sauce or tomato ketchup
2 teaspoons prepared white horseradish
1¼ teaspoons salt
¼ teaspoon freshly ground black pepper

1. Preheat the oven to 375 degrees.
2. Combine all the ingredients in a large mixing bowl. Using your clean hands, work the mixture until it is well combined and all the ingredients are evenly distributed. Pack into a 9-by-5-inch loaf pan, smoothing the top to an even level. Bake in the preheated oven until the meat loaf is nicely browned on top and the meat juices no longer run pink in the center when pierced with the point of a sharp knife, about 55 to 60 minutes. Remove any grease that has accumulated in the bottom of the pan with a bulb baster or by pouring it off.
3. Cut into ¾-inch slices and serve.

YIELD: 6 SERVINGS.

Roast Pork and Thyme Pan Gravy

To hear a roast sputtering away in the oven and to smell its rich aroma as it cooks is really very cozy—and, after it's tantalized you for a couple of hours, is really wonderful to eat!

Pork is one of our favorite meats in almost any form, and so here we offer a recipe for roasting a loin that is simple and delicious. The outside of the roast gets smeared with a paste of mustard and thyme and then the flavorful pan juices are turned into an old-fashioned pan gravy. Add Real Mashed Potatoes (see page 212) or Parmesan Polenta (see page 215), broccoli or Brussels sprouts, and if you're feeling ambitious, Potato Pan Rolls (see page 224), and you've got a real feast. We'd like Hot Brownies with Brandy–Ice Cream Sauce (see page 265) or Candied Gingerbread with Vanilla Cream (see page 256) for a finish.

1 pork loin roast (about 5 pounds), with the bone
1 tablespoon coarse-grained mustard
1 tablespoon minced fresh thyme or
** 1½ teaspoons dried thyme**
1 tablespoon olive oil

Salt and freshly ground black pepper to taste
Butter, as needed
2 tablespoons all-purpose flour
2 cups good-quality canned or homemade (see page 2) chicken stock

1. Ask the butcher to cut through the chine bone of the pork loin to facilitate carving.
2. Preheat the oven to 400 degrees. In a small bowl, stir together the mustard, half the thyme, and the oil. Smear this paste all over the exterior of the meat and sprinkle with salt and pepper.
3. Place the roast, fat side up, on a rack in a shallow roasting pan and place in the pre-heated oven. Immediately reduce the oven temperature to 325 degrees and roast for about 25 to 30 minutes per pound, or until a meat thermometer registers an internal temperature of 145 to 155 degrees. (Pork is

safe to eat when cooked to 140 degrees. We prefer the meat cooked until it is no longer pink.)
4. Remove the meat to a platter, cover loosely with foil, and keep warm.
5. Place the pan with the pork drippings on a stove burner. You should have about 2 tablespoons of fat. If you have more than that, spoon some off; if less, add butter to make up the difference. Sprinkle the flour over the drippings and cook over medium heat, stirring with a wooden spoon, for 2 minutes. Gradually add the stock, stirring to dissolve the browned bits that have adhered to the pan. Gently simmer for 2 min-

utes. Stir in the remaining thyme and season the gravy with salt and pepper to taste.

6. Carve the meat, cutting down between the bones. Stir any accumulated juices into the gravy. Serve the meat with some gravy spooned over the top, and pass the remaining gravy at the table.

YIELD: 6 SERVINGS.

Red Flannel Hash

Hash, a word derived from the French *hacher,* which means "to chop," is considered by some to be a lowly peasant dish made up of leftovers. That's because they have never been fortunate enough to be treated to a good hash. True, the basic ingredients may be the remains from yesterday's boiled dinner, but they are not to be treated lightly. The best hash is carefully seasoned, the meat and vegetables cut into small, but discernible pieces, and the entire mixture cooked in a well-seasoned black cast-iron skillet. Its top and bottom should both have a crust, but since flipping the hash without breaking it is a tricky feat, we prefer to combine stove-top and oven cooking to accomplish the same thing without risk or hassle.

Our purist Yankee friends maintain that Red Flannel Hash must be made only with slab bacon or salt pork, potatoes, onions, and beets, which, of course, give it the characteristic "red flannel" color. Since we live in southern New England, relatively close to New York City, where corned beef is king, most of our tastings of Red Flannel Hash have incorporated that meat, which marries perfectly with the other classic ingredients. The hash mixture may be made early in the day, which leaves only the cooking for the last minute.

This dish is perfectly good on its own, but reaches new heights when topped with a poached egg. It is really a meal in itself, but a hearty lettuce salad with a citrus vinaigrette and a few orange segments tossed in makes it quite special. Black Devil Cupcakes with Double Fudge Frosting (see page 240) or Mocha Pudding with Coffee Cream (see page 254) would be a most appropriate dessert.

Red Flannel Hash (cont.)

3 slices thick bacon
1 large onion, chopped (about 1 cup)
About 1 pound cooked corned beef, cut into
   ½-inch cubes (2½ cups)
2½ cups cooked potatoes, cut into ¼-inch cubes
1½ cups cooked beets (fresh or canned), cut
   into ¼-inch cubes
¼ cup minced parsley
2 teaspoons Worcestershire sauce

1 teaspoon prepared white horseradish
1 teaspoon Tabasco
¼ cup heavy cream
Salt and freshly ground black pepper to taste
1½ tablespoons butter
4 to 6 poached eggs (optional) (see step 6,
   below, for instructions)
Bottled chili sauce (optional)

1. Fry the bacon in a heavy, oven-proof (preferably well-seasoned cast iron) skillet. Remove with a slotted spoon, drain, and crumble. Add the onions to the drippings in the skillet and sauté until softened, about 3 to 5 minutes. Reserve the skillet.

2. Place the bacon, onions, corned beef, potatoes, beets, parsley, Worcestershire sauce, horseradish, Tabasco, and cream in a large mixing bowl and mix gently but thoroughly. Add salt and pepper to taste.

The hash may be made up to 8 hours ahead up to this point. Cover mixture and refrigerate.

3. Preheat the oven to 400 degrees.

4. Add the butter to the reserved skillet and heat. Press the hash mixture into the skillet. Cook on the stove over medium-low heat until a crust forms on the bottom, about 25 minutes.

5. Place the skillet in the preheated oven and bake until the top is crispy and lightly browned, about 15 to 20 minutes.

6. Cut the hash into wedges and serve each topped with a poached egg and some chili sauce if desired.

YIELD: 4 TO 6 SERVINGS.

Lamb Shanks Braised with Cinnamon and Orange Peel

Lamb shanks are an underused cut of meat. They're just delicious braised this way and seasoned with fragrant cinnamon, orange, and oregano—flavors slightly reminiscent of those used in the Middle East.

Serve with yellow rice or steamed couscous, and offer Cranberry-Cointreau Sundaes (see page 269) for dessert.

2 tablespoons olive oil
½ cup all-purpose flour
3 teaspoons dried oregano
¾ teaspoon salt
½ teaspoon freshly ground black pepper
6 lamb shanks (½ to ¾ pound each), trimmed
of any excess external fat
1 large onion, chopped
2 cloves garlic, chopped
1 cup red wine
½ cup orange juice
4 cups water

1 bay leaf
1 cinnamon stick or ½ teaspoon ground
cinnamon
1 pound (about 3 cups) pearl onions
8 carrots (about 1 pound), peeled and cut in
2-inch lengths
1 tablespoon shredded orange zest (thin shreds
made with a zesting tool, or coarsely
grated)
Additional salt and freshly ground black
pepper to taste
¼ cup minced parsley

1. Heat the oil in a large, deep skillet or Dutch oven. Combine the flour, 1½ teaspoons of the oregano, the salt, and the pepper in a paper bag. Shake the lamb shanks in the seasoned flour to coat. Shake off any excess coating. When the oil is hot, brown the meat over medium-high heat, turning frequently so that all sides are well colored, about 10 minutes. (You may need to do this in two batches.) Reduce the heat and add the chopped onion. Cook for 5 minutes, stirring occasionally, until lightly browned. Add the garlic and cook for 1 minute.

2. Raise the heat, pour in the wine, orange juice, and water; stir to dissolve any caramelized juices. Bring to a simmer and add the remaining 1½ teaspoons of oregano and the bay leaf and cinnamon stick or ground cinnamon. Lower the heat, cover, and gently simmer until the meat is almost

tender when pierced with a fork, about 1½ to 2 hours.

3. Meanwhile, peel the pearl onions by pouring boiling water over them and letting them sit for 2 minutes. Drain, cut off the root ends, and slip off the skins.

4. Skim the fat from the surface of the braising liquid. Raise the heat to medium, add the onions, carrots, and shredded orange zest, and simmer, partially covered, until the vegetables are tender, about 25 minutes. If any more fat has accumulated, spoon it off the surface. Discard the bay leaf and cinnamon stick, if using.

The recipe may be made ahead up to this point. Refrigerate for up to 2 days, or freeze for 1 month. Reheat, covered, over low heat on top of stove or oven.

5. Season with salt and pepper to taste. Sprinkle with the minced parsley and serve on warm plates.

YIELD: 6 SERVINGS.

Pear Picadillo

Picadillo, or spiced ground meat, is a specialty of Spain and most of the countries influenced by her vast colonization. Variations of the sweet-sour-spicy meat mixture are found in Mexico and throughout the Caribbean. Depending upon the locale, picadillo may be served over rice, spooned into flour tortillas, or stuffed into whole roasted green chilies, rellenos-style. We like it any of those ways, but you might also like to try it ladled over big squares of Peppery Corn Bread (see page 228) for a tasty break from tradition. An even more heretical (though truly delicious) presentation is to spoon it into romaine lettuce leaves, roll them up, and eat them in your hand or with a fork.

Mixed chopped dried fruit is readily available in the dried fruit or natural-snack section of the supermarket, but if you can't find it, substitute raisins or any chopped dried fruit (such as pears, apples, or apricots) of your choice.

The picadillo benefits from being made ahead to allow its flavors to blend. If you serve rice, tortillas, or corn bread, the only other thing this hearty meal needs is a salad of sturdy greens such as spinach or romaine with a simple, red wine vinaigrette. For dessert, we like Tin Roof Sundaes (see page 270) or Classic Rice Pudding (see page 243).

2 pounds lean ground chuck
1 large onion, chopped
2 cloves garlic, minced
1 large ripe but firm pear, peeled, cored, and
 coarsely chopped
1 16-ounce can plum tomatoes, drained, with
 liquid reserved and tomatoes coarsely
 chopped
1 4-ounce can mild green chilies, chopped
1 fresh or canned jalapeño pepper, seeds and
 ribs removed, finely minced (note: wash
 your hands carefully after working with hot
 peppers)
3 tablespoons cider vinegar
1 tablespoon chili powder

1½ teaspoons salt
1½ teaspoons ground cumin
1 teaspoon brown sugar
1 teaspoon oregano
¾ teaspoon cinnamon
¼ teaspoon cayenne pepper
⅓ cup chopped mixed dried fruit, or golden
 raisins or currants, or chopped dried pears,
 apples, or apricots
⅓ cup toasted chopped or slivered almonds
 (toast for about 10 minutes in a 350-degree
 oven, stirring often)
Cooked rice or warmed, buttered flour tortillas
 or Peppery Corn Bread (see page 228)

1. Brown the ground beef in a heavy skillet or saucepan. When the meat begins to lose its red color, add the onion and continue to cook over medium heat, stirring frequently, until the onion is softened, about 3 to 5 minutes. Add the garlic and sauté about 2 minutes. Spoon or pour off any excess fat.

2. Stir in the pear, plum tomatoes, chilies, jalapeño pepper, chili powder, salt, cumin, brown sugar, oregano, cinnamon, and cayenne pepper. Stir in the dried fruit. Simmer over low heat, partially covered, and stirring often, for about 30 minutes. If the mixture seems to be getting dry, add some of the reserved tomato liquid.

3. Just before serving, stir in the almonds. Spoon over rice or corn bread or onto flour tortillas. If using tortillas, fold up the filled tortillas and eat with a fork or in your hand.

YIELD: 6 SERVINGS.

NOTE: The picadillo, except for the almonds, may be prepared up to 2 days ahead and refrigerated, or frozen up to 1 month. Reheat over low heat on top of the stove.

Roast Leg of Lamb with Rosemary-Mustard Crust

This recipe combines all the tastes we especially like with roasted lamb into a flavorful "crust" that permeates the meat. We always remove the thin tissue called *fell* and as much of the excess fat as we can before roasting and we use an instant-reading meat thermometer (which we believe to be the most accurate type) to tell us when the internal temperature has reached 125 degrees for rare meat and 135 degrees for rosy pink slices.

New breeding techniques and imports have made young, tender lamb available year-round, though we still love to serve roast leg of lamb in the early spring along with Roasted Vegetables (such as asparagus) (see page 218) and some tiny new potatoes, which can either be steamed or cooked right along with the lamb in the roasting pan. A wonderful dessert would be Double Lemon Loaf (see page 236) with some sliced and sweetened strawberries.

1 5- to 7-pound leg of lamb, at room
    temperature
3 tablespoons Dijon mustard
2 cloves garlic, minced

1½ tablespoons cracked black peppercorns
1½ tablespoons fresh rosemary or 1½ teaspoons
    dried rosemary
½ teaspoon coarse salt or sea salt

1. Preheat the oven to 450 degrees. If the butcher has not already done so, trim the papery tissue called *fell* from the leg by making several small cuts and then pulling it off in pieces. This is usually quite easy to do. Then trim off any excess fat from the lamb.

2. In a small dish, combine the mustard and garlic. In another small dish, combine the peppercorns, rosemary, and salt. Spread the lamb with the mustard, and then sprinkle evenly with the peppercorn mixture, patting it in with the palm of your hand.

3. Place the lamb on a low rack in a shallow roasting pan and set in the lower center of the oven. Immediately reduce the oven temperature to 350 degrees. Roast for about 1¼ to 1½ hours until the internal temperature is 125 to 135 degrees depending on the desired doneness. Begin checking the roast after 1 hour of roasting time so that there will be no chance of overcooking it.

4. Remove the roast from the oven and let it rest, loosely covered, for about 10 minutes. To serve, carve the lamb into thin slices and spoon any pan juices over the slices.

YIELD: 6 SERVINGS.

Pan-Grilled Veal Chops with Spicy Paprika Sauce

Veal chops are a delicious treat for when you want a meal in the "I'm worth it" category. The milky-tender meat is enhanced by the subtle hotness of a good paprika. Try to find some imported Hungarian paprika and then store the jar in the refrigerator where it will keep its fresh zing much longer. If you use regular paprika, add a pinch of cayenne pepper to the sauce.

We especially like this dish with our Special Rice (see page 216), braised baby carrots sprinkled with fresh tarragon, and a splashy dessert such as Mixed Fruit–Chocolate Pan Soufflé (see page 264).

4 loin veal chops, each about 6 to 8 ounces
¼ teaspoon salt
⅛ teaspoon freshly ground pepper
2 teaspoons excellent-quality, medium-hot
    paprika
2 tablespoons butter

1 tablespoon vegetable oil
¼ cup minced onion
½ cup white wine
½ cup heavy cream
Salt and freshly ground black pepper to taste

1. Sprinkle the veal on both sides with salt, pepper, and ½ teaspoon of the paprika.

2. Heat 1 tablespoon of the butter and all the oil in a skillet large enough to hold the veal. (You may need to use two skillets. Divide the butter and oil between them.) Sauté the veal over medium heat until golden brown on both sides and cooked through, about 10 to 12 minutes. Do not overcook or the veal will dry out. Remove the meat to a platter and keep warm.

3. Pour off the excess fat from the pan and add the remaining tablespoon of butter. Add the onion and sauté over medium heat until softened, about 3 minutes. Add the remaining 1½ teaspoons paprika and cook, stirring, about 30 seconds. Add the wine and cook over medium-high heat, stirring up browned bits clinging to the pan, until the liquid is reduced by about half, about 3 minutes. Reduce the heat to medium-low and stir in the cream. Simmer, stirring often, until the sauce is slightly thickened, about 3 minutes. Season to taste with salt and pepper.

4. To serve, stir any veal juices accumulated on the platter into the sauce. Serve the veal with the sauce spooned over it.

YIELD: 4 SERVINGS.

Veal Stew in Acorn Squash

Here's a quick and elegant stew that makes great informal party fare because it can be made almost entirely ahead. We've given it a new twist by suggesting that it be served in the hollows of beautiful orange acorn squash.

A nice accompaniment would be a salad of fennel and radicchio with a balsamic vinaigrette, with warm French bread. And for dessert, Double Lemon Loaf (see page 236), Double Crust Apple-Quince Pie (see page 248), or Miss Hulling's Banana-Coconut Cream Pie (see page 246).

2 tablespoons butter or more as needed
2 tablespoons olive oil or more as needed
½ cup all-purpose flour
½ teaspoon salt
¼ teaspoon freshly ground black pepper
2 pounds veal stew meat (shoulder or leg), cut in 1½-inch cubes
2 veal bones, if available
8 ounces fresh mushrooms, such as shiitake or domestic, thinly sliced (about 3 cups)
2 leeks, white parts only, thinly sliced
¼ cup coarsely chopped shallots
1 cup white wine
3 cups good-quality canned or homemade (see page 2) chicken stock

4 teaspoons minced fresh sage or 2 teaspoons crumbled dried sage
1 bay leaf
5 carrots, peeled, halved lengthwise, and cut into 1-inch pieces
About 12 ounces (2 medium) white turnips, peeled and cut in 1-inch cubes
3 tablespoons minced parsley
Sprigs of fresh sage for garnish, if available

BAKED ACORN SQUASH:

3 acorn squash (about 1 pound each)
6 teaspoons butter
Salt and freshly ground black pepper

1. Heat the butter and oil in a large skillet. Combine the flour, salt, and pepper in a paper bag. Dry the veal thoroughly with paper towels and shake it, a few pieces at a time, in the bag with the seasoned flour until each piece is lightly coated with the flour mixture. Brown the pieces of meat over medium heat, making sure not to

crowd the pan. (You will probably need to brown the meat in two batches.) Also brown the veal bones if you have them. Add a little additional butter and oil if necessary. Remove the veal cubes with tongs as they brown and set aside on a plate.

2. If no fat remains in the skillet, add another tablespoon each of butter and oil. Add the sliced mushrooms and cook, stirring, for about 5 minutes. Add the leeks and shallots and cook for 2 minutes. Pour in the wine and stir with a wooden spoon to deglaze and dissolve any flavorful browned bits that have adhered to the bottom of the skillet. (At this point, transfer the contents of the skillet to a large, covered pot or leave it in this skillet if it has a cover and is large enough to hold the entire stew.)

3. Return the veal to the pan. Pour in the chicken stock and add half of the sage and whole bay leaf. Bring to a boil, lower the heat, cover, and simmer over very low heat for 35 minutes, or until the veal is almost tender.

The stew may be prepared ahead up to this point. Remove veal bones and cover stew before storing. Refrigerate it up to 2 days or freeze it for up to 1 month.

4. Add the carrots and turnips, cover again, and continue simmering for another 25 to 30 minutes, until both the meat and the vegetables are tender. Remove the veal bones (if used) and bay leaf. Stir in the parsley and the remaining minced sage.

5. To prepare the squash, preheat the oven to 375 degrees about 1 hour before you are ready to serve the stew. Cut the squashes in half and scoop out their seeds. Do not peel squash. Cut a thin sliver off the bottoms of each half if necessary to make sure it will stand without wobbling. Arrange in a baking pan, place 1 teaspoon of butter in each cavity, and sprinkle lightly with salt and pepper. Pour about ½ cup of water in the bottom of the pan and lay a sheet of foil lightly over the top, but do not seal it around the edges. Bake in the preheated oven until tender when pierced with the point of a sharp knife, about 40 to 50 minutes.

6. Place a squash half on each of six warm plates and fill the centers with the stew, allowing it to cascade over the sides a bit. Garnish the plates with a sprig of fresh sage, if available.

YIELD: 6 SERVINGS.

Sautéed Calf's Liver with Onions, Raisins, and Pecans

One of the best things about calf's liver is that its taste and texture are rich enough to stand up to other assertive and interesting ingredient combinations. Here the complexity of caramelized onions, toasted nuts, and sweet raisins gives the impression that much effort and time have gone into preparation. In fact, it is a quickly cooked recipe that, because of its sophisticated flavors, is best accompanied by a simple dish like Lacy Potato Pancakes (see page 214) and a green salad with a fruit wine vinaigrette. This wintry meal would be further brightened by Hester's Citrus Pudding Cake (see page 242) or Miss Hulling's Banana-Coconut Cream Pie (see page 246) as a finish.

¼ cup raisins
2½ tablespoons bourbon
2½ tablespoons butter
¼ cup broken pecan meats
2 tablespoons oil
3 medium onions, thinly sliced
5 tablespoons all-purpose flour

¼ teaspoon salt
⅛ teaspoon freshly ground black pepper
1 pound calf's liver, cut into 8 slices
4 teaspoons balsamic or red wine vinegar
Pinch of ground cloves
Pinch of freshly ground nutmeg
Salt and freshly ground black pepper

1. Soak the raisins in the bourbon for 10 to 15 minutes.
2. In a large skillet, heat ½ tablespoon of butter. Sauté the pecans over medium heat, stirring constantly, until toasted and fragrant, about 1 minute. Remove from the pan with a slotted spoon. Reserve.
3. Add 1 tablespoon of butter and 1 tablespoon of oil to the skillet. Sauté the onions over low heat, stirring often, until the onions turn golden and begin to caramelize, about 15 minutes. Remove from the pan with a slotted spoon. Reserve.
4. On a shallow plate, combine the flour, salt, and pepper. Lightly dredge the liver pieces in the flour mixture, shaking off any excess coating.

5. Add the remaining butter and oil to the pan. Sauté the liver over medium-high heat until both sides are browned but the interior is still pink, about 5 minutes. Remove the meat from the pan and keep warm on a platter.
6. Add the vinegar to the pan and cook for 30 seconds over medium heat, using a wooden spoon to stir up browned bits clinging to the bottom. Stir in the cloves and nutmeg, onions, raisins with bourbon, and the pecans. Add salt and pepper to taste.
7. Serve the onion mixture spooned over the liver.

YIELD: 4 SERVINGS.

Barbecued Meat Loaves with Iowa Blue Cheese Sauce

This is a uniquely American recipe that combines the nationally loved meat loaf with a favorite method of summer cooking. We form the peppery meat mixture into little individual loaves that grill to a charred exterior and a juicy, moist interior. The simple blue cheese sauce is especially good when made with the excellent American soft blue cheese that originated in and is named after Maytag, Iowa. (Yes, this is also the home of the washing machine.)

Cook a few ears of Corn Grilled in the Husk (see page 227) along with the meat loaves and serve with some thickly sliced, ripe beefsteak tomatoes for a wonderfully easy summer supper. Since the meat mixture can be made in advance and the sauce goes together in seconds, there is ample time to go all out for Red, White, and Blueberry Shortcakes (see page 232), which are, of course, the patriotic ending for this meal.

1 pound ground chuck
½ pound ground pork
½ pound ground veal
1 tablespoon minced parsley
1 teaspoon minced chives
1 teaspoon salt
¾ teaspoon coarsely ground black pepper
Pinch of cayenne pepper
½ cup fine, fresh bread crumbs

1 egg, lightly beaten
2 tablespoons milk

BLUE CHEESE SAUCE:

4 tablespoons unsalted butter, softened
3 tablespoons soft blue cheese, such as
    Maytag Blue
2 teaspoons minced chives
¼ teaspoon lemon juice

1. Build a medium barbecue fire, using some dampened hickory chips if you have them.
2. In a mixing bowl, lightly but thoroughly combine the beef, pork, veal, parsley, chives, salt, pepper, cayenne pepper, bread crumbs, egg, and milk. Gently form the meat into 6 rectangular loaves, each about 1 inch thick.

The meat loaves may be formed early in the day and refrigerated, covered, until ready to grill.
3. Grill the meat loaves until their centers are barely pink and their exteriors are browned and crisp, about 7 minutes on each side.
4. While the meat is cooking, prepare the sauce. Place the butter, cheese, chives, and lemon juice in a small saucepan and mash against the side to combine. Near the end of the meat loaves' cooking time, place the saucepan at the edge of the grill so that the ingredients will just melt.
5. Spoon the sauce over the meat loaves.

YIELD: 6 SERVINGS.

Herbed and Spiced Grilled Butterflied Leg of Lamb

Your butcher or supermarket meat manager will gladly bone a leg of lamb for you and "butterfly" it (trim the meat so that it is spread wide and flat into an approximately even thickness to ensure even cooking). A leg of lamb prepared this way is especially suitable for grilling. We marinate it briefly in a robust, garlicky, Mediterranean mixture and then grill it so that it's beautifully charred on the outside and still pink and juicy within. The marinade is then simmered and used as a sauce to be passed separately if you like. Serve with hollowed-out tomatoes filled with Confetti Rice Salad (see page 211), a side dish of Purple Plum Chutney (see page 229) grilled French bread, and for dessert, Baked Amaretti Nectarines (see page 261) and cold heavy cream.

1 6-pound leg of lamb, boned, trimmed of fat, and butterflied (about 3 pounds trimmed weight)
⅔ cup red wine
⅓ cup olive oil
2 cloves garlic, chopped
4 anchovies, chopped (about 2 teaspoons)

1 tablespoon chopped fresh rosemary or 2 teaspoons dried rosemary
1½ teaspoons ground cumin
½ teaspoon red pepper flakes
½ teaspoon freshly ground black pepper
Rosemary sprigs for garnish, if available

1. Check the lamb to make sure most of the fat is trimmed away. Place in a shallow glass dish.
2. Combine the wine, olive oil, garlic, anchovies, chopped rosemary, cumin, and the 2 peppers in a small bowl and pour over the lamb. Turn the meat to make sure all sides are well coated, cover loosely with plastic wrap, and set aside to marinate for about 1 hour at room temperature. Turn the meat once or twice in the marinade.
3. Meanwhile, build a barbecue fire, light a gas grill, or preheat the oven broiler. When the coals have a coating of gray ash, remove the meat from the marinade and drain on paper towels, leaving some bits of herbs and garlic on the surface if possible. Pour the marinade into a saucepan and simmer over medium heat for 10 minutes or until reduced to about ⅓ cup.
4. Cook the lamb on the grill or under the oven broiler until the outside is nicely charred and the inside is still pink, a total time of about 15 minutes. Let the meat rest for 10 minutes before carving against the grain into thin, diagonal slices. Serve on a platter garnished with rosemary, if available, and pass the sauce for spooning over the meat.

YIELD: 6 SERVINGS.

Pork and Black Bean Chili

Serve with hot corn tortillas, and top with sour cream if you like. A salad of sliced avocado and red onion would be nice on the side. Pineapple drizzled with orange liqueur is a refreshing finish.

1½ pounds boneless pork loin or shoulder,
    trimmed of fat
3 tablespoons oil
1 large onion, chopped
2 cloves garlic, chopped
1½ teaspoons cumin seeds, crushed in a mortar
    with a pestle or with the side of a large
    knife, or 1½ teaspoons ground cumin
1½ tablespoons good-quality chili powder
1 28-ounce can (3 cups) crushed tomatoes in
    purée

1½ teaspoons dried oregano
¾ teaspoon salt or to taste
½ teaspoon freshly ground black pepper
3 cups cooked black beans, pink beans, or
    kidney beans, drained (discard the liquid)
    and rinsed
12 large corn tortillas
¾ cup sour cream (optional)
Sprigs of coriander (optional)

1. Cut the pork into ½-inch cubes. (It is easiest to do this if the meat is very cold or even slightly frozen.) Heat the oil in a large nonreactive skillet. Add the pork and the onion. Cook, stirring frequently, over medium-high heat until the meat loses its pink color and the onions have softened, about 8 minutes. Add the garlic and stir in the crushed cumin and the chili powder. Cook, stirring constantly, for 2 minutes to slightly toast the spices.

2. Stir in the tomatoes, and add the oregano, salt, and pepper. Bring to a boil, lower the heat, and simmer, uncovered, over low heat for 20 minutes, stirring occasionally.

3. Add the beans to the chili and simmer for another 15 to 20 minutes, stirring occasionally. If the chili begins to scorch or to stick to the pan, add ¼ cup or so of water. The chili should be quite thick but not dry.

At this point, the chili may be stored in the refrigerator for 3 days or frozen for up to 1 month.

4. Wrap the tortillas loosely in foil and heat in a 375-degree oven for 10 minutes, or wrap in plastic wrap and heat in a microwave on high for 25 seconds.

5. Serve the chili topped with dollops of sour cream and garnished with sprigs of coriander, with the warm tortillas on the side. Or spoon the chili and its accompaniments into a tortilla and wrap to eat in your hand.

YIELD: 6 SERVINGS.

Pork and Winter Vegetable Stew

Pork, apples, and root vegetables seem to naturally complement one another, so here we've combined them in a succulent stew. It's a great one-pot meal for a party.

Serve with Potato Pan Rolls (see page 224) and a salad of bitter winter greens such as escarole and endive dressed with a vinaigrette made with 1 part sherry vinegar to 3 parts olive oil. For dessert, a platter of Luscious Pecan Pie Bars (see page 266) or Cranberry Bread Pudding with Whiskey Sauce (see page 252) would be perfect.

3 tablespoons vegetable oil
½ cup all-purpose flour
½ teaspoon salt
⅛ teaspoon freshly ground black pepper
2 pounds lean boneless pork, cut in 2-inch cubes (use lean shoulder, leg [fresh ham], or pork butt, and ask the butcher to cut it for you, saving the bone if possible)
2 leeks, washed and sliced
2 cloves garlic, chopped
2 cups sweet cider
2 cups good-quality canned or homemade (see page 2) chicken stock
4 teaspoons minced fresh rosemary or 2 teaspoons dried rosemary

1 bay leaf
8 carrots (about 1 pound), peeled and cut in 2-inch lengths
12 ounces white turnips, peeled and cut in 1-inch cubes
12 ounces parsnips, peeled and cut in ½-inch-thick rounds
1 tablespoon coarse-grained mustard
2 teaspoons cider vinegar or to taste
Additional salt and freshly ground black pepper to taste
Rosemary sprigs for garnish (optional)

1. Heat 2 tablespoons of the oil in a large casserole or stew pot over medium heat. Combine the flour, salt, and black pepper in a paper or plastic bag. Make sure the meat is dry and trimmed of all excess fat. Shake the pork cubes in the flour and cook in a single layer over medium-high heat until browned on all sides, about 10 min-

utes. (This will probably need to be done in two batches. Add an additional tablespoon of oil if necessary for the second batch.) If you have the bone, brown it along with the meat and cook it with the stew for added flavor.

2. Return all meat to the pan, add the leeks and garlic and cook over medium heat for 5 minutes, stirring frequently. Raise the heat to high and pour in the cider and chicken stock, stirring to dislodge the browned bits that have adhered to the bottom of the pan. Add half the rosemary and the whole bay leaf. When the stew has come to a boil, reduce the heat to its lowest setting, cover the pot tightly, and simmer for 1 to 1½ hours, or until the meat is almost tender. (If you have used pork from the leg it will probably take longer to cook than the shoulder or pork butt.)

The stew may be made ahead up to this point and refrigerated for up to 2 days or frozen for 1 month.

3. Lift the excess fat off the stew's surface if chilled or use a large spoon to remove as much as you can if hot. Remove and discard bone (if used) and the bay leaf.

4. Prepare the vegetables. Add the carrots and the turnips to the pot, cover, and simmer for 10 minutes. Add the parsnips and cook for about 15 minutes or more, or until the vegetables and meat are tender.

5. To finish the stew, spoon off any additional accumulated fat on the surface, push the vegetables and meat to one side, and stir in the remaining minced rosemary, the mustard, and the vinegar. Simmer, uncovered, for 5 minutes to blend the flavors, then taste and adjust the seasonings. (If the cider was especially sweet, you may wish to use an additional teaspoon of vinegar to balance the sauce.) Add a generous grinding of black pepper and salt to taste. (You may need little or no salt depending on the saltiness of the chicken stock used.)

6. Serve from a large tureen garnished with sprigs of rosemary, if desired.

YIELD: 6 SERVINGS.

Barbecued Ribs with Red Hot Mama Sauce

Ribs are just about our favorite informal summertime party food. Who doesn't get happy sitting down to a table laden with platters heaped with glistening ribs and all their "fix-in's"?

Until we met our editor, Susan Friedland, author of a delightful gem of a book called *Ribs* (Harmony Books, 1984), we had always simmered our ribs in water to precook them before finishing them on the grill. Susan believes, though—and now we agree—that this tends to toughen them and boils away a good deal of their flavor. She suggests a vinegar marinade instead, which softens the ribs and imparts additional flavor.

Squares of Peppery Corn Bread (see page 228) or The Absolute Best Buttermilk Biscuits (see page 220) and Classic Creamy Coleslaw (see page 223) are the traditional accompaniments. North Sedgwick Grange Baked Beans (see page 210) work well, too. Georgia Peach-Pecan Skillet Cake (see page 234) or Angel Food Cake with Summer Fruit Ambrosia (see page 238) would finish this summer feast most appropriately.

VINEGAR-PEPPER MARINADE:

2 teaspoons salt
1½ teaspoons coarsely ground black pepper
½ teaspoon dried red pepper flakes
3 tablespoons white vinegar

4½ to 5 pounds back ribs (not "country-style" ribs)

1½ cups bottled chili sauce
2 tablespoons cider vinegar
2 tablespoons brown sugar
1 tablespoon dry mustard
1 tablespoon Worcestershire sauce
1 teaspoon Tabasco or other liquid hot-pepper sauce
½ teaspoon cayenne pepper

1. To make the marinade, combine all its ingredients in a small bowl.
2. Cut the racks of ribs into 3- or 4-rib sections by slicing down between the bones. Place them in a large, shallow, glass baking dish and sprinkle the vinegar marinade evenly over the meat. Use your hands to rub the seasonings onto all surfaces of

the ribs. Set aside, loosely covered with plastic wrap, for about 2 hours at cool room temperature or for 2 to 8 hours in the refrigerator.

3. To make the Red Hot Mama Sauce, combine the chili sauce, vinegar, brown sugar, mustard, Worcestershire sauce, Tabasco, and cayenne pepper in a small saucepan. Bring to a boil, lower the heat, and simmer for 15 minutes.

The sauce may be made ahead and stored in a covered container in the refrigerator for up to 3 weeks.

4. Prepare a barbecue fire in a covered grill, and let the coals burn down until they are covered with a gray ash.

5. When the fire is ready, arrange the rib sections on the grill, cover the grill leaving the air vents open, and cook slowly for 30 minutes, turning 2 or 3 times.

6. Transfer about ⅔ cup of the Red Hot Mama Sauce to a plastic container for brushing onto the ribs as they cook. Place the remaining sauce in a bowl for the table.

7. Brush the meat with sauce and continue to cook for another 20 to 30 minutes, turning often, and brushing frequently with more sauce. Cover the grill again if flames flare up. The ribs are done when the sauce on them is lightly caramelized and the meat is no longer pink near the bone when checked with a knife.

8. Cut between each rib to form single-rib portions or provide steak knives so that it can be done at the table. Heap the ribs onto a platter and pass the Red Hot Mama Sauce to use on the side for dipping. Provide plenty of napkins!

YIELD: 4 SERVINGS.

FISH AND SHELLFISH

" . . . but when live fish are brought flouncing into market, you have only to select the kind most agreeable to your palate and the season."

—AMELIA SIMMONS

American Cookery (1796)

"This dish of (fish) is too good for any but anglers or very honest men."

—IZAAK WALTON

The Compleat Angler (1653)

"I don't mind eels
Except as meals."

—OGDEN NASH

Perfect Oven-Fried Fish Fillets

This recipe grew out of our love for the crisp coating on fried seafood that contrasts so beautifully with the smooth fish within—and of the knowledge that most of us would just as soon avoid frying fish at home, preferring to eat it occasionally in a restaurant with a powerful ventilation system. This recipe was developed using a minimum of butter, so the result is a lot less caloric and cholesterol laden than deep-fried fish.

You will need a shallow, rimmed, metal baking sheet or jelly roll pan to make this recipe successfully. The pan must be shallow so that the high heat can circulate freely around the fish; glass does not conduct the heat fast enough to create a crisp coating. Use any type of fillet—flounder, haddock, perch, and so on—as long as it's about half an inch thick. If you use sole, you can sandwich two thin fillets together before dredging them in the crumbs.

Serve this fish with steamed new potatoes, buttered orzo, or our Special Rice (see page 216) and long green beans. Hester's Citrus Pudding Cake (see page 242) or Lemon-Blueberry Mousse (see page 259 or use the same recipe without the blueberries) would be a refreshing dessert.

6 fish fillets (any type), each about 6 ounces and about ½ inch thick
1¼ cups milk
¾ teaspoon Tabasco
1½ cups dry bread crumbs
1 teaspoon grated lemon zest
¾ teaspoon salt
½ teaspoon freshly ground black pepper
½ teaspoon paprika
⅛ teaspoon cayenne pepper
5 tablespoons butter
1½ teaspoons lemon juice
Lemon wedges
Parsley sprigs

1. Preheat the oven to 500 degrees.
2. Rinse the fish and pat dry with paper towels. Combine the milk and Tabasco in a shallow bowl. Combine the bread crumbs with the lemon zest, salt, pepper, paprika, and cayenne papper in another shallow bowl. Work the crumb mixture together with your fingertips to make sure the lemon zest is evenly distributed.
3. Use about 1 teaspoon of the butter to grease a shallow, rimmed, metal baking sheet or jelly roll pan. Dip each fish fillet in the milk mixture, then dredge in the seasoned crumbs, shaking off the excess coating. Place on the baking pan.
4. Melt the remaining butter with the lemon juice. Spoon or drizzle the butter mixture evenly over each piece of fish and bake in the top half of the preheated oven until the outside crust is an attractive

golden brown, about 7 to 9 minutes.

5. Use a large spatula to transfer the fillets to plates and garnish with lemon wedges and parsley.

YIELD: 6 SERVINGS.

Baked Halibut Steaks Creole

Traditional Creole ingredients (tomatoes, peppers, and garlic) are enhanced with some capers and tarragon in this simple topping for baked fish. As the fish cooks and releases its juices, they mingle with the seasoned vegetables and olive oil to produce a light but flavorful sauce. You may substitute almost any other variety of fish steak or thick fillet for the halibut.

Serve with Parmesan Polenta (see page 215) or Special Rice (see page 216) and a green salad. Mixed Fruit–Chocolate Pan Soufflé (see page 264) or Cranberry-Cointreau Sundaes (see page 269) would be a fitting finish.

1½ pounds halibut steaks, cut about 1 inch thick
3 tablespoons olive oil
1 medium tomato, seeded and chopped
1 small green pepper, seeded and chopped
1 clove garlic, minced

1 teaspoon drained capers
1 teaspoon lemon juice
½ teaspoon dried tarragon
⅛ teaspoon freshly ground black pepper
Pinch of red pepper flakes

1. Preheat the oven to 425 degrees.

2. Rinse the halibut and pat dry. Use 1 tablespoon of the oil to coat the bottom of a baking dish large enough to hold the fish comfortably in one layer. Arrange the halibut in the dish.

3. In a small bowl, combine the tomato, green pepper, and garlic. Stir in the remaining 2 tablespoons of olive oil along with the capers, lemon juice, tarragon, black pepper, and red pepper flakes.

4. Spoon the vegetable mixture over and around the fish. Lay a sheet of foil over the top of the dish, but do not seal the edges. Bake in the preheated oven for 10 minutes. Remove the foil and bake for another 10 minutes, or until the fish tests done. Serve directly from the baking dish, spooning the juices over the fish.

YIELD: 4 SERVINGS.

Grilled Salmon with Egg Sauce

In many parts of America, salmon with egg sauce was the focal point of the Independence Day menu during most of the nineteenth and early twentieth centuries. The typical Fourth of July meal consisted of a whole baked salmon with egg sauce, creamed new potatoes and peas, and strawberry shortcake or blueberry pie for dessert. Unfortunately, this delicious culinary tradition began to disappear when the once plentiful salmon started diminishing early in the twentieth century. These days most of us are more apt to think in terms of fried chicken or hamburgers to help us celebrate the Fourth.

Although the high price of salmon forces us to mete it out more carefully, that need not stop us from trying to keep parts of this delicious meal alive. Salmon still makes a wonderful centerpiece for a summer meal, cooked either on the grill or indoors. We think the customary egg sauce is well worth making. But instead of the creamed potatoes and peas, how about our New New-Potato Salad (see page 213) with some blanched sugar peas added for color—and, for old times' sake, Red, White, and Blueberry Shortcakes (see page 232) would be a most patriotic dessert!

4 salmon steaks, each about 6 to 8 ounces and 1 inch thick
2 tablespoons olive oil
Salt and freshly ground black pepper
1 tablespoon butter
1 tablespoon all-purpose flour
½ teaspoon dry mustard

1 cup milk
1 hard-boiled egg, chopped
1 tablespoon chopped parsley
2 teaspoons lemon juice
Salt and freshly ground black pepper to taste
Lemon wedges

1. Prepare and light a fire on a charcoal grill and let the coals burn down so they are covered with gray ash, or preheat a gas grill or an oven broiler.
2. Brush both sides of the salmon steaks with some of the olive oil and sprinkle the fish lightly with salt and black pepper. Set the fish aside while you make the sauce.
3. In a medium saucepan, melt the butter over medium heat. Stir in the flour and the dry mustard and cook, stirring constantly, for 2 minutes. Raise the heat to high and gradually whisk in the milk. Bring to a boil and cook, stirring constantly, for 1 minute until the sauce is smooth and slightly thickened. Remove the pan from the heat and stir in the chopped egg, parsley, lemon juice, and salt and pepper to taste.

The sauce may be made up to 1 hour ahead and reheated gently before serving.
4. Grill or broil the salmon for about 4 minutes on the first side, turn carefully with a large spatula, brush with a little more oil and cook for about 4 minutes on the second side, or until the fish tests done when checked with a small knife. Remove

the salmon to a warm platter and garnish with the lemon wedges. Spoon the sauce over the salmon or pass it separately in a sauceboat.

YIELD: 4 SERVINGS.

Grilled Skewered Swordfish with Mustard-Herb Marinade

Swordfish is one of the few fin fish that takes well to grilling. It is a sturdy fish that can be cut as thick as you want, and it has a high enough fat content so that it stays moist on the grill. Fresh tuna could also be used in this recipe with excellent results.

Here in the Northeast we can often find swordfish "ends" or "chunks," which are the leftovers from the big fish after it has been cut into steaks. They are perfect for skewering and usually cost considerably less than the steaks.

Serve with Confetti Rice Salad (see page 211) or New New-Potato Salad (see page 213) and steamed asparagus or pattypan squash. Green Tomato Cobbler (see page 260) or Purple Plum Crumble (see page 258) would be a beautiful finish to this lovely summer meal.

1½ pounds swordfish, either chunks or steaks cut at least 1½ inches thick
½ cup olive oil
2 tablespoons Dijon mustard
3 tablespoons lemon juice
2 tablespoons minced shallots or scallions

1 clove garlic, minced
1 tablespoon chopped fresh basil or 1 teaspoon dried basil
½ teaspoon salt
¼ teaspoon freshly ground black pepper
Sprigs of fresh basil for garnish (optional)

1. Prepare and light a barbecue fire, or preheat a gas grill or the broiler.
2. Cut the swordfish into 2-inch chunks.
3. In a mixing bowl combine the oil, mustard, lemon juice, minced shallots, garlic, basil, salt, and pepper. Add the fish to the bowl, tossing gently to coat, and marinate for 10 minutes.
4. Remove the swordfish from the marinade and reserve the marinade. Thread the fish chunks onto four metal or dampened bamboo skewers (see note, page 118). Place the skewered fish on the grill over moderately hot coals and cook, turning several times, for a total of about 10 minutes or until the fish tests done. Place on a serving platter, brush with the leftover marinade, and garnish with the sprigs of basil before serving.

YIELD: 4 SERVINGS.

Arkansas Panfried Catfish

Since in the past catfish was one of the few readily available fish in the inland regions of this country, it became a favored staple in places like Arkansas and Missouri, whose slow rivers provided the perfect environment for this fish to thrive. However, with the advent of catfish farming, the rest of the country now gets to enjoy them, too. Their mild, tender, almost sweet flesh tastes quite different from that of saltwater fish.

In this recipe, sesame seeds are mixed into the seasoned flour; these add a subtly nutty flavor and extra crispiness to the crust. Tartar sauce (bottled is fine) is a good, creamy contrast, to the crusty fish.

If catfish hasn't yet reached your fish market, substitute any lean fish fillets, such as sole, perch, or flounder. Steamed new potatoes or Special Rice (see page 216) would be good with this fish, along with the green vegetable of your choice. Black Devil Cupcakes with Double Fudge Frosting (see page 240) would be a terrific finish.

2 tablespoons all-purpose flour
2 tablespoons cornmeal (yellow or white)
1 tablespoon sesame seeds
½ teaspoon salt
⅛ teaspoon cayenne pepper
⅛ teaspoon freshly ground black pepper

2 tablespoons butter
2 tablespoons oil
4 catfish fillets (each about 6 ounces)
1 lemon, cut in wedges
Several sprigs of parsley

1. Combine the flour, cornmeal, sesame seeds, salt, cayenne pepper, and black pepper on a plate. Heat the butter and oil in one very large or two medium-sized skillets. Cut the fish into serving-size pieces and dredge the fillets lightly in the seasoned flour mixture, shaking off the excess coating.

2. When the oil and butter are hot, arrange the fish in a single layer in the pan(s). Cook over medium heat for 2 to 3 minutes on each side to a crusty, golden brown. Use a large spatula to transfer the fish to a warm platter or plates and garnish with lemon wedges and sprigs of parsley. Serve with tartar sauce on the side if desired.

YIELD: 4 SERVINGS.

Broiled Soft-Shell Crabs with Spicy Lime Butter

Soft-shell crabs are a seasonal treat that spells summer for both of us. It is during a short season in late spring that blue crabs shed their hard shells, but modern farming methods today control and extend the season through most of the summer. Crabs are carefully watched, and the "peelers," which are those about to molt, are put in floats or pens and then removed from the water as soon as they shed their hard shells. Soft-shell crabs should be bought live, but unless you are knowledgeable about cleaning them, ask the fishmonger to do it for you. They vary in size, but we prefer the smaller ones that weight about 4 ounces. Allow 2 crabs for each person. After cleaning, the entire crab is deliciously edible.

Traditional methods of cooking these crabs include sautéeing and deep-frying, but we also enjoy them broiled with a lively citrus butter. Serve with Special Rice (see page 216), sautéed snow peas, and The Absolute Best Buttermilk Biscuits (see page 220) or Sky-High Popovers (see page 222). Our favorite dessert with this dish is Red, White, and Blueberry Shortcakes (see page 232).

8 tablespoons butter
1 tablespoon lime juice
¼ teaspoon cayenne pepper
⅓ cup all-purpose flour
¼ teaspoon salt
⅛ teaspoon freshly ground black pepper
8 small soft-shell crabs (about 2 pounds total)
1 teaspoon grated lime zest

1. Preheat the broiler.
2. In a small saucepan, melt the butter and stir in the lime juice and cayenne pepper. Keep the mixture warm over very low heat.

The spicy lime butter may be made several hours in advance. Reheat before using.
3. In a shallow dish, combine the flour, salt, and pepper. Lightly dredge the crabs in the seasoned flour and place them on a rack set over a broiler pan. Drizzle some of the butter over the crabs. Broil about 5 inches from the heat source, turning once and drizzling again with the butter, until the shells turn red and the coating is golden and crisp, a total of about 8 minutes.
4. To serve, drizzle the crabs with the remaining lime butter and sprinkle with the zest. Serve immediately.

YIELD: 4 SERVINGS.

Codfish Cakes with Quick Tomato Sauce

These codfish cakes were derived from a recipe of Brooke's Bermudian grandmother. Fish is, of course, a staple on that isolated island in the Atlantic, and part of each catch was preserved in salt as a hedge against a time when fresh fish and other fresh foods might be in short supply. Potatoes, too, were introduced into Bermuda early in the history of the island—hence, codfish cakes, made with mashed potatoes and salt cod, quickly became an important and popular part of the Bermudian diet.

Codfish cakes can still, of course, be made with salt cod, as the recipes found in such standard cookbooks as *The Joy of Cooking* indicate. We thought, though, that it would be valuable to try to develop a quicker version using fresh fish. Salt cod is somewhat hard to find these days, and it requires many hours (sometimes as long as two days) of soaking and changing the water to rid it of enough salt to make it palatable. We've substituted fresh poached cod and added bacon for a little of that nice, smoky flavor. Even Brooke's father, with his fond childhood memories of the Bermudian original, approved!

A green salad will complete this meal nicely. Hester's Citrus Pudding Cake (see page 242) would be a perfectly appropriate finish.

QUICK TOMATO SAUCE:

1 28-ounce can plum tomatoes
3 tablespoons butter
2 cloves garlic, minced
⅓ cup white wine
½ cup minced scallions, including
     green tops
2 tablespoons minced parsley
Pinch of dried red pepper flakes
Pinch of granulated sugar
½ teaspoon salt or to taste
Freshly ground black pepper to taste

1 pound cod or scrod fillets
1 cup milk
½ teaspoon salt
1 pound all-purpose potatoes
6 slices bacon
2 tablespoons butter
½ cup minced onion
1 egg
1 teaspoon dried thyme
3 tablespoons minced parsley
½ teaspoon freshly ground black pepper
Butter, as needed
¼ cup all-purpose flour, for dredging

1. To make the tomato sauce, slit the tomatoes lengthwise and squeeze out and discard the seeds. Reserve the juice. Chop the tomatoes.

2. Heat the butter in a large skillet. Add the tomatoes and the garlic and cook, stirring, for 2 minutes. Add the wine and about ¼ cup of the reserved tomato juice.

Simmer, uncovered, for 10 minutes. Stir in the scallions and parsley and season with the red pepper flakes, sugar, salt, and pepper. Simmer for a few more minutes to combine the flavors. If the sauce is thick, add a little more of the juice.

The sauce may be made 2 to 3 hours ahead and kept at room temperature. Reheat before serving.

3. Check the fish to make sure that all bones have been removed. Cut the fillets into pieces if necessary and place them in a saucepan with the milk and the salt. Bring to a simmer, cover, and cook gently until the fish is opaque, about 4 to 5 minutes. Remove the fish to a plate with a slotted spoon (it will probably be falling apart) and reserve the poaching milk to use in the mashed potatoes.

4. Peel the potatoes and cut them into 2-inch chunks. Cook in salted water until very tender, about 20 minutes. Drain well and mash with the butter and just enough of the poaching milk to make stiff mashed potatoes. (You will need 2 to 4 tablespoons of the liquid.)

5. Place 3 strips of bacon in each of two large skillets. Cook the bacon over me-dium-low heat until crisp. Drain on paper towels, leaving the fat in the skillets.

6. Crumble the bacon and add it to the mashed potatoes along with the cooked cod, onion, egg, thyme and parsley. Mix together with a wooden spoon until well combined. The mixture should not be perfectly smooth, but should have a few small but identifiable chunks of fish left. Season with the pepper and about ¼ teaspoon of salt, or to taste. (The amount of salt needed will depend on the saltiness of the bacon.)

7. Heat the bacon fat in the two skillets. There should be about 2 tablespoons of fat in each one. If there is less, add enough butter to make up the difference.

8. Use about ½ cup of the potato mixture to make each cake. Form into 3-inch cakes with your hands and dredge very lightly in the flour, brushing all the excess off with your fingers. When the bacon fat is hot, add the codfish cakes to the pan. Cook them over medium heat until they are crusty and a dark golden brown and are heated through, about 6 minutes on each side.

9. Serve the hot potato cakes with the tomato sauce spooned on the side.

YIELD: 4 SERVINGS.

Panfried Shad Roe with Spring Peas and Bacon

Shad, a member of the herring family, was for years an abundant and cheap fish found along the entire Atlantic Coast of the United States. The fish are born in early summer in rivers and migrate to the sea in autumn. There they remain for five years before swimming again upstream in the spring to spawn. As the rivers and streams are being cleaned up, shad are returning. The fresh shad season follows the advent of springtime: It begins in Florida in February and peaks in the Northeast in May. Shad festivals abound in small towns from the Carolinas to Connecticut.

The fish is as much prized for its wonderful roe as it is for the meat itself. Pairs of the orange-red roe sacs vary greatly in size, but a weight of between 8 and 12 ounces is most common and, we think, most desirable for cooking and presentation. Since the membrane covering the roe is quite delicate, rough handling in a skillet can result in rupturing the membrane and causing a big mess. We have found that a preliminary simmering in salted water solves this problem.

Many shad roe lovers eat them sautéed for breakfast, but we think the rich flavor is better suited to a light springtime supper. The traditional white toast accompaniment is just fine in the evening, too, but Sky-High Popovers (see page 222) are a nice alternative. Serve with Special Rice (see page 216) and a salad of young spinach leaves tossed with a fruity vinaigrette. Double Lemon Loaf (see page 236) with sliced and sugared strawberries is an appropriately seasonal finish.

1 tablespoon lemon juice

2 pairs shad roe (a total of 1 to 1½ pounds)

4 slices bacon, diced

Butter, as needed

3 tablespoons all-purpose flour

Salt and freshly ground black pepper to taste

1 egg

½ cup fine dry bread crumbs

¼ teaspoon grated lemon zest

⅓ cup white wine

⅔ cup heavy cream

½ cup cooked fresh green peas or frozen baby peas, thawed

4 thin lemon slices

1. Bring a medium saucepan of salted water to a boil, add the lemon juice and gently lower the roe into the water. Add more boiling water if the shad roe are not completely covered. Reduce the heat and simmer gently until the roe begins to firm up, about 5 to 7 minutes. Remove from the water with a slotted spoon and drain well on paper towels. Trim the membranes and carefully cut each roe pair into 4 pieces so that you have a total of 8 pieces.

The recipe may be prepared a few hours in advance up to this point. Chill the roe, but bring it back to room temperature before frying.

2. While the roe is cooking, sauté the bacon in a large skillet until crisp. Drain the bacon and reserve the drippings in the pan. There should be about 4 tablespoons drippings; if there is less, add enough butter to make up the difference.

3. In a shallow dish, combine the flour with a pinch each of salt and pepper. In another shallow dish, lightly beat the egg. In a third shallow dish, combine the bread crumbs with the lemon zest. Dip the roe pieces into the flour and shake off the excess coating, then dip into the egg, and finally into the bread crumbs to coat.

4. Heat the reserved bacon drippings and fry the roe over medium heat, carefully turning once, until browned and crisp, a total of 5 to 6 minutes. Transfer to a warm serving platter and cover lightly with foil.

5. Add the wine to the pan and cook over medium-high heat for about 1 minute, scraping up browned bits clinging to the bottom. Add the cream and simmer until the sauce is thickened, about 3 minutes. Add the peas and salt and pepper to taste, and simmer about 1 minute.

6. To serve, spoon the sauce over the roe and garnish with the reserved bacon and lemon slices.

YIELD: 4 SERVINGS.

Anthony's Mussels

Anthony's is a marvelous and beautiful restaurant in downtown St. Louis, a city that is a relatively unknown culinary mecca. This interpretation of his inspired yet simple dish raises the lowly mussel to ethereal heights.

Because mussels in the shell are a natural work of art, they are served that way, heaped in a shallow bowl with the fennel- and Pernod-scented cooking liquid ladled over them. After the mussel meat has been extracted and enjoyed and the shells discarded into a separate bowl, Anthony recommends breaking off big chunks of crusty warm French rolls to sop up the remainder of the excellent broth. The restaurant serves this in smaller portions as an appetizer, but Melanie has been known to order a double serving and a tossed green salad, and consider it the perfect main course.

At home, we make the recipe often, especially since it can be completed in about 30 minutes. A fitting dessert would be the very beautiful Georgia Peach-Pecan Skillet Cake (see page 234) in summer or Cranberry Bread Pudding with Whiskey Sauce (see page 252) in winter.

2 leeks, white parts only, thoroughly rinsed and cut in julienne strips about 1½ inches long

1 small (about 8 ounces) fennel bulb, chopped

2 tablespoons butter

2 cloves garlic, minced

4 dozen (about 4 pounds) mussels, scrubbed and debearded

1½ cups white wine

1½ cups bottled clam juice or fish stock

½ cup water

1 bay leaf, broken

2 cups heavy cream

2 tablespoons Pernod or other anise-flavored liqueur (optional)

3 tablespoons minced flat-leaf parsley

Freshly ground black pepper

Salt to taste

1. In a 3-quart saucepan, sauté the leeks and fennel in the butter over medium-low heat until softened, about 5 to 8 minutes. Add the garlic and sauté about 1 minute. Take the pan off the heat and reserve.

2. Place the mussels, wine, clam juice, water, and bay leaf in a large pot. Cover and steam the mussels over medium-high heat until the shells open, about 5 minutes.

Remove the mussels in the shell from the pot with tongs or a slotted spoon and place in a large bowl, covering it with plastic wrap to keep the mussels warm. Discard any mussels that have not opened.

3. Strain the broth through a coffee filter or several layers of cheesecloth into the pan with the vegetables. Add the cream, bring to a simmer, and cook uncovered for 5 to

8 minutes until liquid is somewhat reduced. Stir in the optional Pernod, parsley, and pepper. Add salt to taste. (Bottled clam juice is salty, so be careful.) Add the mussels to the pot, cover, and place over low heat for about 1 minute to reheat the mussels and infuse them with some of the broth.

4. To serve, evenly divide the mussels among 4 large, shallow soup dishes. Ladle ¼ of the broth and vegetables over each dish of mussels.

YIELD: 4 SERVINGS.

Oyster-Thyme Pan Roast

Melanie first tasted an oyster pan roast at the Grand Central Oyster Bar & Restaurant, a New York City culinary landmark. Opened in 1913 on the lower level of Grand Central Terminal, the cavernous but gracious dining room has managed to maintain its quality and reputation. Many New Yorkers feel that there is no better place in town for seafood. Indeed, the Oyster Bar has a seemingly unlimited menu and often boasts more than a dozen varieties of sparkling fresh clams and oysters daily.

Most of the seafood served at the Oyster Bar is simply prepared and presented, a trick that is successful only if a restaurant starts with the freshest and best ingredients. Of the many savory dishes we have sampled there, one of our favorites is still the oyster pan roast. It is nothing more than oysters stewed gently in butter and cream, lightly seasoned, and spooned over white toast. We think it is comfort food at its best.

Oyster pan roast is also ridiculously easy to prepare at home. Just be sure you start with good oysters. If you live in an area where fresh oysters are available, call in advance and ask the fishmonger to shuck them and reserve the liquor since they are tricky to shuck at home. Refrigerated, pasteurized oysters in a sealed can are nationally marketed and found in most fish markets and seafood departments of good supermarkets. These are perfectly delicious in a pan roast and are usually somewhat less expensive than oysters in the shell. Depending upon the region of the country where the oysters are harvested, they may range from the tiny dime-size Pacific Olympias to the two- or three-bite-size East Coast

Oyster-Thyme Pan Roast (cont.)

varieties. Thus, the numbers of oysters you will need depends on where you live, though about 6 average-size oysters for each person is a good rule of thumb.

After you have the oysters ready, this dish takes less than ten minutes to prepare. Its rich simplicity demands very few accompaniments. But we like a lively salad of radicchio and Belgian endive dressed in a white wine vinaigrette and a lightly steamed seasonal green vegetable such as broccoli or zucchini. The Oyster Bar is also renowned for its confections, and they would surely be proud to serve something as good as Georgia Peach-Pecan Skillet Cake (see page 234) for dessert.

6 tablespoons butter
⅓ cup finely chopped celery
3 tablespoons minced shallots
1½ pints (about 36) shucked oysters and their liquor
¼ cup white wine
1¼ cups heavy cream
¾ teaspoon Tabasco

1 tablespoon minced fresh thyme or 1 teaspoon dried thyme
Salt to taste
Cayenne pepper to taste
6 slices white toast
6 small sprigs fresh thyme for garnish (optional)

1. Melt the butter in a heavy saucepan and sauté the celery over medium-low heat for about 2 minutes. Add the shallots and sauté about 2 minutes. Add the oysters, their liquor, the wine, cream, Tabasco, and thyme, and simmer until the edges of oysters just curl, about 2 to 3 minutes. Add salt and cayenne pepper to taste.

2. To serve, place a slice of toast in each of six shallow soup bowls and ladle the oysters and the broth over the toast. Garnish with a sprig of fresh thyme.

YIELD: 6 SERVINGS.

Southern-Style Shrimp Boil

One version or another of this method of cooking shrimp (or crawfish or crab) is used up and down the entire southern Atlantic and Gulf coasts—from Maryland, Virginia, and the Carolinas, all the way down through Georgia and Louisiana. Each region has its own variation, but the eating experience always epitomizes informal dining at its best. The shellfish is simmered in a highly seasoned court bouillon and served with a dipping sauce. Sometimes shrimp boil is cooked outdoors in huge vats or half-barrels and dumped out in heaps onto long, newspaper-lined tables as part of a community supper. It also makes great bar food, where it is set out in bowls on the long counters to be washed down by the local brew.

We think it's a wonderful idea for a casual summer supper in any part of the country! Guests are invited to peel the unshelled shrimp themselves and then dunk them into a seasoned butter dipping sauce. Serve with Classic Creamy Coleslaw (see page 223), Confetti Rice Salad (see page 211), or Old-Fashioned Picnic Potato Salad (see page 207), and Peppery Corn Bread (see page 228) or The Absolute Best Buttermilk Biscuits (see page 220). Either Red, White, and Blueberry Shortcakes (see page 232) or Maggie Valley Buttermilk Pie (see page 244) would be a fine dessert.

3 pounds medium or large shrimp, in their shells
6 cups water
1 tablespoon black peppercorns
2 teaspoons salt
2 teaspoons whole cloves
1 teaspoon celery seed
1 teaspoon dry mustard
1 teaspoon cayenne pepper
3 bay leaves
1 rib celery, including leaves, broken in half

4 sprigs parsley, including stems

SEASONED BUTTER DIPPING SAUCE:

12 tablespoons butter
¼ cup lemon juice
1 tablespoon Worcestershire sauce
1 tablespoon white wine vinegar
1 teaspoon salt
½ teaspoon coarsely ground black pepper
½ teaspoon Tabasco

1. Rinse the shrimp well under cold running water and set aside. In a large saucepan, combine the water and the remaining ingredients for the shrimp boil. Bring to a boil, reduce the heat, and simmer, covered, for 20 minutes so that the flavors have a chance to permeate the water.

2. Meanwhile, make the dipping sauce. Melt the butter over low heat in a small saucepan with the lemon juice, Worcestershire sauce, vinegar, salt, and pepper. Remove the pan from the heat and stir in the Tabasco.

The dipping sauce may be made up to 2 hours ahead and kept at room temperature. Reheat before serving.

3. Bring the seasoned water back to a rapid boil and add the shrimp to the pot. Cook the shrimp for 1 to 3 minutes, depending on their size, until they turn pink but are not tightly curled. Do not overcook since they will continue to cook a bit after they are out of the water. Drain them into a colander and discard the celery and the parsley sprigs. Do not discard the rest of the whole spices since they look nice amidst the shrimp.

4. Dump the hot shrimp onto the center of a table that has been covered with several layers of newspaper. Pour the Seasoned Butter Dipping Sauce into 2 or 3 small bowls and invite your guests to peel the shrimp themselves and dip them into the sauce.

YIELD: 6 servings.

Crawfish Étouffée

Every year on the first weekend in May, the tiny Louisiana Cajun community of Breaux Bridge attracts up to 300,000 people for its annual International Crawfish Festival. Until Cajun cooking became an international food craze, due in large part to the immensely talented chef Paul Prudhomme, crawfish were a relatively unknown ingredient outside of Louisiana. There, they were long considered to be poor-man's fare and more of a pest than a delicacy. Now, with a nation that can't seem to get enough of Cajun cooking, they have become much prized and are available up North, both fresh and frozen.

Fresh crawfish tails need to be shelled and the meat will weigh about half as much as the whole tail. Save the shells and any fat that you can extract. Make a stock from the shells according to our recipe (see below) and add the fat to the étoufée along with the stock. If you use frozen crawfish meat, use fish stock or bottled clam juice in place of crawfish stock. If you can't find crawfish at all, a delicious and equally authentic étouffée can be made with shrimp. Again, don't waste those wonderful shells.

Étouffée literally means "smothered," and this dish is indeed smothered with vegetables in an aromatic roux and an enrichment of butter, making it one of the more elegant and delicious repasts in the Cajun repertoire. The roux is crucial to the depth of flavor and color of the étouffée. Old recipes require the cooking of a medium-dark roux over low heat with constant stirring for up to 45 minutes. We favor a new, quicker version that cooks in about 5 minutes over medium-high heat. Use a heavy pot and a wooden spoon, and don't stop stirring even for a second lest the roux burn. We think the final flavor of the "quick" roux is just as good, and the time and energy saved is substantial. Have the vegetables ready and at hand; adding them at the very moment that the roux reaches the proper color helps to stop the roux from further cooking. The entire roux base can be made in advance, which makes this a terrific last-minute dish for entertaining. The étouffée is traditionally served over rice or, nontraditionally, over pasta. Nothing else is needed other than a spinach salad lightly dressed with a fruit or sherry wine vinaigrette, French rolls, and Maggie Valley Buttermilk Pie (see page 244) or Luscious Pecan Pie Bars (see page 266) and vanilla ice cream for dessert.

THE ROUX:

2 cups crawfish or shrimp stock (recipe
   follows) or bottled clam juice
4 tablespoons vegetable oil
6 tablespoons all-purpose flour
About 1 large onion, chopped (1 cup)
About 1 large green pepper, chopped (1 cup)
About 1 large rib celery, chopped (⅔ cup)
3 cloves minced garlic
½ teaspoon dried thyme leaves
½ teaspoon dried basil leaves
½ teaspoon cayenne pepper
Salt to taste

8 tablespoons butter

2 pounds crawfish tails, peeled or 1½ pounds medium shrimp, shelled and deveined (save all shells for stock; recipe follows)

1 cup thinly sliced scallions, including most of the green tops (about 1 bunch)

½ teaspoon dried thyme leaves

½ teaspoon dried basil leaves

2 tablespoons lemon juice

1 tablespoon Worcestershire sauce

½ cup minced parsley

Salt to taste

2 to 3 drops Tabasco or other hot sauce

12 ounces cooked fettuccine or 4 cups cooked long-grain white rice

1. If you are using crawfish or shrimp stock, make it first and reserve. (You will need 2 cups. If you do not have enough, add water to make up the difference.) Chop all the vegetables before beginning the roux.

2. Heat the oil in a heavy 3- to 4-quart saucepan until nearly smoking. Using a long-handled wooden spoon, stir in the flour, breaking up any lumps. Continue to cook, stirring constantly over medium-high heat until the roux turns a rich mahogany color, abut 3 to 5 minutes. Watch carefully since the roux color changes quickly after a few minutes. It should be a rich brown, but not burned.

3. When the proper color is reached, immediately stir in the onion, green pepper, and celery. Reduce the heat to low and cook, stirring, for about 2 minutes. Stir in the garlic, thyme, basil, and cayenne pepper. Cook over low heat, stirring, about 2 minutes. Stir in the stock or clam juice and bring to a simmer, stirring. Cover and cook over low heat, stirring frequently, for about 15 minutes. Add salt to taste.

The roux may be made up to 1 day ahead. Gently reheat before using.

4. While the roux base is simmering, heat 4 tablespoons of the butter in a large skillet. Add the crawfish tails (or shrimp), scallion, thyme, and basil and cook over medium heat, stirring constantly, until the shellfish redden and are just cooked through, about 2 to 3 minutes. (Do not overcook either the crawfish or shrimp since they are very delicate.) Stir in the lemon juice and Worcestershire sauce.

5. Stir the crawfish mixture into the roux base. Set the saucepan over the lowest possible heat or partially remove it from the burner. Using a wooden spoon, stir in the remaining 4 tablespoons of butter, ½ tablespoon at a time, adding another piece only as the previous one is incorporated. (The object is to produce a creamy mixture, not to melt the butter.) Stir in the parsley, and season with salt and Tabasco to taste.

6. Serve the étouffée ladled over hot fettuccine or mounds of cooked rice.

YIELD: 6 SERVINGS.

CRAWFISH OR SHRIMP STOCK:

1 medium onion, quartered
1 carrot, quartered
1 small rib celery, quartered
4 whole peppercorns

1 bay leaf, broken in half
1 1-inch piece lemon peel, colored part only
Shells from 2 pounds crawfish tails or from
    1½ pounds medium shrimp
3 cups water
¼ cup white wine

1. To make the stock, place all the ingredients in a nonreactive saucepan and bring to a boil, stirring often. Lower the heat and simmer, uncovered, for 25 to 30 minutes.

2. Pour the stock through a fine mesh strainer, pushing on the solids with the back of a spoon to extract the flavor.

YIELD: ABOUT 2 CUPS.

NOTE: The stock can be made a day ahead and refrigerated, or frozen up to 2 months.

Clam-and-Scallop Risotto

Although it takes a good deal of hands-on attention to make risotto, it is worth every minute of stirring and watching. The rice of choice is Italian Arborio since its short grain can absorb a lot of liquid. The rice is widely available in specialty or Italian markets; if you cannot find it, substitute regular long-grain rice.

A basic risotto recipe can be varied with herbs, vegetables, sausage, fish, or small amounts of any cooked meat. Here we use clams (look for the smallest available for the prettiest presentation), scallops, and tomatoes.

In Italy, risotto is often served in small portions as a "prima" course; we think it can star as the main event. Almost a meal in itself, the risotto only needs Roasted Vegetables (such as broccoli) (see page 218) dressed with a garlic, white wine vinegar, and olive oil vinaigrette and some crunchy breadsticks to round it out. End a summer meal with Lemon-Blueberry Mousse (see page 259) and in other seasons, finish with raspberry sherbet and Giant Anise Sugar Cookies (see page 267).

3½ cups good-quality canned or homemade (see page 2) chicken stock
1 cup bottled clam juice
¾ cup white wine
4 tablespoons butter
½ cup minced onion
1½ cups Arborio or long-grain rice
12 ounces fresh plum tomatoes, peeled, seeded, and diced or 1 16-ounce can plum tomatoes, drained, seeded, and diced
8 ounces bay scallops or quartered sea scallops
16 small cherrystone or other fresh clams in the shell, scrubbed
⅓ cup chopped flat-leaf parsley
Salt and freshly ground black pepper to taste

1. In a saucepan, bring the chicken stock, clam juice, and wine to a simmer. Keep at a low simmer throughout the cooking procedure.

2. In a heavy, nonreactive, 3-quart saucepan, heat 3 tablespoons of the butter and sauté the onion over medium-low heat, about 3 minutes. Add the rice and sauté, stirring with a wooden spoon, until all grains are coated with butter and the rice becomes translucent, about 2 minutes.

3. Add about ¾ cup of the simmering stock or enough to cover the rice. Cook over medium heat, stirring nearly constantly and keeping the mixture at an even, gentle simmer until most of the liquid has been absorbed, about 5 minutes. Continue this process of adding stock to cover and cooking until nearly absorbed until there is only ½ to 1 cup of stock left, about 15 minutes more. At this point, the mixture should look creamy and the rice should be almost tender, but firm in the center of the grain. Add another ¼ cup simmering stock, the tomatoes, and the scallops. Cover the pan and simmer until the scallops are cooked through, about 3 minutes.

4. Meanwhile, bring the remaining ½ cup or so of stock to a rolling boil, add the clams, and cover the pot. Lower the heat and steam until the clams open, about 3 to 5 minutes. Remove the clams and discard the liquid, or strain and add to the risotto, if desired.

5. To serve, stir the parsley and remaining 1 tablespoon butter into the risotto. Season to taste with salt and pepper. Ladle the risotto into shallow soup dishes or rimmed serving plates. Arrange the clams on top. Serve immediately.

YIELD: 4 SERVINGS.

White Clam Personal Pizzas

The world's best pizzas come out of New Haven, Connecticut. Now we realize that this is a personal opinion and open to dispute. Still, even the most jaded would be impressed at the lengthy queues night after night outside several local establishments that serve the authentic New Haven "apizza."

One of the most popular and most famous of these is Pepe's, which attracts legions of locals, Yalies, and tourists who have heard tales of the succulent wonders of the white clam pizza. Longtime fans but culinary "fidgets" as well, we just had to slightly personalize the original. We shaped the dough into single-serving portions and added more clams, more herbs, and a sprinkling of hot pepper—all of which enchance rather than change the marvelous simplicity of this dish. Our crust is just as thin as Pepe's, but we use quick-rise yeast to produce a wonderful dough in minutes. Canned clams can be used here, but we wouldn't be so heretical (we do live in New England, after all) as to suggest that they are quite as good as the real thing. Serve the pizzas with lots of beer, a big green salad, and Purple Plum Crumble (see page 258) or Hester's Citrus Pudding Cake (see page 242) for dessert.

PIZZA DOUGH:

3 cups all-purpose flour
1 package quick-rise yeast
1 teaspoon granulated sugar
1 teaspoon salt
1 tablespoon olive oil
1 cup warm (about 120 degrees) water
About 2 tablespoons yellow cornmeal for
    sprinkling on the baking sheet

3 cloves garlic, minced
¼ teaspoon dried red pepper flakes
4 tablespoons olive oil
2 dozen littleneck clams, shucked and chopped
    (about 1 cup) or 2 6½-ounce cans chopped
    clams, drained and juices reserved
1 tablespoon minced fresh oregano or
    1 teaspoon dried oregano
1 tablespoon minced fresh basil or 1 teaspoon
    dried basil
3 tablespoons grated Parmesan cheese

1. To make the dough, place the flour, yeast, sugar, and salt in the workbowl of a food processor. Pulse 2 or 3 times to mix. With the machine running, add the oil and water through the feed tube. When the dough forms a ball, process about 45 seconds to knead. (If making the dough by hand, mix the dry ingredients in a large bowl. Beat in the liquids until a smooth dough forms. On a lightly floured surface, knead the dough for 10 minutes until smooth and elastic.) Place the dough in an oiled bowl, turning to coat the top with oil, cover lightly with a towel, and let rise in a warm place until doubled in bulk, about 30 minutes.

2. Preheat oven to 500 degrees. Sprinkle 1 tablespoon of the cornmeal on each of two large, noninsulated baking sheets.

3. Steep the garlic and red pepper flakes in the oil for about 15 minutes.

4. Punch down the risen dough and divide it into 4 parts. On a lightly floured surface, roll each part into a circle roughly 8 inches in diameter and place on the prepared baking sheets. Brush each pizza equally with the garlic oil and sprinkle with the clams and a small amount of clam juice. Then sprinkle each pizza with the oregano, basil, and cheese.

5. Bake the pizzas on the lower and center racks of the oven for 12 to 14 minutes, switching the positions of the baking sheets halfway through for even cooking, until their crusts are crisp and speckled with brown. Serve immediately.

YIELD: 4 SERVINGS.

New England Boiled Lobster

There's a lot of debate about the proper way to cook lobsters. We think that boiling them New England–style in a large pot of well-salted water not only results in tender and moist meat but is the most practical method for a home cook.

The crucial factor in producing lobster with succulent meat is the cooking time. Undercooked lobster clings to the shell and is quite disgusting and inedible. Dry, overcooked meat is a crying shame—especially given lobsters' price per pound. Although we've always used minutes per pound as a guideline to a lobster's doneness, we sometimes have been uncertain of the timing if the cooking water takes some time to come back to a boil. Recently, Melanie's friends at the fish market have taught us a terrific test for doneness. If, after the allotted cooking time, you can pull one of its antennae out fairly easily, the lobster is cooked. If not, test again after a few minutes. The cooking water needs to be quite salty. Salt raises the boiling point of the water so that the lobsters cook faster; the meat also tastes best if it has a slightly salty tang.

We like the Maine practice of serving vinegar along with the melted butter for dipping. It nicely cuts the richness of the lobster meat. Our personal preferences for rounding out a lobster feast are buttered corn on the cob, Classic Creamy Coleslaw (see page 223) and Great Garlic Bread (see page 225). Be sure to provide side plates for these accompaniments since the dinner plate will be too full of delicious lobster to accommodate anything else! We like blueberry pie with a scoop of vanilla ice cream or Red, White and Blueberry Shortcakes (see page 232) for a sufficiently grand finale.

6 live lobsters (1¼ to 1½ pounds each)
12 tablespoons unsalted butter, melted

1 tablespoon cider vinegar (or more or less to taste)

1. Fill two 8-quart pots ⅔ full of water. Cover, bring to a boil, add 2 tablespoons of salt to each, and return to a boil. Grasp the live lobsters with tongs and plunge them headfirst into the rapidly boiling water, three to a pot. Immediately cover again and begin timing, allowing 10 minutes per pound (for example, approximately 15 minutes for a 1½-pounder). When the water has come back to a rolling boil, uncover the pots. At the end of the allotted time, test a lobster for doneness by lifting one out of the water with tongs and pulling on one of its antennae. If the antenna pulls out after it has been given a quick shake or two, then the lobster is done. If it doesn't pull out easily, return the lobster to the pot, cook for another 2 minutes, and test again.

2. Remove the lobsters from the water with tongs and drain in a colander. Place them on a large, rimmed baking sheet, split them down the centers of their tails, and drain as much water as possible from their cavities. Transfer to individual plates and serve. Provide nutcrackers and small picks for extracting the meat from the claws.

3. Divide the melted butter among two bowls or among six individual bowls. Add vinegar to all of the butter, or to only one of the bowls, or pass it at the table so that people can add it as desired.

YIELD: 6 SERVINGS.

Shellfish Paella

The word *paella* refers to a large, shallow, 2-handled pan and not to a specific recipe. Depending upon the region in Spain, there are paellas made with chicken, seafood, meat, and combinations thereof. There are even all-vegetable paellas. The common ingredient, though, is a saffron-flavored rice base. Because paella is, to our minds, one of the great dishes, we think it is well worth the rather steep price of saffron. It is also well worth searching out good Spanish chorizo, for its flavor is incomparable.

Since most recipes for paella seem extraordinarily complicated and time-consuming, in our early years of cooking we were both rather intimidated by the long lists of ingredients, cooking instructions, and various pans required for separate sautés and simmers. But, being real fans of rice dishes in general and paella in particular, we attempted several of these marathons and quickly realized that the preparation of a shellfish paella need take only minutes instead of hours and one pan instead of several. We make our paellas without any problem in large skillets or sauté pans, but the traditional utensil, if you have one, makes a very pretty table presentation.

As in most shellfish combination dishes, the seafood mixture can be varied according to preference and availability. In fact, we don't usually make our choice until we are in the fish market and check both our wallets and the fresh catch of the day. If you feel rich, you may want to add some lobster but we think that paella is every bit as good (and good looking) made entirely with mussels, which are inevitably one of the best buys.

Paella is a one-dish meal that needs only a salad of romaine lettuce and orange sections in a sherry or red wine vinaigrette, crusty peasant bread, and Mocha Pudding with Coffee Cream (see page 254) to finish.

½ teaspoon saffron threads

½ cup white wine

½ pound chorizo sausage or hot Italian sausage

4 tablespoons olive oil

1 large onion, chopped

1 small red bell pepper, chopped

1 small yellow bell pepper, chopped

2 cloves garlic, minced

1½ cups raw long-grain white rice

¼ to ½ teaspoon red pepper flakes (depending upon the spiciness of the sausage and personal taste)

1½ cups fish stock or bottled clam juice

1 16-ounce can plum tomatoes, drained and coarsely chopped (reserve the liquid)

12 small clams, scrubbed

12 small mussels, scrubbed and debearded

18 medium (about ½ pound) shrimp, peeled and deveined if necessary

½ pound sea scallops, halved or quartered if they are large

1 cup frozen green peas, thawed

¼ cup pitted and sliced good-quality green olives

3 tablespoons minced parsley

Salt to taste

1. Place the saffron threads on a saucer or piece of wax paper and crush with the back of a spoon. Soak the crushed saffron in the wine for 10 minutes.

2. Slice the chorizo into pieces about ¼ inch thick. Sauté the sausage in a 12- to 14-inch skillet, a sauté pan with a lid, or a paella pan, stirring often until browned, about 5 to 8 minutes. Remove to a plate with a slotted spoon. Pour off the excess fat from the skillet but leave the browned drippings in the bottom of the pan.

3. Add the oil to the skillet and sauté the onion and red and yellow peppers over medium-low heat until just softened, about 5 minutes. Add the garlic and sauté about 1 minute. Stir in the rice and red pepper flakes and cook, stirring, until the rice is coated and begins to turn translucent, about 1 minute. Stir in the saffron and wine mixture, the fish stock or clam juice, tomatoes, and ½ cup of the reserved tomato liquid. Bring to a boil, while continuing to stir, then lower heat, cover pan and simmer for 12 minutes.

4. Remove cover from skillet and arrange clams and mussels in rice, pushing them into the mixture with a spoon. Replace cover and simmer for 10 minutes. Add the shrimp, scallops and peas, stirring them in gently. Cover and simmer until clams and mussels are opened, shrimp and scallops are cooked through, and most of the liquid is absorbed into the rice, about 3 to 5 minutes. Stir in the olives, taste and add salt as needed.

5. Sprinkle with the parsley and serve directly from the skillet.

YIELD: 6 SERVINGS.

Maque Choux–Stuffed Trout

Maque choux is a highly seasoned Cajun corn dish. It usually includes bell peppers, onions, tomatoes, and a touch of cream. We particularly like a variation on this theme as a colorful and savory stuffing for boned trout. In summer, use fresh corn cut from the cob and ripe, red tomatoes, but this is a wonderful winter dish as well since frozen corn and good canned tomatoes are just as delicious.

Small trout are widely available in most fish markets and they make an attractive and easy presentation, especially when coated with a cornmeal mixture and then quickly panfried to a golden-brown crispness. The sauce is made in minutes in the same skillet.

We like to serve this assertive main dish with some plain rice, a simple salad with a lemon and oil dressing, and a wonderful dessert, such as Cranberry Bread Pudding with Whiskey Sauce (see page 252).

⅓ cup yellow cornmeal

⅓ cup all-purpose flour

½ teaspoon salt

¼ teaspoon freshly ground black pepper

5 tablespoons butter

1 medium onion, chopped (½ cup)

3 tablespoons thinly sliced scallions, including some of the green tops

About ½ small green pepper, chopped (¼ cup)

About 1 rib celery, chopped (⅓ cup)

¾ cup corn kernels, cut from the cob or frozen

1 ounce prosciutto or smoked ham, shredded

¼ teaspoon cayenne pepper

½ teaspoon Tabasco

Salt and freshly ground black pepper to taste

1½ cups bread cubes made from about 3 slices day-old French bread

⅓ cup heavy cream

1 egg, beaten

4 whole boneless trout, each about 8 ounces

2 tablespoons vegetable oil

½ cup white wine

1 pound ripe tomatoes, peeled and seeded or 1 16-ounce can plum tomatoes, drained

¼ teaspoon ground cumin

2 tablespoons minced parsley

1. Combine the cornmeal, flour, ½ teaspoon salt, and ¼ teaspoon black pepper in a shallow dish. Set aside.

2. Heat 3 tablespoons of the butter in a large skillet. Over medium–low heat, sauté the onion, scallions, green pepper, celery, corn, and prosciutto until the onion is softened, about 5 minutes. Season with cayenne pepper, Tabasco, and salt and pepper. Turn into a mixing bowl and toss with the bread cubes, cream, and egg until well blended.

3. Divide the vegetable mixture into 4 parts and stuff one part into the cavity of each of the trout. If necessary, use small skewers or toothpicks to close the cavities. Coat both sides of the trout with the cornmeal mixture.

4. Heat the remaining 2 tablespoons butter and the oil in a large skillet. (You may need to use two skillets with half the oil and butter in each if you don't have one large enough for all the trout. Or you may cook the trout in two batches in a single skillet.) Sauté the trout over medium heat, carefully turning once with a spatula, until golden brown and just cooked through, about 5 to 6 minutes on each side. Remove the trout to a warm platter.

5. Add the wine to the skillet and cook over high heat for about 45 seconds, scraping up any browned bits that are clinging to the bottom. Add the tomatoes and cumin and cook over medium-high heat until the sauce is slightly thickened, about 2 minutes. Stir in the parsley. Season to taste with salt and pepper.

6. To serve, spoon the sauce around the trout.

YIELD: 4 SERVINGS.

Smoked Fish Cakes with Herbed Tartar Sauce

Smoked salmon is readily available and, combined with fresh salmon, makes a colorful, summery, delicate, and memorable alternative to traditional fish cakes. Since the smoked salmon will be chopped, there is no need to buy perfect thin slices. Instead, ask for the end pieces and trimmings, which are usually much less expensive.

We especially favor the distinctive tarragon flavor in the simple tartar sauce that accompanies this dish. Corn on the cob served with Parmesan cheese–seasoned melted butter and blanched sugar snap peas sprinkled with a fruit vinegar would be delicious complements. Angel Food Cake with Summer Fruit Ambrosia (see page 238) or Lemon-Blueberry Mousse (see page 259) would be a lovely finale to this light meal for a warm evening.

HERBED TARTAR SAUCE:

¾ cup good-quality commercial or homemade mayonnaise
1½ tablespoons sweet pickle relish (India relish)
1 tablespoon chopped fresh tarragon or 1 teaspoon dried tarragon
¾ teaspoon lemon juice
⅛ teaspoon Tabasco

2½ cups fine fresh bread crumbs made from 5 to 6 slices good-quality, firm white bread
½ cup chopped flat-leaf parsley, including some of the tender stems

12 ounces skinless and boneless fresh salmon fillet
4 ounces smoked salmon
4 tablespoons butter
½ cup chopped onion
½ cup chopped red bell pepper
1 egg
1 egg yolk
1 teaspoon Dijon mustard
1 teaspoon Worcestershire sauce
½ teaspoon Tabasco
¼ teaspoon freshly ground black pepper
2 tablespoons vegetable oil

1. To make the tartar sauce, combine the mayonnaise, relish, tarragon, lemon juice, and Tabasco in a small bowl. Cover and refrigerate 30 minutes or up to 2 days before using.

2. To make the fish cakes, place 1¼ cups of the bread crumbs and the parsley in a mixing bowl. Reserve the remaining crumbs in a shallow dish to coat the fish cakes.

3. Coarsely chop both the fresh and smoked salmon by hand or by pulsing in a food processor. Add to the crumbs in the mixing bowl.

4. Heat 2 tablespoons of the butter in a small skillet and sauté the onion and bell pepper over medium-low heat until softened, about 5 minutes. Add to the mixing bowl.

5. In a small bowl, whisk together the egg, the yolk, mustard, Worcestershire Sauce, Tabasco, and pepper. Add to the mixing bowl and toss with a fork to blend all ingredients. Chill the mixture, covered, for at least 30 minutes or up to 4 hours.

6. Using about ⅓ cup for each fishcake, form the fish mixture into 8 patties, each about 2½ to 3 inches in diameter. Coat both sides of the fish cakes with the reserved bread crumbs, patting the crumbs into the cakes.

7. Using two skillets, heat 1 tablespoon of the remaining butter and 1 tablespoon of the oil in each. Sauté the fish cakes over medium heat until crusty brown, about 5 minutes on each side, flattening them slightly with a spatula when they are turned.

8. Serve immediately, accompanied by the tartar sauce.

Yield: 4 servings.

SEMIVEGETARIAN

Aubergine aubergine
Lettuce pray for the marrow
For no one radishes the end
We have all cucumbered our unworthy chives
With foul swedes
It ill beetroots us to publicly sprout peas
From the endive our fennels
None escapes the cabbages of thyme
Even the wisest sage comes to a spinach
Celery celery I say unto you
This is the cauliflower
When salsifiers all
Artichoke and kale

—B. C. LEALE

A Vegetation to Be Read by the Parsnip

Grits-and-Greens Spoon Bread

Spoon bread is a thoroughly American dish. With its roots in the Deep South, it was regularly served in Colonial times both at country peasant tables and in the sophisticated dining room of Thomas Jefferson's Monticello.

Spoon bread is aptly named, for it is a cross between a soufflé and a moist, dense baked pudding—truly a bread that must be eaten with a spoon. Depending upon the ingredients added to the basic mixture, spoon bread can be a bread, a starchy vegetable substitute, or a main course.

Traditionally made with a base, or "rick," of cornmeal cooked in milk and enriched with egg yolks, the batter is then lightened with beaten egg whites. All manner of flavorings from cheese to vegetables or from ham to sausage can be added. Here, we have taken a further liberty in substituting quick grits for the cornmeal—a bit heretical, perhaps, but exceedingly good. We also like the distinctive flavor of collard greens, but other similar greens such as turnip or dandelion can be used as well.

This hearty main course is especially suited to accompaniments of stewed tomatoes, and confirmed meat eaters might enjoy an extra slice of sautéed ham on the side. Either Baked Ginger–Bay Leaf Apples (see page 262) or vanilla ice cream with sliced, sweetened strawberries would be a terrific dessert choice.

1 tablespoon dry bread crumbs
1 pound fresh young collard greens or
   1 10-ounce package frozen collard greens
3½ cups milk
¾ teaspoon salt
¼ teaspoon freshly ground black
   pepper
¾ cup quick grits (do not use instant grits)

5 tablespoons butter
6 tablespoons grated Parmesan cheese
3 egg yolks, lightly beaten
1 medium onion, chopped (½ cup)
About 4 ounces smoked ham, diced finely
   (1 cup)
1 large clove garlic, minced
4 egg whites

1. Generously butter a deep, 2-quart casserole or soufflé dish and sprinkle with the bread crumbs.

2. If using fresh collard greens, wash them well and trim and discard the stems and any particularly tough outer leaves. Blanch the leaves in boiling water until just tender, about 4 to 5 minutes. Drain very thoroughly, pressing out as much excess moisture as possible, and coarsely chop the greens. If using frozen greens, thaw and squeeze out as much moisture as possible.

The greens may be prepared a day in advance and refrigerated.

3. Preheat the oven to 350 degrees.

4. Bring the milk, salt, and pepper to a gentle boil in a heavy 3-quart saucepan. Slowly stir in the grits and return the mixture to a boil, stirring constantly. Lower the heat and cook, stirring, until the mixture is quite thick, about 3 to 4 minutes. Take the pan off the heat and stir in 4 tablespoons of the butter and 4 tablespoons of the cheese. Beat in the egg yolks. Set the mixture aside to cool slightly.

5. In a large skillet, sauté the onion and ham in the remaining 1 tablespoon of butter until the onion is beginning to soften and the ham is beginning to brown, about 3 minutes. Add the garlic and collards and sauté 1 minute. Gently stir the collards mixture into the grits mixture.

6. Beat the egg whites until stiff, but not dry. Stir about ¼ of the whites into the grits and greens mixture to lighten it, then fold in the remaining whites.

7. Turn the mixture into the prepared casserole and sprinkle with the remaining 1 tablespoon of cheese. Bake in the center of the oven for 35 to 50 minutes, depending upon the depth of the casserole, until the bread is puffed and its top is browned and a knife inserted in the center comes out clean. Spoon Bread should be soft in the center with a more crusty edge.

8. Serve immediately.

YIELD: 4 TO 6 SERVINGS.

Ratatouille Pan Pizza

Ratatouille is one of those dishes that always seem to yield gargantuan quantities and ample leftovers. Since deep-dish pizzas are an integral part of Melanie's Sicilian heritage, it was only natural that extra ratatouille, a wonderfully savory southern Mediterranean vegetable stew, should be used as a filling for this hearty pie. In fact, the colorful and tasty combination of vegetables, cheese, and a yeasty crust is such a hit that she now makes the ratatouille expressly for the pizza.

Rich with the meatiness of eggplant, the heady aroma of garlic, and the salty tang of capers, this knife-and-fork pizza is a wonderful main dish that makes us think of summer, even when the snow is falling. Precede it with a light first course of ripe melon wedges, sprinkled with coarse ground pepper, draped with paper-thin slices of prosciutto, and accompanied with a slice of lime. Finish with Baked Amaretti Nectarines (see page 261) for a supper with a Mediterranean accent.

RATATOUILLE:

4 tablespoons olive oil
1 large onion, thinly sliced
3 cloves garlic, minced
About 2 small (8 ounces) zucchini, sliced about
    ¼ inch thick
1 small eggplant (about 12 ounces), unpeeled
    and cut into ¾ inch cubes
1 green bell pepper, seeded and sliced ¼ inch
    thick
½ teaspoon salt
½ teaspoon coarsely ground black pepper
About 6 (12 ounces) fresh plum tomatoes or
    1 1-pound can plum tomatoes, drained and
    sliced about ¼ inch thick
1 teaspoon minced fresh rosemary or
    ¼ teaspoon dried rosemary
2 teaspoons bottled capers

PIZZA DOUGH:

1 package active dry yeast (see note)
1 teaspoon granulated sugar
1 cup lukewarm water (105 to 110 degrees)
2½ cups all-purpose or bread flour, plus up to
    ¼ cup more as needed
½ cup yellow cornmeal
1 teaspoon salt
4 tablespoons olive oil

ASSEMBLY:

1 tablespoon yellow cornmeal
About 8 ounces provolone cheese, shredded
    (2 cups)
¼ cup grated Parmesan cheese
1 teaspoon minced fresh rosemary or
    ¼ teaspoon dried rosemary

1. To make the ratatouille, heat the olive oil in a large skillet. Sauté the onions over medium-low heat until just softened, about 3 to 5 minutes. Add the garlic and sauté about 1 minute. Add the zucchini, eggplant, and bell pepper and cook, stir-

ring, until all ingredients are coated with the oil, about 2 minutes. Add the salt and pepper and stir well. Cover the pan and cook over very low heat for about 30 minutes. Add the tomatoes, rosemary, and capers and simmer over low heat, covered, for 10 minutes. Remove from the heat and let the mixture cool slightly.

The ratatouille can be made 2 days ahead. Bring it back to room temperature before filling the pizza.

2. To make the pizza dough, dissolve the yeast and sugar in the warm water. Let it stand until it begins to look frothy, about 5 to 8 minutes. Place the 2½ cups flour, cornmeal, and salt in a food processor. Pulse 2 or 3 times to blend. With the motor running, pour the yeast mixture and olive oil through the feed tube. Process until a soft ball forms, then continue to "knead" by processing for about 45 seconds. (If the dough does not form a ball, add more flour, 1 tablespoon at a time, until a ball does form.) (If making the dough by hand, mix the dry ingredients in a large bowl. Beat in the liquids until a smooth dough forms. On a lightly floured surface, knead the dough for 10 minutes until smooth and elastic.) Turn the dough into an oiled mixing bowl, cover lightly with a towel or plastic wrap, and let rise until doubled in bulk, about 1 hour at room temperature or about 6 hours in the refrigerator.

3. To assemble and bake the pizza, preheat the oven to 450 degrees. Use an 11-by-15-inch metal jelly roll pan. (If using two pans see note.) Sprinkle the pan with the cornmeal.

4. Punch the dough down and place on a lightly floured surface. Let the dough rest for about 5 minutes, then roll it into a circle or rectangle that extends about 2 inches beyond the sides of the pan. Ease the dough into the pan, patting it so it fits evenly in the bottom and about 1 inch up the sides of the pan.

5. Combine the provolone and Parmesan cheeses and sprinkle about ⅓ of the mixture over the dough. Spoon in the ratatouille.

6. Place the pizza on the lowest rack of the oven and immediately lower the temperature to 425 degrees. Bake until the crust is golden brown and the ratatouille is bubbly, about 25 to 30 minutes. Sprinkle with the remaining cheese mixture and the rosemary. Return the pizza to the oven, baking it until the cheese is melted and begins to be lightly flecked with brown, about 5 minutes.

7. Let the pizza stand for about 5 minutes, then cut in wedges to serve.

YIELD: 6 SERVINGS.

NOTE: The pizza dough can be made using 1 package "quick-rise" yeast. The rising time will be about half as long.

If using two pans, use deep, round pizza pans, cast-iron skillets, or springform pans that are 9 or 10 inches in diameter. Divide the dough and toppings between each pan.

Red Beans 'n' Rice

When Brooke visited New Orleans a few years ago, she managed to eat at least five meals a day—partly because she was egged on by one of her fellow tasters, who kept reminding her that it was okay because, after all, she hadn't eaten a thing on the plane! Meal number three (after the hot boudin on the trip from the airport, and the oysters at Acme's, and the preceding dinner at LeRuth's) was a plate of red beans and rice at Buster Holmes's on Burgundy Street. It was heaven.

Here's a quick version, which uses canned red beans, and it is really a very close facsimile. Use good-quality beans, and if you can't find red beans, kidney beans are a fine substitute. Serve with a large green salad and maybe chocolate sundaes or Tin Roof Sundaes (see page 270) for a truly terrific meal.

2 tablespoons olive oil
1 pound flavorful sausage in casing, such as andouille, kielbasa, chorizo, linguisa, hot Italian sausage, or other spicy smoked or unsmoked sausage
1 cup chopped onion
¾ cup chopped green pepper
1 clove garlic, minced
2 1-pound cans (3½ cups) red beans or kidney beans, drained

2 cups water
1 bay leaf, broken in half
½ teaspoon dried oregano
¼ teaspoon dried thyme
¼ teaspoon black pepper
⅛ teaspoon cayenne pepper
1 cup raw long-grain rice
¼ teaspoon Tabasco or to taste
Cider vinegar or white wine vinegar and additional olive oil (optional)

1. Heat the oil in a large skillet. Cut the sausage on the diagonal into ¾-inch lengths and cook the pieces in the oil over low heat until well browned, about 10 to 12 minutes. If you use unsmoked sausage, check to make sure that it is no longer pink inside. Remove the pieces of sausage with tongs and set them aside, leaving the drippings in the pan.

2. Add the onion, green pepper, and garlic to the pan drippings and cook for 3 minutes over medium heat until softened. Add the beans to the skillet, along with the water, bay leaf, oregano, thyme, black

pepper, and cayenne pepper. Simmer, partially covered, over low heat for 20 minutes, stirring occasionally.

3. Meanwhile, prepare the rice using 2 cups water to which ¾ teaspoon salt has been added and following package directions for cooking time.

4. Using the back of a large spoon, mash about one quarter of the red beans against the side of the pan. This will thicken the sauce slightly and help give it the proper creamy consistency. Stir well and continue to simmer, uncovered, for 5 to 10 minutes more. The beans should still be somewhat

soupy, so add a little more water if they seem dry. Discard the two pieces of bay leaf and season with the Tabasco to taste.

5. Place the reserved sausage on top of the beans, cover the pot, and cook for 2 to 3 minutes over low heat to allow the sausage to heat through.

6. Ladle the beans and sausage over the plain hot rice. Pass cruets of vinegar and oil as condiments if desired.

YIELD: 4 TO 6 SERVINGS.

Garlic-and-Mustard–Fried Eggs with Frizzled Pastrami

This quick little supper dish is perfect for last-minute guests. If you don't have any pastrami on hand, use very thinly sliced smoked ham, prosciutto, or Canadian bacon. A light main course, it is well rounded out with Scalloped Potatoes Our Way (see page 209) or Lacy Potato Pancakes (see page 214), Roasted Vegetables (see page 218), and Classic Creamy Coleslaw (see page 223) or a salad of leafy greens dressed with a red wine vinaigrette. For a hungry group, you might wish to double the recipe and serve 2 eggs to each person. Consider Mocha Pudding with Coffee Cream (see page 254) or Double Crust Apple-Quince Pie (see page 248) for dessert.

3 tablespoons butter
4 ounces pastrami, thinly sliced
4 slices seeded rye bread, toasted and buttered
4 extra-large eggs

Salt and freshly ground black pepper to taste
1 clove garlic, minced
1 tablespoon grainy Dijon mustard

1. Heat 1 tablespoon of the butter in a large skillet and sauté the pastrami over medium-high heat until golden and "frizzled," about 2 minutes. Remove the meat from the pan and arrange it over the warm, buttered toast on individual plates.

2. Add the remaining 2 tablespoons of butter to the skillet and heat. When the foam subsides, carefully break the eggs into the skillet. Fry over medium-low heat until the whites have just set, about 3 minutes. Season the eggs with salt and pepper to taste. Place atop the pastrami.

3. Stir the garlic into the butter in the skillet and cook, stirring, for about 30 seconds. Stir in the mustard. Drizzle over the eggs.

4. Serve immediately.

YIELD: 4 SERVINGS.

Enchiladas Norteno

When Brooke moved to California and tasted her first bite of Mexican food, she knew she was permanently hooked! Fortunately, our mobile society and cross-country travel have produced many millions of Tex-Mex addicts like ourselves, and by now we have all spread the gospel from Maine to Alaska, insisting that at least the bare minimum in the way of Mexican ingredients be stocked on our market shelves. Now, when the craving strikes, most of us can find tortillas and canned green chilies and dried cilantro (which will do fine in a pinch)—and it's fairly easy to improvise from there.

These simplified cheese enchiladas call on those basic ingredients and some other readily available items like ricotta and Monetery Jack cheeses. Serve the enchiladas with their suggested vegetable garnishes for a complete meal. Sliced pineapple and papaya and a plate of Molasses-Ginger Crinkles (see page 268) would make a nice dessert.

2 tablespoons vegetable oil
½ cup chopped onion
1 clove garlic
1 16-ounce can (2 cups) tomato purée
¾ cup water
1 tablespoon minced fresh cilantro or
   1 teaspoon dried cilantro
½ teaspoon dried oregano
½ teaspoon salt or to taste
¼ teaspoon freshly ground black pepper
Pinch of granulated sugar

2 teaspoons red wine vinegar
About 7 ounces Monterey Jack cheese, grated
   (1¾ cups)
1¼ cups ricotta cheese
1 3- or 4-ounce can chopped green chilies,
   drained
8 corn tortillas
Optional garnishes: sliced black olives, diced
   tomatoes, shredded lettuce, sliced scallions,
   wedges of lime

1. Preheat the oven to 425 degrees.
2. Heat the oil in a large nonreactive skillet or saucepan. Sauté the onion and garlic over medium heat until the onion begins to soften, about 3 minutes. Stir in the tomato purée, water, cilantro, oregano, salt, pepper, and sugar. Bring to a boil, lower the heat, and simmer, uncovered, for 10 minutes. Stir in the vinegar.
3. While the sauce is simmering, combine 1¼ cups of the Monterey Jack cheese, the

ricotta cheese, and the chilies in a mixing bowl.
4. On the countertop, line up the pan of sauce, the tortillas, and the filling. To make the enchiladas, briefly dip each tortilla in the sauce to soften it, then place 2 rounded tablespoons of cheese filling on the tortilla, roll loosely, and place seam side down in a single layer in a 7-by-11-inch baking dish. Pour the remaining sauce over the enchiladas, sprinkle with the re-

maining ½ cup of cheese, and bake, loosely covered with foil, in the preheated oven for 15 minutes, or until the cheese is melted and the sauce is bubbly.

5. Serve the hot enchiladas with the sliced black olives, chopped tomato, shredded lettuce, sliced scallions, and lime wedges. Pass bottled red or green hot sauce on the side if desired.

YIELD: 4 SERVINGS.

Scrambled Eggs with Cheddar and Thyme

Scrambled eggs are among the most homey and familiar of breakfast dishes. Properly cooked over low heat, they are sublimely creamy and moist. When enlivened with a touch of piquant mustard and herbs and covered with a coating of melting cheddar, they become an outstanding quick main course for supper. Roasted Vegetables (see page 218) and Lacy Potato Pancakes (see page 214) would make the meal special, and Black Devil Cupcakes with Double Fudge Frosting (see page 240) would make it memorable, indeed.

12 eggs
1 tablespoon Dijon mustard
1½ teaspoons minced fresh thyme or
　½ teaspoon dried leaf thyme
⅓ cup milk
3 tablespoons butter

About 6 ounces sharp cheddar cheese, grated
　(1½ cups)
¼ cup thinly sliced scallions, including most of
　the green tops
¼ teaspoon freshly ground black pepper
Salt to taste

1. Lightly beat the eggs with the mustard, thyme, and milk.
2. Heat the butter in a large skillet and pour in the eggs. Cook over very low heat, stirring almost constantly, until the eggs have formed into a creamy, moist mass, about 5 to 8 minutes.

3. Sprinkle the eggs with the grated cheese, scallions, and pepper. Serve directly from the skillet. Pass salt separately since the saltiness of the cheese may be enough in the dish. (The eggs may be transferred to a warm serving dish before sprinkling with the cheese if desired.)

YIELD: 6 SERVINGS.

Quick Hoppin' John

Hoppin' John originated with slaves living on South Carolina plantations, its name probably stemming from the ritual of having the children hop once around the dinner table for good luck. In most southern states, you still risk being dogged by misfortune if you don't begin the new year with a heaping plate of rice and black-eyed peas, and since we love to perpetuate this kind of tradition, we always try to have this on New Year's Day up North, too.

Offer Hoppin' John as a warming and soulful supper that might also include sliced country ham, Peppery Corn Bread (see page 228), and Baked Ginger–Bay Leaf Apples (see page 262) for dessert.

½ pound bacon cut into ½-inch pieces
3 medium onions, chopped (1½ cups)
1 cup chopped celery, including some celery
    leaves
1 clove garlic, minced
2 10-ounce packages frozen black-eyed peas or
    2 1-pound cans drained black-eyed peas

1 bay leaf, broken in half
4 cups water
1 cup raw long-grain rice
¾ teaspoon salt
¼ teaspoon freshly ground black pepper
Chopped red onion, vinegar, and olive oil as
    condiments, if desired

1. In a large, heavy pot, cook the bacon over medium heat until the fat is rendered and the bacon is nicely browned, about 10 minutes. Remove the pieces of bacon with a slotted spoon and set aside to use later. Pour off all but 3 tablespoons of the bacon drippings.

2. Add the chopped onion to the drippings and cook over medium heat for 3 minutes. Add the celery and garlic and stir. Add the beans, along with the bay leaf, water, rice, salt, and pepper. Bring to a boil, lower the heat, cover, and cook over very low heat for 20 minutes or until the rice is tender. The Hoppin' John should be somewhat on the soupy side.

3. Scatter the reserved browned bacon over the top and stir it in gently with a fork. Discard the two pieces of bay leaf, taste for seasoning, and serve.

YIELD: 4 TO 6 SERVINGS.

Mother's Magnificent Cheese Scallop

We consider this casserole—in a word—magnificent! This was a frequently requested favorite in Brooke's house when she was growing up. We've followed that recipe, which her mother called cheese scallop, fairly closely, although we've added ham, which is certainly optional. Other cookbooks call it cheese bread pudding or cheese strata or just plain cheese casserole; but, with slightly shifting proportions, it usually amounts to about the same thing.

This also makes a terrific brunch or lunch dish. For supper, we'd add some steamed broccoli, a salad of hearty lettuces and sliced tomatoes, and sesame breadsticks. Peanut Butter–Chocolate Chip Brownies (see page 263) would do splendidly for dessert.

10 slices firm white bread, preferably day-old
3 tablespoons butter, softened
About 10 ounces cheddar cheese, grated
    (2½ cups)
About 4 ounces ham, preferably smoked, diced
    (1 cup)
3 tablespoons thinly sliced scallions, including
    green tops

4 eggs
2½ cups milk
1½ teaspoons dry mustard
Scant ½ teaspoon salt
⅛ teaspoon coarsely ground black pepper
Paprika for dusting top

1. Cut the crusts from the bread. Spread one side of each slice of bread with butter and cut each slice into 3 strips. Layer half the bread strips in the bottom of a buttered 1½- to 2-quart baking dish, and sprinkle with half of each of the cheese, ham, and scallions. Layer the rest of the bread strips over this, scattering the remaining cheese, ham, and scallions over the bread.
2. Preheat the oven to 350 degrees.
3. In a mixing bowl, whisk together the eggs, milk, mustard, salt, and pepper.

Pour the custard mixture evenly over the bread in the baking dish. If any bread sticks up out of the custard, push it down with your fingers or a spatula to make sure it gets saturated with the liquid. Lightly dust the top of the casserole with paprika.
4. Bake in the preheated oven until the scallop is evenly puffed and golden brown and a sharp knife inserted near the center comes out clean, about 55 to 65 minutes. Serve immediately.

YIELD: 6 SERVINGS.

NOTE: The cheese scallop may be put together up to 2 hours ahead, covered with plastic wrap, and weighted with a bowl to keep bread submerged. Uncover and sprinkle with paprika before baking.

Chorizo-Cornmeal Pudding

Corn bread is one of our favorite things to eat. This dish is based on an old-fashioned recipe that uses baking soda and cream of tartar instead of the more modern double-acting baking powder for leavening. We have tried the latter and somehow the pudding isn't quite as delicious. Here we have enriched the already moist bread with cheese and sour cream and given it a southwestern twist with the marvelous flavor of spicy chorizo sausage. The accompanying Tomato-Chili Sauce, which can be prepared a day ahead, makes this a colorful, zesty dish for all seasons. It is easily prepared and needs little else except a spinach salad with a few strawberries tossed in, if you have them. Tin Roof Sundaes (see page 270) would be a great finish.

½ pound chorizo sausage, sliced and then
    coarsely chopped
Vegetable oil, as needed
1 medium green bell pepper, chopped
½ cup thinly sliced scallions, including most of
    the green tops
1 cup yellow cornmeal
1 cup all-purpose flour
1 tablespoon granulated sugar
2 teaspoons cream of tartar
1 teaspoon baking soda
¾ teaspoon salt
¼ teaspoon freshly ground black pepper
3 eggs
1 cup sour cream
½ cup milk

4 tablespoons butter, melted
4 ounces Monterey Jack cheese, shredded
    (about 1 cup)
¾ cup cooked corn, cut from the cob or
    ¾ cup frozen corn, thawed

TOMATO-CHILI SAUCE:

1 medium onion, chopped (½ cup)
1 tablespoon butter
1 clove garlic, minced
1 teaspoon chili powder
1 28-ounce can plum tomatoes in purée
1 4-ounce can chopped green chilies
1 teaspoon granulated sugar
Salt and freshly ground black pepper to taste

1. Preheat the oven to 400 degrees. Butter a 2-quart baking dish.

2. In a large skillet, sauté the chorizo over medium-low heat, stirring frequently, until browned, about 4 to 5 minutes. Remove the sausage from the skillet with a slotted spoon and place in a bowl. Pour off all but 1 tablespoon drippings from the skillet. (If there is not 1 tablespoon drippings, add vegetable oil to make up the difference.) Sauté the green pepper until just softened, about 3 minutes. Add the scallions and sauté for 1 to 2 minutes more. Add to the chorizo and reserve.

3. Sift the cornmeal, flour, sugar, cream of tartar, baking soda, salt, and pepper into a large mixing bowl. In another mixing bowl, whisk together the eggs, sour cream, milk, and melted butter until well blended and smooth.

4. Make a well in the center of the dry ingredients and add the liquid ingredients all at once. Stir until blended and smooth, but do not overmix. Stir in the cheese, corn, and chorizo mixture.

5. Turn into the prepared baking dish, smoothing the top. Bake in the center of the oven until set, if a knife inserted in the center comes out clean, and the top is golden brown, about 30 minutes.

6. While the corn pudding is baking, pre-pare the Tomato-Chili Sauce. In a large skillet, sauté the onion in the butter for 3 to 4 minutes. Add the garlic and chili powder and sauté 1 minute, stirring constantly. Add the tomatoes, green chilies, and sugar. Bring to a boil, stirring. Lower the heat and simmer gently, uncovered, stirring often, until the sauce is sightly thickened, about 10 minutes. Season to taste with salt and pepper. Keep warm until ready to serve.

The sauce can be made a day ahead and reheated before serving.

7. Cut the pudding into squares and serve with some of the sauce spooned over it. Pass the remaining sauce separately.

YIELD: 6 SERVINGS.

Triple Cheese and Macaroni

Our version is rendered especially creamy by the ricotta cheese, colorful by the freshness of red and green bell peppers, and distinctly adult by the liberal lacing of white wine. The crunchy, toasted, fresh bread crumb topping is a pleasant textural contrast to the smoothness of the pasta and sauce. By using a fine-quality, sharp yellow cheddar and freshly grated Parmesan cheese you'll make this dish a hit with even the fussiest of guests. Finish off with Angel Food Cake with Summer Fruit Ambrosia (see page 238) in season, or Cranberry-Cointreau Sundaes (see page 269) for a cold-weather party.

Triple Cheese and Macaroni (cont.)

4 tablespoons butter
½ cup chopped onion
½ cup coarsely chopped red bell pepper
½ cup coarsely chopped green bell pepper
2 tablespoons all-purpose flour
¼ teaspoon freshly ground black pepper
1 cup heavy cream
⅔ cup white wine

1 cup ricotta cheese
4 ounces sharp cheddar cheese, grated (1 cup)
10 tablespoons grated Parmesan cheese
12 ounces small pasta tubes, short fusilli, or
    elbow macaroni, cooked and drained
Salt to taste
½ cup fine fresh bread crumbs made from
    1 slice firm white bread

1. Generously butter a 2-quart baking dish.

2. In a large skillet, heat the butter and sauté the onion and both bell peppers over medium-low heat until softened, about 5 minutes. Sprinkle the flour and pepper over the vegetables and cook, stirring, for about 2 minutes.

3. Add the cream and wine and bring to a boil, stirring constantly. Lower the heat and simmer, stirring, until the sauce is somewhat thickened, about 3 minutes. Remove from heat and stir in the ricotta, cheddar, and 6 tablespoons of the Parmesan cheese.

4. Add the sauce to the pasta and blend well. Season with salt to taste. (Cheeses can be quite salty, so no salt may be needed.) Turn into the prepared baking dish. Combine the bread crumbs with the remaining 4 tablespoons of Parmesan cheese and sprinkle over the top of the casserole.

5. If the dish is to be served immediately, preheat the broiler. If you wish to serve it several hours later, cover and refrigerate; then bring the casserole back to room temperature and reheat in a preheated 350-degree oven before continuing.

6. Broil about 4 inches from the heat source until the casserole is bubbly and the crumbs are browned, about 1 to 2 minutes, or bake in a preheated 350-degree oven until the casserole is heated through and the crumbs are browned, about 30 to 35 minutes. (If the crumbs are not browned, run the casserole under a broiler for a few seconds.)

7. Serve while hot.

YIELD: 6 SERVINGS.

Farmhouse Ham-and-Potato Frittata

A peasant-style baked omelet, the frittata is far better suited to entertaining than its more elegant French cousin, the classic pan omelet. Rather than requiring last-minute, one-at-a-time cooking on the stove top, a frittata to serve six can be assembled in a casserole, baked without watching and immediately eaten hot or enjoyed later at room temperature.

Filling ideas for frittatas are limited only by availability and imagination, but we especially like the homeyness of potatoes and flavorful ham, and the sharpness of Gruyère cheese for an informal supper. Appropriate country-style accompaniments might be sautéed or steamed young dandelion or mustard greens or spinach, Peppery Corn Bread (see page 228) and Green Tomato Cobbler (see page 260).

12 ounces (2 or 3) red-skinned potatoes,
  unpeeled
3 tablespoons olive oil
⅓ cup thinly sliced onion
4 ounces country ham, sliced thin and cut in
  1-inch squares
10 eggs

¼ cup minced parsley
2 teaspoons minced fresh rosemary or
  ¾ teaspoon dried rosemary
About 6 ounces Gruyère or other Swiss-style
  cheese, grated (1½ cups)
⅛ teaspoon freshly ground black pepper

1. Halve the potatoes if they are large and cook them in lightly salted, boiling water until just tender, about 15 to 18 minutes. Drain and set aside to cool.

2. Meanwhile, preheat the oven to 400 degrees. Coat the bottom of a 2-quart baking dish with the olive oil. Lay the onion slices evenly in the oil and place the dish in the preheated oven for 10 minutes, or until the onion is wilted and beginning to turn golden. Remove the dish from the oven.

3. Reduce the oven temperature to 350 degrees. Arrange the ham over the onions. Slice the unpeeled potatoes between ⅛ and ¼ inch thick and layer over the ham. Whisk the eggs with the parsley and rosemary and pour over the potatoes. Sprinkle the frittata first with the cheese and then with the pepper.

4. Bake until the frittata is puffy and light golden brown, and the eggs are set, about 25 minutes. Serve hot or at room temperature, cut in squares or spooned out of the dish.

YIELD: 6 SERVINGS.

Summer Squash and Feta Pie

This Grecian version of a classic savory custard pie is robustly flavored with salty feta cheese, but the mint, colorful squashes, and plum tomatoes also make it delicate and summery. Because of the abundant filling, be sure to use a deep pie plate or a fluted 10-inch quiche pan if you have one. The pie pastry and most of the filling ingredients can be prepared far ahead, and the pie itself is easily assembled just before baking. Since it is good served warm or at room temperature, this is an excellent party dish. Add a lemon vinai-grette–dressed salad of leafy romaine lettuce with a few orange sections tossed in and a dessert of Baked Amaretti Nectarines (see page 261) for a lovely, light supper.

PASTRY:

1¼ cups all-purpose flour
½ teaspoon salt
8 tablespoons unsalted butter, chilled and cut
    into 12 pieces
4 tablespoons ice water

FILLING:

3 tablespoons olive oil
About 1 small (4 ounces) zucchini, sliced thin
About 1 small (4 ounces) yellow crookneck
    squash, sliced thin

1 medium onion, thinly sliced (about ½ cup)
2 tablespoons chopped fresh mint or
    2 teaspoons dried mint
1 tablespoon chopped fresh marjoram or
    1 teaspoon dried marjoram
¼ teaspoon salt
¼ teaspoon freshly ground black pepper
4 ounces feta cheese, crumbled (about 1 cup)
1 plum (about 2 ounces) tomato, thinly sliced
3 eggs
1½ cups light cream or half-and-half

1. To make the pastry, stir the flour and salt together in a mixing bowl. Cut in the butter using your fingertips or two knives until the butter is the size of small peas. Sprinkle with the water and toss with a fork until all ingredients are moistened.

Gather into a ball, wrap completely in plastic wrap, and chill 30 minutes or up to 24 hours. (The pastry can also be made in a food processor.)

2. On a lightly floured surface roll the pastry into a 12- or 13-inch circle. Ease into a deep 10-inch pie plate or fluted quiche pan and crimp the edges. (If using a straight-sided quiche pan, be sure to secure the pastry edges so that they won't slide down during baking by folding them over the top edge before crimping.) Prick the pastry all over and then place the prepared shell in the freezer for 15 to 20 minutes.

3. Preheat the oven to 450 degrees.

4. Bake the pastry in the lower center of the oven until golden brown, about 12 to 15 minutes. If the pastry puffs up during baking, gently push it down with the back of a spoon or with a pot holder. Let cool completely.

The pastry can be baked early in the day and kept at room temperature until ready to fill.

5. When ready to bake, preheat the oven to 350 degrees.

6. To make the filling, heat the oil in a large skillet and sauté the zucchini, crookneck squash, and onion until just softened, about 3 minutes. Stir in the mint and marjoram, and season with salt and pepper. Cool slightly and then spread the mixture in the cooled pie shell. Sprinkle with the cheese and lay the tomato slices over the top.

7. In a mixing bowl, whisk together the eggs and cream. Place the pie shell on the center rack of the oven. Carefully pour the custard over the vegetables and cheese in the pie shell. (The dish will be very full.) Slide the pie into the oven and bake until lightly browned and a knife inserted 1 inch from the center comes out clean, about 45 minutes.

8. Let cool about 10 minutes before cutting into wedges. Serve while still warm or at room temperature.

YIELD: 4 TO 6 SERVINGS.

Baked Stuffed Eggplant Mike Elia

Brooke's friend Mike Elia has been plying her with recipes for years—all of them wonderful! This is an adaptation of one from his mother, whose family came from the Barese region of Italy, and it has become a treasured favorite at Brooke's house. The savory stuffing cooks to a nice, firm, sliceable texture that is almost meatlike, and it stays beautifully moist as it stews in the sauce. Small cubes of potato add body and an unexpectedly delicious flavor to the sauce.

Serve with a salad of arugula and peppers dressed with a balsamic vinaigrette and salted breadsticks. Mocha Pudding with Coffee Cream (see page 254) makes a lovely finish to this meal.

1 large (1¼ pounds) eggplant
3 tablespoons olive oil
½ cup chopped onion
1 cup fresh bread crumbs
¼ cup Parmesan cheese
3 eggs, lightly beaten
2 tablespoons minced parsley
¼ teaspoon salt
⅛ teaspoon freshly ground black pepper

POTATO-TOMATO SAUCE:

2 tablespoons olive oil, plus 2 teaspoons for
   drizzling on top
1 1-pound can plum tomatoes and juice
2½ cups water
6 ounces (1 medium) all-purpose or Idaho
   potato
1 clove garlic, minced
⅛ teaspoon oregano
¼ teaspoon salt
Freshly ground black pepper to taste
1½ tablespoons Parmesan cheese

1. Do not peel the eggplant. Slice off the green cap and cut the eggplant in half lengthwise. Use a sharp knife to score the meat into ½-inch cubes, leaving a ½-inch rim around the edge. Scoop out the flesh with a spoon and coarsely chop it.

2. Heat the olive in a large skillet. Add the eggplant cubes and the onion to the skillet

and sauté over low heat, stirring frequently, until the eggplant is softened and lightly browned, about 8 to 10 minutes. Remove the pan from the heat and stir in the bread crumbs, Parmesan cheese, eggs, and parsley. Season with the salt and black pepper.

3. Preheat the oven to 350 degrees.

4. Sprinkle the eggplant shells lightly with salt and pepper and divide the stuffing between them.

The recipe may be made ahead up to this point and wrapped and refrigerated for up to 3 hours.

5. To make the Potato-Tomato Sauce, coat the bottom of a 7-by-11-inch baking dish with the 2 tablespoons olive oil. Pour the can of tomatoes into the baking dish and cut them into quarters with a sharp knife or the side of a spoon. Add the water to the pan. Peel the potato and cut it into thin (no more than ¼ inch thick) slices. Stack the slices, cut them into ¼-inch strips, and cut the strips into small cubes. Add them to the tomato mixture in the baking dish, along with the garlic, oregano, salt, and pepper. Set the stuffed eggplant shells on top of the tomato mixture. Sprinkle the Parmesan cheese over the tops of the eggplant and into the sauce, and spoon a few pieces of tomato from the sauce onto the tops of the eggplant to help keep it moist. Drizzle a teaspoon or two of olive oil over the tops of the eggplant.

6. Bake, uncovered, in the preheated oven until the potatoes are tender and the tops of the eggplant are lightly browned, about 1 to 1¼ hours. The sauce will reduce quite a bit as it cooks. Cut each stuffed eggplant in half, and serve one piece on each of four individual plates with some sauce spooned around and over it.

YIELD: 4 SERVINGS.

Huevos Rancheros with Warm Salsa

In Mexico and in the American Southwest, huevos rancheros are served up with gusto for breakfast. This spicy, savory egg dish is quite filling and is indeed wonderful for a leisurely late breakfast or brunch, but we happen to think that it makes an even better supper.

Infinite variations on the basic huevos rancheros recipe abound since it seems to invite any number of flourishes in the hands of a creative cook. This version uses the typical southwestern ingredients. Our salsa, though, is something of a hybrid since it's really a fresh raw salsa *cruda* that is just barely cooked. It retains its beautiful fresh flavor, yet doesn't cool down the eggs when it goes on top.

Serve these huevos rancheros with refried beans on the side (there are some very good ones in a can) and a salad of dark greens with some thinly sliced oranges, red onion, and crisp jicama, if you can find it. Pass additional warm, buttered tortillas if desired, and offer Mocha Pudding with Coffee Cream (see page 254) for dessert.

WARM SALSA:

1 tablespoon vegetable oil
1 pound fresh tomatoes, peeled, seeded, and
  chopped (about 1¾ cups)
¼ cup chopped onion
1 small clove garlic, minced
1 fresh or canned jalapeño, seeds removed and
  minced, or ⅛ teaspoon dried red pepper
  flakes (note: wash your hands carefully after
  working with hot peppers)
½ teaspoon salt, or to taste
Freshly ground black pepper to taste

¼ teaspoon ground cumin
2 tablespoons minced fresh cilantro or
  1½ teaspoons dried cilantro

¼ cup plus 1 tablespoon vegetable oil
8 corn tortillas, 5 or 6 inches in diameter
Salt to taste
2 tablespoons butter
8 eggs
About 6 ounces cheddar cheese, grated
  (1½ cups)
1 avocado, peeled and sliced (optional)

1. To make the warm salsa, heat the oil in a skillet and add the chopped tomato, onion, garlic, jalapeño or red pepper flakes, salt, pepper, and cumin. Cook over medium-high heat until the juices of the tomatoes just start to run, about 2 minutes. Stir in the cilantro and set aside until ready to use.

The salsa may be made ahead and held at room temperature for 1 hour or refrigerated for 1 day, but the fresher it is, the better.

2. Heat the ¼ cup of oil in a 7- or 8-inch skillet. Press each tortilla into the oil with a spatula and cook over medium-high heat about 20 seconds on each side, or until the tortilla begins to fleck with brown and becomes somewhat crisp. Drain on paper towels and sprinkle lightly with salt. The tortillas will crisp a bit more after they are removed from the oil.

3. Heat half of the remaining oil and half of the butter in each of two large skillets. Fry the eggs over low heat until the whites are set. Leave the eggs sunny-side up. When the eggs are almost cooked, scatter the cheese over them and cover the pans for about 30 seconds, or until the cheese starts to melt.

4. Meanwhile, reheat the salsa over low heat.

5. Place two tortillas on each of four warm plates. Slide an egg onto each tortilla and spoon over with the warm salsa. Garnish with the sliced avocado, if desired.

YIELD: 4 SERVINGS.

ACCOMPANIMENTS

"For a home dinner, it is always desirable to serve for first course a soup; second course, meat or fish with potatoes and two other vegetables; third course, a vegetable salad with French dressing; fourth course, dessert; fifth course, crackers, cheese, and café noir."

—*FANNIE MERRITT FARMER*

The Boston Cooking-School Cook Book (1912 edition)

"Trifles make perfection, but perfection is no trifle."

—*SHAKER APHORISM*

The Best of Shaker Cooking (1985)

"Let the sky rain potatoes."

—*WILLIAM SHAKESPEARE*

The Merry Wives of Windsor

Our Favorite Vinaigrette Dressing

This is our version of the classic French dressing for green salads. It is weighted on the slightly tart side. If you are using very mild salad greens or a sharp vinegar, you may wish to decrease the amount of vinegar by up to 1 tablespoon. This vinaigrette is also wonderful as a dressing for warm roasted vegetables.

The success of this, or any vinaigrette, depends wholly upon the quality of oil and vinegar. Our basic dressing uses red wine vinegar and a light olive oil. Other options are given in the variations at the end of the recipe.

3 tablespoons red wine vinegar
¼ teaspoon salt
⅛ teaspoon freshly ground black pepper

1 teaspoon Dijon mustard
8 tablespoons olive oil

Mix the vinegar and salt in a small bowl and let stand 1 minute. Whisk in the pepper and mustard. Slowly whisk in the oil until well blended.

YIELD: ABOUT ⅔ CUP.

NOTE: Use the dressing soon after preparation for the freshest flavor. Any extra dressing can be refrigerated a day or two in a covered container. Reblend before using.

VARIATIONS

Add 1 tablespoon minced shallots, parsley, chives, or cilantro with the mustard.

Add 1 clove minced garlic with the mustard.

Increase the mustard to 1 tablespoon for a mustard dressing.

Add 1½ teaspoons minced fresh herbs or ½ teaspoon dried herbs of your choosing, such as basil, tarragon, oregano, marjoram, or mint.

Use a fruit vinegar, such as blueberry, raspberry, or strawberry, in place of the wine vinegar. Use 2 tablespoons nut oil, such as walnut or hazelnut, or 6 tablespoons safflower oil in place of the olive oil. Use to dress light, summery lettuces and green salad with fruit.

Use balsamic vinegar in place of wine vinegar and increase the amount to 4 tablespoons if desired since the flavor is pronounced and mellow. Use to dress sturdy greens such as romaine.

Use 2 tablespoons lemon juice to replace 2 tablespoons of the vinegar. Use all safflower oil or a combination of 2 tablespoons nut oil, such as walnut or hazelnut, and 6 tablespoons safflower oil to replace the olive oil. Use to dress light lettuces.

Old-Fashioned Picnic Potato Salad

An outdoor feast in summer isn't really a picnic unless you have potato salad. This recipe is a lot like the one our Moms used to make—though they probably used dried mustard in the dressing instead of our preferred Dijon.

There are many variations on this theme. Some people like to add a little of the sweet pickle juice to their salad; some a sprinkling of celery seed. Others love to garnish theirs with a sliced hard-boiled egg and tomato. This is a great basic recipe. Do what you will to put your own stamp on it.

2 pounds waxy potatoes
3 tablespoons cider vinegar or white wine vinegar
3 tablespoons vegetable oil
Salt and freshly ground black pepper to taste
½ cup thinly sliced celery
½ cup chopped red onion

3 tablespoons chopped gherkins
3 tablespoons chopped parsley
¾ cup mayonnaise
1 tablespoon Dijon mustard
2 tablespoons cream or milk
½ cup thinly sliced radishes (optional)

1. Boil the potatoes in their skins in salted water to cover until just fork tender, about 15 to 30 minutes, depending on their size. Drain well. When cool enough to handle, peel the potatoes and slice them or cut them into ½-inch cubes. Mix the vinegar and vegetable oil and toss with the warm potatoes. Add salt and pepper to taste. Set aside so the potatoes can cool and absorb the vinegar and oil, about 15 minutes.
2. When the dressed potatoes are cool, add the celery, onion, chopped gherkins, and parsley to the bowl and gently combine.
3. In a small bowl, whisk together the mayonnaise and mustard and thin with the cream or milk. Season with additional salt and pepper. Pour the dressing over the potatoes and toss gently but thoroughly. Chill at least 1 hour.
4. When ready to serve, stir the salad again gently and garnish the bowl with the sliced radishes if desired.

YIELD: 6 SERVINGS.

Marianne's Macaroni Salad

Melanie's mother is a marvelous cook who believed in "fresh and simple" long before they became buzzwords among fashionable foodies. Thus, her macaroni salad is uncomplicated and unadorned except for a sprinkling of parsley. Though the basic ingredients remain fairly constant, she varies the vegetables, according to what looks good in the market. Also, she might add a chopped hard-boiled egg or 1 tablespoon minced fresh basil either into the salad or sprinkled on top with the parsley. For really special occasions, she would stir about ¼ cup crumbled Gorgonzola or other blue cheese into the mayonnaise dressing, but the straightforward version was enjoyed at least once a week during the warm months throughout Melanie's growing-up years.

The real secret to this salad, though, is mixing the warm macaroni (and we always use elbow macaroni, but you can develop your own tradition) with about half of the dressing and then chilling for at least a couple of hours. The prepared vegetables are added with the remaining dressing no more than 1 hour before serving, thus preserving their crunchiness and bright color.

Serve this wonderful "go with" at meals featuring simple barbecued chicken, steak, or burgers, or as part of a buffet that might include a sliced ham or cold roast beef.

8 ounces elbow macaroni
1 cup mayonnaise
2 tablespoons lemon juice
1 tablespoon Dijon mustard
½ teaspoon salt
¼ teaspoon freshly ground black pepper
1 to 2 tablespoons milk
1 cup diced celery

½ cup shredded carrots
½ cup thinly sliced small radishes
½ cup diced red bell pepper
½ cup thinly sliced scallions, including most of the green tops
Salt and freshly ground black pepper to taste
3 tablespoons minced parsley

1. Cook the macaroni in a large pot of boiling, salted water until al dente. Drain well and let cool slightly.
2. Meanwhile, in a small bowl blend together the mayonnaise, lemon juice, mustard, salt, pepper, and enough milk to thin the dressing to a pourable consistency.

3. In a large bowl, combine the macaroni with ½ of the dressing. Cover and chill about 2 hours.
4. Add the celery, carrots, radishes, bell pepper, scallions, 2 tablespoons of the parsley, and the remaining dressing to the macaroni. Stir gently but thoroughly to

blend well. Season with salt and pepper to taste. Sprinkle with the remaining parsley.

5. Serve immediately or cover and chill up to 1 hour.

YIELD: 6 TO 8 SERVINGS.

Scalloped Potatoes Our Way

One of the most soothing dishes of all, scalloped potatoes can also be one of the most satisfying accompaniments to simple suppers of grilled meats or roasts. We like the pristine, clear flavors of potato and onion heightened with garlic and smoothed out with cream, so "our way" is to add no flour to thicken the sauce and mask the tastes. In contrast to the mellow smoothness of the casserole, we like a simple sprinkling of bread crumbs that bake to a golden crunch. The dish can be assembled a couple of hours ahead and refrigerated. Bring it back to room temperature before baking.

1 large onion, sliced thin (about 1 cup)
1½ tablespoon butter
1 large clove garlic, minced
1½ pounds all-purpose potatoes, peeled and sliced thin

½ teaspoon salt
¼ teaspoon pepper
1½ cups heavy cream
1 slice firm white bread

1. Preheat the oven to 400 degrees.
2. In a large skillet, sauté the onions in 1 tablespoon of the butter over medium-low heat until the onion begins to soften, about 3 minutes. Add the garlic and sauté about 1 minute more.
3. Place the onion mixture in a shallow 2-quart baking dish or gratin dish. Add the potatoes, add salt and pepper, and toss gently until well combined. Use a spatula or large spoon to spread the potatoes in an even layer in the baking dish. Pour the cream over the potato mixture.
4. Use a food processor to make crumbs from the bread and sprinkle evenly over the potato mixture. Dot with the remaining ½ tablespoon of butter.
5. Place in the center of the oven and bake 10 minutes, then lower the heat to 350 degrees. Continue to bake until the potatoes are tender, the crumbs are richly browned, and the mixture is bubbly, about 35 to 40 minutes.
6. Serve directly from the baking dish.

YIELD: 6 SERVINGS.

North Sedgwick Grange Baked Beans

Every summer the grange hall in North Sedgwick, Maine, holds a baked-bean casserole supper. The menu, which is parceled out to be cooked by women members of the organization, consists of casseroles of various kinds, coleslaw, biscuits, iced tea or coffee, and blueberry pie or chocolate pie for dessert. But the focal point is the beans, and since good baked beans have a long history in Maine, each cook prides herself on contributing beans made her special way. Hence, we've tasted quite a number of bean styles over the years and have come to some firm conclusions about our preference.

We like them to be well seasoned and slightly sweet, with some tomato to help cut the starchy richness, and we like plenty of sauce. The recipe that follows conforms to these strictures. We suggest using three different kinds of beans in the casserole for variety of color and texture, but just one or two will work fine, also. We have found that the quality of canned beans varies greatly, so try to buy the best even if they cost a little more. You may, of course, substitute home-cooked beans if you prefer.

One other thing that makes a big difference is the shape of the casserole dish. For this recipe you need a 2-quart baking dish that's at least 3 inches deep. When a shallower baking dish is used, too much liquid evaporates, and the beans get dry.

1 large onion, chopped (1 cup)	½ teaspoon curry powder
1 clove garlic, chopped	¼ teaspoon salt
1 tablespoon butter	⅛ teaspoon freshly ground black pepper
¾ cup bottled chili sauce	1 16-ounce can cooked white beans, drained
½ cup real maple syrup	1 16-ounce can cooked red beans, pink beans,
½ cup water, or more as needed	pinto beans, or kidney beans, drained
3 tablespoons dark rum or bourbon	1 16-ounce can small lima beans, drained or
1 tablespoon cider vinegar	1 10-ounce package small frozen lima beans,
2 teaspoons Worcestershire sauce	cooked
2 teaspoons dry mustard	3 to 4 strips bacon

1. Preheat the oven to 350 degrees.
2. In a large skillet, sauté the onion and garlic in the butter over medium-low heat for 3 minutes until softened. Add the chili sauce, maple syrup, water, rum, vinegar, Worcestershire sauce, mustard, curry powder, salt, and pepper to the skillet and

bring to a simmer over medium heat. Cook for about 2 minutes to blend flavors.
3. Put the beans in a deep 2-quart casserole (not a shallow baking dish), pour the sauce over them, and stir gently to combine. The beans will look very soupy at this point, but the sauce thickens a lot as it cooks. Lay

3 or 4 strips of bacon over the top of the casserole and place in the preheated oven. Bake for 1 hour, or until the sauce is bubbly and the bacon is cooked. If the bacon is not crisp enough, run the casserole under the broiler for about 1 minute to brown. The beans should have plenty of sauce. If they look at all dry, add up to ½ cup of water as they finish cooking.

YIELD: 6 TO 8 SERVINGS.

NOTE: If the beans are made ahead and reheated, the extra water should be added before reheating.

Confetti Rice Salad

This rice salad is a colorful addition to many meals. The vegetables evoke the flavors of spring, though they are all readily available year-round. We especially like to serve the salad with almost any plain grilled meat, chicken, or fish. Since the quantities can be easily increased and the salad tastes best at room temperature, it is a terrific buffet or party dish.

2 cups water
1 cup raw long-grain white rice
1 teaspoon salt
7 tablespoons olive oil
1 cup thawed frozen green peas
1½ tablespoons lemon juice
1 teaspoon Dijon mustard

¼ teaspoon pepper
1 small red bell pepper, cut in ½-inch cubes
1 small yellow bell pepper, cut in ½-inch cubes
4 scallions, incuding most of the green tops, sliced thin
2 tablespoons minced parsley

1. Bring the water to a boil, add the rice, ¾ teaspoon of the salt and 1 tablespoon of the olive oil. Cover the pan, lower the heat, and simmer until the liquid is absorbed and the rice is tender, about 20 to 22 minutes. About 2 minutes before the rice is cooked, add the peas, but do not stir.
2. While the rice is cooking, whisk together the remaining oil, lemon juice, mustard, pepper, and the remaining ¼ teaspoon salt.
3. Turn the rice into a large mixing bowl, add the bell peppers, scallions, and the dressing, and toss to combine. Add the parsley and toss again. Serve at room temperature.

YIELD: 4 TO 6 SERVINGS.

Real Mashed Potatoes

We cheered when trendy New York restaurants started serving mashed potatoes a couple of years ago. One establishment even went so far as to brag about their marvelous old-fashioned mashed potatoes "with real lumps!"

For a long time, potato dishes of all kinds were in eclipse, having unfairly garnered a reputation for being too high in calories. Sensible people felt unable to eat them with a clear conscience. Then, as we became aware that we should cut down on animal fats and fill up on carbohydrates, suddenly it was okay to consider eating potatoes again. Hooray! But in the meantime, cooking anything other than a baked potato or frozen fries had become something of a lost art. Maybe people thought they needed special equipment to make mashed potatoes, like grandma's potato ricer, long since given away to the second-hand shop.

We don't think you need anything special. Just start with good, starchy, all-purpose, Idaho or russet potatoes. (Never use waxy boiling potatoes for making mashed potatoes.) Make sure they're cooked until they're good and tender, and mash them right in the pot with a hand-held masher or a portable mixer or both, adding a minimum of butter and milk and seasoning well with salt and pepper.

Mashed potatoes are great with anything that's even remotely saucy or juicy—and perfection, of course, with gravy.

2 pounds potatoes (all-purpose, Idahos, or russets)	**½ teaspoon salt or to taste**
3 tablespoons butter	**Generous pinch of white pepper**
½ cup milk	**Pinch of grated nutmeg, if desired**

1. Peel the potatoes, making sure to peel away any green parts of the flesh under the skin since they can make the potatoes taste bitter. Cut into 2-inch chunks. Boil in a nonreactive saucepan in lightly salted water to cover for 20 minutes, or until the potatoes are very tender when pierced with the point of a sharp knife.

2. Drain the potatoes and return them to the hot saucepan. Place the saucepan over the lowest possible heat for 1 minute to evaporate any remaining moisture.

3. Using a potato masher or a large fork, begin mashing the potatoes. Cut the butter into 3 pieces, and add it, along with most of the milk, to the saucepan. Continue mashing, trying to get the potatoes as smooth as possible, adding the remaining milk as you go. At this point, to get perfectly smooth, lump-free potatoes, switch to a portable electric mixer, beating at a high speed right in the saucepan until the potatoes are smooth and fluffy. This can be done on the stove over a low burner, or

the saucepan can be returned to the low heat and rewarmed gently.

4. Season with the salt and pepper, and nutmeg if desired, and serve.

YIELD: 4 TO 6 SERVINGS.

New New-Potato Salad

This is a lighter potato salad, dressed primarily with a white wine vinaigrette that includes a little sour cream for richness. The potatoes look nice with their red skins left on, and lots of bright green herbs lend their fresh color as well as their flavor.

2½ pounds red-skinned potatoes
6 tablespoons olive oil
3 tablespoons dry white wine or white vermouth
2 tablespoons white wine vinegar
3 tablespoons sour cream
1 teaspoon Dijon mustard

3 tablespoons minced shallots
¾ teaspoon salt or to taste
⅛ teaspoon freshly ground black pepper or to taste
¼ cup minced parsley
1 tablespoon snipped chives

1. Scrub the potatoes. Leave them whole if small. If larger, cut into 2-inch chunks. Cook in boiling salted water until just tender when pierced with a metal skewer or the point of a sharp kinfe, about 20 minutes. Drain, and when cool enough to handle, slice the potatoes about ⅛ inch thick. Place the warm potato slices in a large bowl and toss with the olive oil, wine, and vinegar. Set aside until the potatoes are tepid and the liquid is absorbed.

2. In a small bowl, whisk together the sour cream, mustard, shallots, salt, and pepper. Pour this dressing over the potatoes and toss gently so that it evenly coats them. Sprinkle the minced parsley and chives over the salad and gently toss again. Taste for seasoning, adding more salt and pepper if necessary. Serve the salad tepid or chilled and sprinkled with some additional parlsey if desired.

YIELD: 6 SERVINGS.

Lacy Potato Pancakes

We absolutely love potato pancakes but have always felt a bit guilty about them since most recipes call for cooking them in copious amounts of fat. So, in order to "have our [pan] cake and eat it too," we set out to perfect a tasty, yet reasonable version that we could happily eat often. We season with goodly amounts of onion and pepper, then cook in a minimal amount of a mixture of butter and oil, though bacon drippings (if you have some) or peanut oil can be substituted for an entirely different flavor.

Although undisputably traditional as an accompaniment to dishes such as our Braised Sweet-and-Sour Brisket (see page 131), potato pancakes are also marvelous set alongside Pan-Grilled Veal Chops with Spicy Paprika Sauce (see page 141), Pork Chops with Caraway Cream (see page 129), Roast Pork and Thyme Pan Gravy (see page 134), or Peppered Beef and Red Wine Vinegar Sauce (see page 124). These pancakes and Scrambled Eggs with Cheddar and Thyme (see page 191) would also make a terrific supper. We also like them made in miniature and served as a first course with a dab of caviar and a spoonful of sour cream, or for breakfast with poached eggs set on top.

1 pound (about 3 medium) all-purpose potatoes
1 medium onion
1 tablespoon all-purpose flour
½ teaspoon salt
¼ teaspoon coarsely ground black pepper

1 egg, lightly beaten
1½ tablespoons vegetable oil or bacon
    drippings
1½ tablespoons butter

1. Peel and coarsely grate the potatoes and the onion. Place the mixture in a tea towel, wrap tightly and squeeze out as much excess moisture as possible. Turn the potato and onion mixture into a large mixing bowl and toss with the flour, salt, and pepper. Add the egg and stir to blend well.

2. Using two large skillets, heat half of the oil and butter in each. When the foam has subsided, spoon about 2 tablespoons of the potato mixture into the skillet and flatten with a spatula or the back of a mixing spoon to make flat patties about 2½ inches in diameter. Cook over medium heat until golden brown, about 4 to 5 minutes. Turn and cook for another 4 or 5 minutes or until golden brown on the other side. (The pancakes may also be cooked in two batches in a single skillet keeping the finished pancakes warm in a 300-degree oven until all are cooked.

3. Serve immediately, or may be held up to 30 minutes in a single layer on a baking sheet set in a 300-degree oven to maintain crispiness.

YIELD: 4 TO 6 SERVINGS.

Parmesan Polenta

Polenta is the Italian answer to grits and is prepared in as many different ways. Simple polenta is a soothing cornmeal mush, while the baked and deep-fried versions are absolutely elegant. Our method combines the best of both since the finished polenta remains somewhat soft but has a firm crustiness around the edge. The flavoring depends upon the quality of the cheese—be sure it is fresh!

Serve this with any simple grilled or broiled meat. It is also excellent with meats or fish topped with a tomato-based sauce since the same sauce will be delightful spooned over the polenta.

3 cups good-quality canned or homemade (see page 2) chicken stock
¼ teaspoon salt (omit if using salted chicken stock)
¼ teaspoon freshly ground black pepper
1¼ cups yellow cornmeal

3 tablespoons minced flat-leaf parsley
3 tablespoons butter
5 tablespoons excellent-quality grated Parmesan cheese
6 sprigs flat-leaf parsley for garnish

1. Bring the stock, salt, and pepper to a rolling boil in a 3-quart saucepan. Very slowly, pour in the cornmeal, stirring constantly. (If you add it too fast, it will clump.) Lower the heat and stir until the mixture becomes very thick, about 2 minutes. Stir in the minced parsley, 1 tablespoon of the butter, and 4 tablespoons of the cheese.

2. Heat ½ tablespoon of the remaining butter in a heavy 8- or 9-inch broiler-safe skillet. Scrape the cornmeal into the skillet. Smooth the top and cook on the stove top, uncovered and without stirring, over medium-low heat until the polenta is nearly firm and lightly crusty around the edges, about 15 to 20 minutes.

3. Preheat the broiler.

4. Sprinkle the top of the polenta with the remaining 1 tablespoon of cheese and dot with the remaining 1½ tablespoons of butter. Place under the broiler until lightly browned, about ½ to 1 minute.

5. Let cool in the pan for a few minutes, then cut into wedges and serve from the skillet. Garnish with parsley sprigs.

YIELD: 4 TO 6 SERVINGS.

Special Rice

All rice, really, is quite special. And there are plenty of occasions when you want absolutely plain, boiled white rice: under a spicy gumbo; with any highly seasoned oriental stir-fry; or alongside a rich and flavorful Crawfish Étouffée (see page 168). But most other times a heap of pure white grains holds little in the way of culinary or visual interest.

Our master recipe sets out easy and basic guidelines for lifting rice from the category of simple into that of sublime. It calls for sautéeing a little onion and the raw rice in a small amount of butter before adding liquid. This initial cooking gives the rice a flavor boost and coats the grains, allowing them to retain their identity in the final steaming process. We call for chicken stock in the master recipe, but almost any flavored liquid can be used, depending on what you intend to serve with the rice. (Our many flavor variations follow.) In this one instance, even a chicken bouillon cube dissolved in water is preferable to using plain water.

The other thing that makes this recipe a little "special" is that we suggest baking the rice in the oven. This allows for greater flexibility, particularly when entertaining, because the finished rice will keep warm beautifully in the turned-off oven if it has to wait for dinner. Also, the amounts can easily be multiplied and cooked in large pans if you are serving a crowd. If you prefer to cook the rice in a saucepan on top of the stove, there is no need to bring the liquid to a boil before adding it, and decrease the cooking time to about 20 minutes.

2 tablespoons butter
½ cup chopped onion
1 cup raw rice (see note)

2 cups good-quality canned or homemade (see page 2) chicken stock or other liquid
Salt and freshly ground black pepper to taste

1. Preheat the oven to 350 degrees.
2. Melt the butter in a medium saucepan. Add the chopped onion and sauté gently for 2 minutes, or until it begins to soften. Stir in the rice and cook, stirring with a wooden spoon, until all the grains are coated with butter and the rice has turned translucent, about 2 minutes more.
3. Heat the chicken stock, water, or other liquid to a simmer. Scrape the rice mixture into a 1½- or 2-quart baking dish, pour the hot liquid over the rice, and stir once with

a fork. Cover the baking dish, either with a lid or with a piece of foil, tightly sealing the edges, and place in the preheated oven. Bake for about 35 minutes, or until the rice is just tender and the liquid has been absorbed. (It will keep hot in the turned-off oven for up to 30 minutes.)

The rice may be made ahead up to this point and the casserole reheated in a water bath in the oven for 20 minutes.

4. Fluff with a fork and season with salt and pepper to taste before serving. If any other additions are being made, stir them in gently.

YIELD: 4 TO 6 SERVINGS (3 CUPS RICE).

NOTE: Use any type of rice: long- or short-grain, Arborio, Basmati, Texmati, for example. Brown rice can also be substituted, but increase the cooking time to about 60 minutes in the oven, about 45 minutes on top of the stove.

VARIATIONS

Use clam juice as part of the liquid if serving the rice with seafood.

Stir in 1 to 2 tablespoons butter at the end of the cooking time for richer rice.

Substitute olive oil for the butter for a heartier, slightly Mediterranean flavor. Add flavor variations such as minced garlic, pepper strips, sliced green or black olives, chopped tomatoes, and sauté along with the onions.

Stir in minced fresh herbs at the end of the cooking time or crumbled dried herbs at the beginning.

Sauté 1 cup sliced mushrooms along with the onion.

Add a teaspoon or so of grated lemon or orange zest and replace about ¼ cup of the liquid with lemon or orange juice.

Sauté ¼ cup golden or black raisins and 3 tablespoons pine nuts along with the onion. Add a pinch of cinnamon or allspice for a Middle Eastern twist.

Add ½ teaspoon crushed saffron to the liquid for a brilliantly colored and distinctly flavored result.

Stir in 3 strips cooked and crumbled bacon at the end of the cooking time.

Stir in ¼ cup grated Parmesan cheese at the end of the cooking time.

Add 1 tablespoon minced jalapeño peppers to the cooked rice. (Note: Wash your hands carefully after working with hot peppers.)

Stir 1 tablespoon sesame oil and ¼ cup minced scallions into the cooked rice.

Roasted Vegetables

This method of cooking can be used with several different vegetables and the result—a slightly charred, smoky flavor and the vegetables done to crisp-tender perfection—is absolutely delicious. You may dress the cooked vegetables with a vinaigrette, coat them with melted butter, sprinkle them with herbs, or simply enjoy them plain with a bit of salt and pepper.

1 to 1½ pounds fresh vegetables (see variations at end of recipe)

4 to 6 tablespoons olive oil
Salt and freshly ground pepper to taste

1. Preheat the oven to 500 degrees.
2. Prepare the vegetables as instructed in Variations. Brush all sides of the vegetables with some of the olive oil. Sprinkle with salt and pepper.

3. Roast on a baking sheet or baking dish in a single layer for the recommended time, turning often during roasting.
4. Serve while hot, either plain, buttered, or sprinkled with herbs.

YIELD: 4 TO 6 SERVINGS.

VARIATIONS

Broccoli: cut head into florets, each with about 2 inches of stem. Roast for 8 to 10 minutes.

Asparagus: use slender asparagus and snap off the tough ends. Roast for 3 to 5 minutes.

Zucchini and yellow summer squash: use small squashes and cut them in half lengthwise or slice them. Roast for 5 to 7 minutes.

Bell peppers: use any color; quarter the peppers and discard the ribs and seeds. Roast for 6 to 8 minutes.

Sweet onions: peel and cut crosswise into ½-inch-thick slices. Roast for 6 to 8 minutes.

Scallions: use whole scallions. Roast for 2 to 4 minutes.

Fennel: cut it into ½-inch-thick slices. Roast for 6 to 8 minutes.

Eggplant: use small eggplants and cut diagonally or lengthwise into ½-inch-thick slices. Roast for 6 to 8 minutes.

Plain Muffins

This plain muffin makes a terrific quick dinner bread. The brown and white sugars in the recipe help to round out the flavor, but it's not enough sweetness to make the bread taste like a breakfast roll. These are wonderful with soups, stews, and salads.

Just be sure not to overmix the batter or the muffins will be tough. The batter, in fact, should really not be smooth enough to fall ribbonlike from the spoon as cake batter does; but it should fall in blobs with a few lumps remaining.

2 cups all-purpose flour
3 teaspoons double-acting baking powder
¾ teaspoon salt
1½ tablespoons granulated sugar
1½ tablespoons brown sugar
1 egg
1 cup plus 2 tablespoons milk
4 tablespoons butter, melted

1. Preheat the oven to 400 degrees. Lightly butter or oil with vegetable spray a muffin tin with 12 cups, each with about ⅔ cup capacity.
2. In a large bowl, sift together the flour, baking powder, salt, and both sugars, and set aside.
3. In a small bowl, whisk together the egg, milk, and melted butter.
4. Make a well in the center of the dry ingredients and pour the liquid ingredients in all at once. Combine with no more than 15 or 20 strokes of a wooden spoon until the flour is moistened and no white specks are visible. The batter will be quite thick and a few lumps may remain.
5. Spoon into the prepared muffin tins, filling the cups three-quarters full, and bake in the middle of the preheated oven until the tops are rounded and a speckled golden brown, about 18 to 20 minutes.
6. Let cool in the pan for 3 to 4 minutes before removing the muffins by lifting each one out with a knife. Serve hot in a napkin-lined basket.

YIELD: 12 MUFFINS.

The Absolute Best Buttermilk Biscuits

We took the best of everything to develop this recipe for one of the most versatile quick breads. Buttermilk produces a very tender, slightly tangy biscuit. Butter adds rich flavor, while vegetable shortening gives a flaky, light texture. An initially high oven temperature assures a preliminary boost to a high rise. Food-processor directions make this quick bread even quicker. The result, we modestly believe, is The Absolute Best Buttermilk Biscuits.

Be sure to note the many variations at the end of the recipe. By the time you run through all your ideas, you will be a superb biscuitmaker and can write to us with your own inspirations.

2 cups all-purpose flour
2 teaspoons double-acting baking powder
1 teaspoon salt
½ teaspoon baking soda
½ teaspoon granulated sugar
¼ cup chilled butter
¼ cup vegetable shortening
¾ cup cold buttermilk

1. Preheat the oven to 450 degrees.
2. Place the flour, baking powder, salt, baking soda, and sugar in the workbowl of a food processor and process about 10 seconds to blend. (To prepare dough by hand, see note.) Cut the butter and shortening into small pieces and distribute evenly over the flour mixture. Pulse 10 to 12 times until the mixture resembles coarse meal. With the motor running, slowly pour the buttermilk through the feeding tube. Stop the motor as soon as the buttermilk is poured in and the mixture begins to clump.
3. Remove the steel blade from the workbowl and gather the dough into a ball with your hands. Turn it out onto a lightly floured surface. Roll or pat it to an even ½-inch thickness. Cut the dough with a 2-inch biscuit cutter and place the bicuits 2 inches apart on an ungreased baking sheet. (You can gather the scraps together and reroll, but be as gentle with the dough as you can or the biscuits will be tough.)
4. Place in the center of the oven and bake for 5 minutes. Lower the temperature to 425 degrees and bake for 8 to 10 minutes longer until the biscuits are a rich golden brown and well risen. Serve while warm.

YIELD: ABOUT 16 BISCUITS.

NOTE: The biscuit dough may also be prepared by hand. Place the flour, baking powder, salt, baking soda, and sugar in a mixing bowl and stir well. Cut up the butter and shortening and then rub with your fingers until the mixture resembles coarse meal. Add the buttermilk all at once and stir with a fork to make a dough. Turn out onto a lightly floured surface and knead 30 seconds. Proceed to roll, cut, and bake biscuits as above.

VARIATIONS

Add 1 teaspoon dried herbs or 1 tablespoon minced fresh herbs of your choosing, such as dill, basil, oregano, marjoram, rosemary, or sage to the dry ingredients.

Replace up to 1 cup of the all-purpose flour with whole wheat flour.

Add 1 tablespoon minced parsley or chives with the buttermilk.

Add 1 teaspoon cumin, celery, poppy, caraway, or fennel seeds with the dry ingredients.

Brush the tops of the unbaked biscuits with melted butter for extra richness.

Add 4 slices cooked and crumbled bacon with the milk.

Add 2 tablespoons grated Parmesan or Romano cheese with the dry ingredients.

Increase the sugar to 2 tablespoons and use a 2½-inch cutter to make dessert shortcakes. Increase baking time by about 2 minutes.

For softer pan rolls, place the unbaked cut biscuits in two ungreased 8- or 9-inch round baking pans. Increase baking time by 1 or 2 minutes.

To make square biscuits and to avoid re-rolling the trimmings, pat the dough into an 8-inch square that is about ½ inch thick. Use a sharp knife to cut it into 16 squares. Bake as directed in the basic recipe.

Sky-High Popovers

Leavened only by eggs, popovers are just about the easiest and fastest of breads to mix and make. In our experience, though, they can often be dismal failures—sometimes turning out doughy and far from the "sky-high" hollow and crispy puffs that characterize this lovely, light, and airy roll.

There are several widely divergent schools of thought on making popovers. Some people place the filled muffin or popover tins in a cold oven and then raise the heat to about 450 degrees. Others begin with the hot oven and then lower the heat. We like the latter idea, believing that the initial burst of heat is what puffs the dough. We even like to preheat the tins or cups before pouring in the batter.

We have found that the size and shape of the pan makes an enormous difference, too. Classic popover tins are made of heat-conducting metal and are usually about twice as deep as they are wide. Since most people do not own these tins, we tried other pans. Standard 5-ounce Pyrex custard cups are an ideal shape and muffin tins can be used as well, provided they are deeper than they they are wide.

Popovers are a most versatile bread, and you are almost certain to have the ingredients on hand. In addition, their extremely light texture and slightly eggy flavor provide a fine accompaniment to almost any meal. The batter can be made a couple of hours ahead and refrigerated. Be sure to stir it to recombine the ingredients just before pouring it into the pans. Popovers are best eaten hot from the oven when their crusty, golden exterior can be broken open to expose a moist, hollow interior that cries out to be spread with a little sweet butter. Popovers also make a terrific breakfast bread served with jam or drizzled with honey or maple syrup.

---

1 cup sifted all-purpose flour
½ teaspoon salt
1 cup milk

1 tablespoon butter, melted
2 eggs, slightly beaten

1. Preheat the oven to 450 degrees. Generously butter 6 popover pans, 8 5-ounce Pyrex custard cups, or 8 deep muffin tins.
2. In a mixing bowl, stir together the flour and salt. Whisk in the milk, butter, and eggs until well blended. The batter should be the consistency of thick cream.

3. Place the buttered tins or pans in the preheated oven until heated, about 2 minutes. (If you are using custard cups, they are easiest to handle if you set them in muffin tins so that they are stable and do not wobble around.) Watch carefully so that the butter used to grease the tins of the

pans does not begin to burn. Remove the preheated pans from the oven and immediately divide the batter evenly among the tins, filling each no more than two-thirds full.

4. Bake in the center of the oven for 15 minutes. Lower the heat to 350 degrees and continue to bake until the popovers are well risen, a rich golden brown, and crisp, about 15 to 20 minutes longer. (Do not open the oven door until near the end of the baking time.)

5. Serve hot.

YIELD: 6 TO 8 POPOVERS.

Classic Creamy Coleslaw

There are countless versions of coleslaw, the simple cabbage salad of Pennsylvania Dutch origin. Though there is indeed a place for coleslaw dressed with vinaigrette, tossed with apples, and seasoned with herbs, we think that a simple basic blend of thinly sliced cabbage and a dressing of mayonnaise, a little sour cream for tang, and a minimum of extras is the best of all.

¾ cup mayonnaise
¼ cup sour cream
1 tablespoon red wine vinegar
1 tablespoon granulated sugar
1 tablespoon minced onion
2 teaspoons Dijon mustard

1 teaspoon salt
¼ teaspoon freshly ground black pepper
1 small head (1½ pounds) green cabbage, thinly sliced
1 carrot, grated

1. In a large bowl, combine the mayonnaise, sour cream, vinegar, sugar, onion, mustard, salt, and pepper. Add the cabbage and carrot and toss thoroughly.

2. Refrigerate the coleslaw for at least an hour, but not more than 4 hours before serving to allow the flavors to blend.

YIELD: 6 TO 8 SERVINGS.

Potato Pan Rolls

The potato in these rolls helps produce a smooth-textured grain and somehow adds a certain subtle tang to their taste. In other words, they taste so good that they're worth the effort—especially if you are also yearning for the smell of bread baking in your kitchen.

1 4- to 5-ounce all-purpose potato
1 envelope active dry yeast (see note)
1 tablespoon plus ¼ teaspoon granulated sugar
2 tablespoons warm water
1 cup milk
1¼ teaspoons salt

4 tablespoons butter
3¼ to 3½ cups unbleached or all-purpose flour
1 egg, slightly beaten
4 tablespoons butter, melted, for brushing on the rolls

1. Peel the potato and cook it in a small saucepan of boiling water until tender. Drain, discard the water, and mash with a fork. You should have about ½ cup of mashed potato.

2. Dissolve the yeast with ¼ teaspoon of the sugar in the 2 tablespoons warm water and set aside until the yeast is bubbly, about 5 minutes.

3. Heat the milk with the remaining tablespoon of sugar and the salt. Remove from the heat, add the butter, and stir until melted. Stir in the mashed potatoes.

4. Place 3 cups of the flour in a large mixing bowl and add the milk mixture, the yeast mixture, and the egg. Stir to combine well. Knead on a well-floured board or with a dough hook in a heavy-duty mixer until the dough is smooth and elastic, about 8 minutes. Add enough additional flour to make a soft, workable dough.

5. Transfer the dough to a greased bowl, cover, and let rise in a warm place until doubled in bulk, about 1½ hours.

6. Punch the dough down. Lightly butter two 8- or 9-inch round cake pans. Divide the dough into 24 equal pieces and shape each piece into a round ball. Arrange the balls of dough in the cake pans side by side, leaving about ¼ inch between each roll. Brush the rolls with some of the melted butter. Let rise for 30 minutes at room temperature before baking, or cover loosely with plastic wrap and let rise in the refrigerator for 8 hours or overnight.

7. Preheat the oven to 375 degrees. Brush the rolls again with the remaining melted butter and bake in the preheated oven until a beautiful golden brown, about 25 to 30 minutes. Serve hot.

YIELD: 24 ROLLS.

NOTE: These rolls freeze very well after baking. Wrap them in foil to reheat. Quick-rise yeast may be substituted. Rising times will be about half as long.

Great Garlic Bread

We decided this recipe had to be included after more than a couple of our friends said, "Be sure to write a recipe for garlic bread. I've had so many awful versions in restaurants and at friends' homes." No doubt this is because too many people use garlic powder or dried garlic flakes or the stuff crushed in oil in a jar.

We really believe that fresh garlic is the only way to go. And use real butter, or a combination of butter and olive oil. Beyond that, there are a couple of ways to make the garlic bread, the choice depending on the circumstances. If you're serving a crowd, then wrapping the loaves in foil to heat in a hot oven is the most practical method. If you're making garlic bread for just a few people, then the broiled bread works fine.

The option of combining butter and olive oil, given below, is particularly delicious with any dishes that have a highly seasoned tomato sauce.

5 tablespoons butter or 3 tablespoons butter
   plus 2 tablespoons olive oil
1 large clove garlic

1 1-pound Italian or French bread
1 tablespoon Parmesan cheese (optional)
Sprinkling of paprika (optional)

1. Remove the butter from the refrigerator to soften. Peel the garlic, cutting off any brown spots, and split the clove in half to remove the green sprout in the center, if there is one. Mince the garlic fairly fine and beat it into the softened butter. (Alternatively, melt the butter together with the olive oil and minced garlic.)
2. Preheat the broiler.
3. Split the loaf of bread in half lengthwise and spread with the garlic butter or brush with the butter–olive oil mixture. Sprinkle the cheese evenly over the bread and dust lightly with paprika if desired. Place on a baking sheet and broil about 5 inches from the heating element until lightly toasted. Cut the loaf into slices and serve in a napkin-lined basket. (Alternatively, cut the loaf diagonally into slices almost but not quite all the way through the bottom of the loaf. Spread or brush the cut sides of the bread with the garlic butter. Wrap the loaf in a large sheet of foil and place on a rack in a preheated 400-degree oven for 5 minutes or until hot.)

YIELD: 4 TO 6 SERVINGS.

Spiced and Pickled Watermelon Rind

This delicious sweet-and-sour accompaniment has several advantages: It keeps for about a week in the refrigerator, making it a fine do-ahead condiment; it will cost you almost nothing since you will undoubtedly have more than enough watermelon rind available several times during the summer; and, despite the lengthy soaking time, the recipe is a breeze and requires only a few minutes of actual work to make. These, along with the fact that watermelon pickles taste wonderful, are reasons enough to make them!

Serve them at almost any barbecue, especially with hamburgers or chicken. Or give them as little hostess gifts when you are invited away for a summer weekend. The recipe can also be doubled or tripled and then processed in a boiling-water bath according to standard directions provided by manufacturers of canning jars.

Rind from about ¼ large watermelon
2 tablespoons kosher salt or sea salt
Water
¾ cup white cider vinegar
10 tablespoons granulated sugar
4 whole cloves

4 whole allspice
4 whole black peppercorns
1 stick cinnamon, broken in half
1 thin slice fresh gingerroot
1 large strip lemon peel, colored part only

1. Remove and discard all of the pink flesh from the watermelon rind. Cut the rind into ¾- to 1-inch cubes. You should have about 4 cups. Place the cubes in a large, nonreactive pot or bowl. Dissolve the kosher salt in 2½ cups of water and pour it over the watermelon cubes, being sure that they are submerged. (If necessary, weigh down the cubes with a plate.) Chill at least 6 or up to 24 hours.

2. Drain the watermelon cubes and rinse in several changes of cold water. Simmer the cubes in water to cover until just barely

fork tender, about 20 to 25 minutes. Drain.

3. In a heavy, nonreactive saucepan, bring the vinegar, sugar, and ¼ cup of water to a boil, stirring to dissolve the sugar. Tie the cloves, allspice, peppercorns, cinnamon, gingerroot, and lemon peel in a spice bag or piece of cheesecloth and add to the saucepan. Add the drained watermelon cubes. The liquid should just barely cover the cubes. If it does not, add a small amount of water.

4. Bring the mixture back to a boil, partially cover the pan, lower the heat, and

briskly simmer until the cubes are tender and translucent (about 20 to 30 minutes).

5. Cool watermelon in the syrup, then discard the spice bag. Chill the watermelon in the syrup, covered, for up to 1 week.

6. Serve chilled in a dish.

YIELD: ABOUT 6 SERVINGS (2½ TO 3 CUPS PICKLES AND LIQUID).

Corn Grilled in the Husk

This is a terrific way to cook corn when you've got the grill going anyway, and maybe it's too hot to even think about boiling a big pot of water on the stove inside. Soaking the unhusked ears in water first allows the corn to steam on the grill and helps to keep it from drying out. As the husks char, the corn acquires a slight smokiness making for a different and quite delicious corn-eating experience!

4 to 6 ears of corn
Butter

Salt and freshly ground black pepper
  to taste

1. Prepare and light a barbecue fire or preheat a gas grill.

2. Carefully pull the husks of the corn down to the stem end and remove and discard as much of the corn silk as possible. Wrap the husks back up around the ears, securing them at the tip with a twist tie or a piece of string. Place the wrapped corn in a large bucket of water to soak for 10 to 15 minutes.

3. Arrange the corn on the grill over a moderately hot fire and cook, turning frequently with tongs, until the kernels are tender when tested, about 30 minutes. If the husks begin to blacken too much, brush them with some more water.

4. Remove the ears to a platter. When cool enough to handle, strip off the husks and spread the corn with some butter and sprinkle with salt and pepper.

YIELD: 4 SERVINGS.

Peppery Corn Bread

We love this peppery corn bread with casseroles, soups, and stews in the winter and with salads and grilled meats in the summer. It's just rich enough to be a substantial element in any meal, and the black pepper adds a really pleasant zippy kick. If you're having it for breakfast, though, you might want to leave the pepper out.

1 cup yellow cornmeal
1 cup all-purpose flour
2 tablespoon granulated sugar
4 teaspoons double-acting baking powder
¾ teaspoon salt

½ teaspoon freshly ground black pepper
1 egg
1 cup milk
4 tablespoons butter, melted

1. Preheat the oven to 425 degrees.
2. In a large bowl, sift together the corn-meal, flour, sugar, baking powder, salt, and pepper.
3. In a small bowl, whisk together the egg, milk, and melted butter.
4. Make a well in the center of the flour mixture. Pour in the liquid ingredients and stir to combine. Spread the batter evenly into a 9-inch-square baking pan. Bake in the preheated oven until the corn bread is a mottled golden brown all over the top and a cake tester inserted in the center comes out clean, about 18 to 20 minutes.
5. Cut into 12 or 16 squares and serve hot in a napkin-lined basket.

YIELD: 12 TO 16 SQUARES OF CORN BREAD.

NOTE: The batter may also be made into corn sticks or corn muffins.

Purple Plum Chutney

Fresh fruit chutneys are easy to make, and sometimes a little homemade relish like this is just the thing to lift a main course of broiled or roasted meats or fish from the ordinary to the special.

1½ pounds purple or red plums, pitted and
    coarsely chopped
1 large onion, chopped (1 cup)
¼ cup light brown sugar
3 tablespoons white vinegar
1 tablespoon lemon juice
¾ teaspoon grated lemon zest
1 teaspoon dry mustard

1 teaspoon salt
½ teaspoon ground ginger
¼ teaspoon cayenne pepper
1 cinnamon stick, broken in half
Pinch of ground cloves
½ to ¾ cup water, depending on juiciness of
    plums

1. Place all the ingredients, including the ½ cup of water, in a medium, nonreactive saucepan. Bring the mixture to a simmer and cook, uncovered, over low heat, stirring occasionally, until the fruit and onion are soft and most of the liquid has been absorbed, about 30 to 40 minutes. Watch carefully toward the end of the cooking time. If the chutney seems in danger of scorching, add up to ¼ cup or so more water.

2. Remove and discard the pieces of cinnamon stick. Cool the chutney.

YIELD: 2 CUPS.

NOTE: The chutney will keep, stored in the refrigerator, for at least 1 month. Allow it to age for at least 1 day before serving to give the flavors a chance to develop.

DESSERTS

"The way not to die is to keep on livin'."
"I always like something sweet."

—BUSTER HOLMES
Handmade Cookin' (1980)

"And suddenly the memory returns. The taste was that of a little crumb of madeleine . . . which my aunt Léonie used to give me. . . ."

—MARCEL PROUST
Remembrance of Things Past (1913–1926)

"When we're dressing up to go to someone's house for dinner, Alice often tries to persuade me that there are ways of showing appreciation to the hostess other than having thirds."

—CALVIN TRILLIN
Alice, Let's Eat (1978)

" . . . and when the whole Escape was finished, there was Pooh, sitting on his branch, dangling his legs, and there, beside him, were ten pots of honey. . . ."

—A. A. MILNE
Winnie-the-Pooh (1926)

Red, White, and Blueberry Shortcakes

Chocolate mousse is decadent. Gâteau Saint-Honoré is impressive. Sacher torte is elegant. Tarte Tatin is a classic. But we would walk past these pastry-cart temptations straight toward a homespun creation of warm, tender biscuits, split and slathered with sweet butter, sandwiched with brilliant berries, and topped with an outrageous dollop of whipped cream. Yes, we firmly believe that strawberry shortcake is America's contribution to the list of the world's greatest desserts.

Typical of Yankee ingenuity, it is also one of the world's easiest desserts to make. The rich biscuits taste best when baked at the last minute, but they can be mixed, rolled, cut, and chilled on the baking sheet several hours ahead. (Leftover biscuits can be reheated in a 350-degree oven for about 5 minutes.) The fruit mixture and even the sweetened whipped cream will hold just as long in the refrigerator.

One summer, we were the happy recipients of a basket of just-picked blueberries from a neighbor's patch. At the risk of gilding the lily, we added them to our own strawberries and found that the result was even better than the original. It is now our favorite Fourth of July (or anytime in July) dessert. It is also terrific any time that fresh strawberries are available, but frozen, unsweetened blueberries are just fine.

BERRY FILLING:

2 pints strawberries, rinsed and drained on
    paper towels
1 pint blueberries, rinsed and drained on
    paper towels
½ cup granulated sugar
1 teaspoon lemon juice

BISCUITS:

2 cups sifted all-purpose flour
3 tablespoons plus 2 teaspoons granulated
    sugar
1 tablespoon double-acting baking powder
½ teaspoon salt
10 tablespoons unsalted butter, chilled and
    cut into 20 pieces
¾ cup cold milk

ASSEMBLY:

3 tablespoons unsalted butter, softened
1 cup heavy cream softly whipped with
    1 tablespoon confectioners' sugar

1. To prepare the berry filling, choose 6 to 8 of the most perfect strawberries and set aside for the garnish. Hull the remaining strawberries. Crush half of them using a fork or the back of an spoon and slice the remaining half; put both the sliced and crushed berries in a mixing bowl along with half of the blueberries. Place the remaining blueberries in a small saucepan, stir in the sugar and the lemon juice, and set the pan over medium-low heat. Stir, crushing the blueberries with the back of a spoon, until the juices are released and the sugar is dissolved to form a syrup, about 3 to 5 minutes. Let cool and then stir into the berries in the mixing bowl. Let stand at room temperature for about 20 minutes. If not using immediately, cover and chill for several hours, but remove the berries from the refrigerator about 30 minutes before using.

2. To make the biscuits, preheat the oven to 450 degrees.

3. Sift the flour, 3 tablespoons of the sugar, baking powder, and salt into a mixing bowl. Use your fingertips to cut the chilled butter into the flour until the mixture resembles coarse crumbs. Make a well in the center and add all but 1 tablespoon of the milk. Mix gently with a fork or wooden spoon just until the dough holds together.

4. Turn the dough out onto a lightly floured surface and knead 5 or 6 times. Roll or pat the dough to a ¾-inch thickness and cut with a 2¾- or 3-inch biscuit cutter. Gently gather the scraps together and re-roll. You should have 6 to 8 biscuits. Place the biscuits 2 inches apart on an ungreased baking sheet.

The biscuits may be covered with plastic wrap and refrigerated for several hours at this point.

5. When ready to bake, brush the biscuits with the remaining 1 tablespoon of milk and sprinkle with the 2 teaspoons of sugar. Place in the center of the oven and immediately lower the temperature to 375 degrees. Bake the biscuits until they are a pale golden brown, about 15 to 18 minutes. Remove to a rack to cool slightly.

6. To assemble the shortcakes, split the warm biscuits and spread the bottom halves with the softened butter. Spoon some of the berries and accumulated juices over the buttered halves and replace the tops. Spoon more berries and juices over the top, dollop with the whipped cream, and garnish with the reserved whole berries. Serve immediately.

YIELD: 6 TO 8 SERVINGS.

Georgia Peach-Pecan Skillet Cake

We developed this recipe because we confess to a fond memory of the pineapple ring–maraschino cherry upside-down cakes of our childhood. It seemed like magic to invert a perfectly plain, innocent-looking cake to disclose that brightly colored, syrupy sweet topping that had been hidden on the bottom of the pan. This is a sophisticated updated version of the classic and clever skillet cake. We use fresh peaches and a good shot of bourbon in the syrup and ground pecans in the cake to produce a mildly sweet dessert with southern flavors.

¼ cup pecan pieces
6 tablespoons butter
½ cup packed light brown sugar
2 tablespoons bourbon
¾ pound peaches
1 tablespoon all-purpose flour
3 eggs

½ cup granulated sugar
1 teaspoon vanilla extract
¾ cup all-purpose flour
¾ teaspoon double-acting baking powder
Pinch of salt
Unsweetened whipped cream as an
　　accompaniment

1. Preheat the oven to 375 degrees. Spread the pecans on a baking sheet and toast until dark brown and fragrant, about 5 to 6 minutes. Set aside to cool. Reduce the oven temperature to 350 degrees.
2. Place the butter in a 9-inch skillet with an ovenproof handle or in a 9-inch layer-cake pan. Set the pan over low heat on top of the stove to melt the butter. Raise the heat to medium, stir in the brown sugar, and cook, stirring, until the sugar is dissolved and the mixture is bubbly. Remove

from the heat and stir in 1 tablespoon of the bourbon.

3. Peel the peaches by plunging them into boiling water for 1 minute and then slipping off their skins. Thinly slice the peaches and scatter the slices in an even layer over the brown-sugar syrup. Set aside while you make the cake.

4. Place the cooled pecans in the workbowl of a food processor with the tablespoon of flour. Process by pulsing the motor on and off until the nuts are finely ground. Pecans may also be finely chopped by hand. Set aside.

5. Beat the eggs and the granulated sugar with an electric mixer until very light and almost tripled in volume, about 5 minutes. Stir in the remaining 1 tablespoon of bourbon and the vanilla extract.

6. Sift the flour, baking powder, and salt into a bowl. Add the ground pecans and toss to combine well with the flour. Sprinkle the flour mixture over the beaten eggs and gently but thoroughly fold the two together with a rubber spatula.

7. Pour the cake batter over the peaches, smooth the top, and bake in the center of the preheated oven for 30 to 40 minutes, or until the cake has set and a cake tester inserted in the center comes out clean. (If using a cast-iron skillet, check the cake after the 30 minutes since it will cook faster than one baked in an aluminum layer-cake pan.)

8. Run a sharp knife around the edge of the cake to loosen the sides. While still warm, invert the cake onto a serving platter. Leave the pan on the cake for a few minutes and then lift it off. Serve warm or at room temperature, topped with a dollop of whipped cream.

YIELD: 6 TO 8 SERVINGS.

NOTE: The cake may be made earlier in the day and held at room temperature. Leftovers are delicious for breakfast.

Double Lemon Loaf

If you love lemon, here's a wonderfully rich, very moist—and *intensely* lemony—loaf cake. A double hit of lemon—both juice and zest—goes into the cake batter *and* the soaking syrup, resulting in a lovely yellow-flecked cake with threads of glazed lemon zest on the top. It slices beautifully and is great on its own or served with berries or other fruit on the side.

Try to make this dessert a day or two ahead; it seems to improve if allowed to age (well wrapped) in the refrigerator, deepening and intensifying its lemoniness.

⅔ cup milk
1 tablespoon lemon juice
2 cups all-purpose flour
1 tablespoon double-acting baking powder
½ teaspoon baking soda
¼ teaspoon salt
¼ teaspoon nutmeg
8 tablespoons butter, softened
1¼ cups granulated sugar
3 eggs

1 teaspoon vanilla extract
2 tablespoons grated lemon zest

SOAKING SYRUP:

⅓ cup lemon juice
½ cup granulated sugar
1 teaspoon slivered or coarsely grated lemon zest (see note)

1. Butter a 9-by-5-inch loaf pan. Line the bottom with wax paper or baking parchment and butter the paper. Flour the pan, knocking out all the excess. Preheat the oven to 350 degrees.

2. Combine the milk and the lemon juice and set aside for 5 minutes. (The lemon juice will "clabber" the milk, thickening and slightly curdling it, to make sour milk.)

3. Sift together the flour, baking powder, baking soda, salt, and nutmeg; set aside.

4. With an electric mixer, cream the butter and sugar until light and fluffy. Beat in the eggs, one at a time, then beat on high speed for 1 minute. Beat in the vanilla extract and the grated lemon zest. With the mixer on low speed, add the flour mixture, alternating with the sour milk, in 3 additions. Beat until smooth but do not overmix.

5. Turn the batter into the prepared cake pan. Smooth the top evenly with a rubber spatula and bake on the center rack of the preheated oven until a skewer inserted in the center comes out clean, about 55 to 60 minutes.

6. Meanwhile, make the soaking syrup. Heat the lemon juice, sugar, and lemon zest in a small saucepan over medium heat, stirring until the sugar dissolves.

7. Let the cake cool in the pan for 10 minutes. Begin spooning the hot syrup (rewarm the syrup if necessary) over the warm cake in the pan. As the cake absorbs the syrup, spoon more of it evenly over the top until all the syrup is used. (It may seem like a large quantity of syrup, but the cake should absorb it all.) Let the cake cool to room temperature in the pan.

8. Run a sharp knife around the edges of the cake to loosen it. Invert the cake onto a plate, peel off the paper, and turn it right side up. Wrap well in plastic wrap and refrigerate for at least 3 hours to allow for easier slicing, or for as long as 3 to 4 days. Bring to room temperature before serving.

The cake may be made ahead and frozen for up to 1 month.

YIELD: 8 TO 10 SERVINGS.

NOTE: Remove the lemon zest with a vegetable peeler and cut it crosswise into thin slivers; or use the specially designed zesting tool available in kitchenware shops; or grate on the large holes of a grater.

Angel Food Cake with Summer Fruit Ambrosia

Angel food is a great American cake. Its exact origin is obscure, but it was developed in the nineteenth century. Some say it was the invention of thrifty Pennsylvania Dutch housewives who wanted to put leftover egg whites to good use. Others feel that a St. Louis restaurateur should be credited for the heavenly discovery. (If the latter is true, the man in question was a bit devilish since he went to extraordinary lengths to keep the recipe secret.)

However it began, angel food cake was enormously popular in the 1800s and is today experiencing a comeback. And well it should be, for it is virtually fat and cholesterol free and far lower in calories than any other kind of cake. Unlike some things that are good for you, though, angel food cake tastes terrific.

We like it plain, but its texture also makes it a perfect sponge for fruit juices. We often serve it with an updated streamlined version of southern-style summer fruit ambrosia. The splash of seltzer water or club soda added to the ambrosia just before serving is the inspiration of Melanie's mother-in-law, and it gives a fresh sparkle to any fruit salad.

Because angel food cake contains no fat, it is best served on the day it is baked. However, it keeps well, sealed in an airtight container kept in a very dry place, for a day or so at room temperature. It can also be frozen for a few weeks if very well wrapped.

1¼ cups sifted cake flour	**2 teaspoons vanilla extract**
1⅔ cups granulated sugar	**½ teaspoon almond extract**
14 egg whites (1¾ to 2 cups)	**2 teaspoons lemon juice**
½ teaspoon salt	**Summer Fruit Ambrosia (recipe follows)**
1½ teaspoons cream of tartar	

1. Preheat the oven to 300 degrees. Have ready an ungreased 10-inch, tube, angel-food cake pan, preferably one with a removable bottom and "feet" on the top.
2. Resift the flour onto a piece of wax paper. Sift the sugar onto a separate piece of paper or process the sugar for a few seconds in a food processor.
3. In a large, grease-free mixing bowl, beat the egg whites until frothy. Add the salt and cream of tartar and beat until soft, not stiff, peaks form. Using the mixer,

beat in about 4 tablespoons of the sugar. By hand, fold in the remaining sugar, 2 tablespoons at a time, using a gentle, but deep, over and under motion with a wide spatula.
4. Place the flour back into the sifter and sift over the batter, 2 to 3 tablespoons at a time. Fold in each addition, gently but thoroughly. Fold in the vanilla, almond extract, and lemon juice.
5. Turn the batter into the pan and smooth the top with a spatula. Rap the pan on the

counter 2 or 3 times to remove any air bubbles.

6. Bake in the center of the oven until the top is golden brown and springy to the touch, about 70 minutes.

7. Remove the cake from the oven and, if using a pan made for angel food cakes, invert onto the "feet." If using a different tube pan, invert onto the neck of a bottle to allow the cake to cool upside down without touching the counter. Let cool completely for at least 3 hours, then turn out onto a wax paper–lined plate. Turn right side up onto a serving plate. (If the cake does not come out of the pan easily, you may loosen the edges with a sharp knife, but be careful not to dislodge the golden crust.)

8. To cut the cake, use a gentle sawing motion with a serrated knife or cut by pulling a taut thread back and forth through the cake. Serve with the fruit ambrosia.

YIELD: ABOUT 12 SERVINGS.

Summer Fruit Ambrosia

Use any combination of ripe fruits that appeals to you and are the best available. We choose our fruits according to color and texture as well as contrasting flavors. Use ripe, but not overly soft fruit, so the ambrosia will not become mushy. The recipe may be adjusted to yield almost any quantity. It is especially nice with Angel Food Cake (see page 238), but it is also a delicious dessert by itself.

¼ cup packaged flaked coconut
⅓ cup orange juice
1½ teaspoons grated orange zest
3 tablespoons granulated sugar
2 tablespoons crème de cassis or orange liqueur (optional)

8 cups cut-up fresh summer fruit, such as sweet cherries, melon balls, nectarines, peaches, apricots, plums, raspberries, or blueberries, or a combination.
½ cup seltzer or club soda

1. Toast the coconut in a 325-degree oven for about 5 minutes, stirring often, until golden brown and fragrant. Let cool.

The coconut may be toasted several days ahead and stored in an airtight container.

2. Stir together the orange juice, zest, sugar, and optional liqueur until the sugar is dissolved. Toss with the cut-up fruit. Chill at least 1 hour or up to 4 hours.

3. Just before serving, add the club soda and stir gently. Sprinkle with the toasted coconut.

YIELD: 12 SERVINGS (8 CUPS).

Black Devil Cupcakes with Double Fudge Frosting

Who can possibly resist a moist, almost black devil's food cupcake topped with a swirl of double fudge frosting? This cake, which is neither too rich nor too sweet, is made even more intensely chocolatey by the addition of a pinch of black pepper and a little coffee powder. It will probably knock your socks off!

¼ teaspoon instant coffee
1½ cups water
1½ cups all-purpose flour
½ cup unsweetened cocoa
1⅓ cups granulated sugar
1½ teaspoons double-acting baking powder

1½ teaspoons baking soda
½ teaspoon salt
Pinch of freshly ground black pepper
8 tablespoons unsalted butter, melted
3 eggs
1½ teaspoons vanilla extract

1. Preheat the oven to 350 degrees. Lightly grease and flour 24 standard-size (about 2½ inches in diameter) muffin cups, or place a paper cupcake liner in each cup.
2. Place the instant coffee in a 2-cup measure. Add 2 tablespoons boiling water and stir until dissolved. Add the remaining water to measure 1½ cups and set aside.
3. Sift the flour, cocoa, sugar, baking powder, baking soda, salt, and pepper into a mixing bowl. Add the melted butter, the eggs, and coffee water, and the vanilla. Combine with a whisk, beating the batter about 60 strokes or until smooth.
3. Pour into the prepared cupcake cups, filling each one about ⅔ full. Bake in a preheated oven until the cupcakes have risen evenly and their tops spring back when touched, about 20 to 25 minutes. Cool in pans for 5 minutes, then turn out onto a wire rack to cool completely. Frost with Double Fudge Frosting.

YIELD: 24 CUPCAKES.

NOTE: The cupcakes will keep if well wrapped for 1 day, or will freeze well, either before or after frosting. When thawing the cupcakes, keep the plastic wrap on until they are thawed or condensation will collect on the surface.

DOUBLE FUDGE FROSTING:

4 ounces semisweet chocolate
1 ounce unsweetened chocolate
6 tablespoons unsalted butter

Pinch of salt
2 egg yolks
1⅓ cups confectioners' sugar
2 tablespoons cream or milk

Melt the chocolates, butter, and salt together in a double boiler, or in a bowl set over simmering water, or in a microwave. Cool until the chocolate is lukewarm, about 5 minutes. With an electric mixer, beat in the egg yolks, sugar, and cream or milk, until the frosting has a smooth, creamy consistency, about 1 minute. Use immediately to frost the cupcakes.

YIELD: 2 CUPS (ENOUGH FOR 24 CUPCAKES).

NOTE: If the frosting is stored in the refrigerator, it will become too firm to spread and should be brought back to room temperature before using.

Hester's Citrus Pudding Cake

Brooke's mother, Hester, has a repertoire of delicious desserts, including great custards and fruit crisps and gingerbread—but this citrus pudding cake is probably the most frequently requested of them all. These ingredients combine and bake like a pudding, yet when the dessert is done it has separated as if by magic into a fluffy sponge layer on top with a rich, custardy sauce beneath.

1¼ cups granulated sugar
3 tablespoons all-purpose flour
5 eggs, separated
1¼ cups milk
1½ teaspoons grated lemon zest

1½ teaspoons grated orange zest
⅓ cup lemon juice
⅓ cup orange juice
Pinch of salt

1. Preheat the oven to 350 degrees.
2. In a large mixing bowl, combine the sugar and the flour and stir with a wire whisk until well combined. In a small bowl, whisk together the egg yolks and the milk. Slowly pour the egg yolk–milk mixture over the sugar mixture, and stir with a whisk to blend. Stir in the lemon and orange zests and juices.
3. In a separate bowl, beat the egg whites with the pinch of salt until stiff but not dry. Pour the egg yolk mixture over the beaten egg whites and stir together gently with a large wire whisk. The mixture should be well blended but still light and frothy. (The egg base is so light that it is difficult to fold the two together with a rubber spatula in the traditional manner.)
4. Pour the batter into a shallow 2-quart baking dish and set the dish into a larger baking pan. Pour hot water into the larger pan to come halfway up the sides of the pudding pan. Bake in the preheated oven until the top is colored a rich golden brown and the pudding is firm to the touch in the center, about 30 to 35 minutes. Serve warm, at room temperature, or cool.

YIELD: 6 SERVINGS.

Classic Rice Pudding

There are many, many versions of rice pudding, ranging from the perfectly ethereal *riz imperatrice* of France to the perfectly awful plastic containers of white glue sold in some supermarket delis. Some rice puddings are dense and starchy while others are light and puffy. Some have little or no seasoning and others are (dreadfully) filled with candied fruit.

For us, rice pudding is a creamy custard, as soothing as a nursery memory but livened for adult tastes with a splash of bourbon and a sprinkling of currants. We have tried it with fancy rice and exotic flavorings, but we agree that this simple, pleasing version is our favorite.

Rice pudding is a marvelous dessert after a simple meal of broiled meat or chicken or as a cooling finish to a hot and spicy main course.

2 tablespoons bourbon	**3 egg yolks**
⅓ cup currants	**1 whole egg**
1½ cups milk	**⅔ cup granulated sugar**
⅛ teaspoon salt	**2 cups light cream or half-and-half**
¼ cup long-grain rice	**1 tablespoon vanilla extract**

1. Warm the bourbon and pour it over the currants. Soak for 30 minutes.
2. Bring the milk to a simmer and stir in the salt and rice. Cover the pot and simmer over very low heat, stirring occasionally, until the rice is nearly tender, about 12 to 15 minutes. (All the liquid will not be absorbed.)
3. Preheat the oven to 325 degrees. Lightly butter an 8-inch-square baking dish.
4. Whisk together the egg yolks, whole egg, sugar, cream, and vanilla until blended but not frothy. Gently whisk in the cooked rice and milk. Stir in the currants and any unabsorbed bourbon. Pour the pudding into the prepared dish and place the dish in a larger pan. Fill the larger pan with hot water to come halfway up the sides of the pudding pan. Just before placing in the oven, stir the pudding mixture again to evenly distribute the solid ingredients. Bake in the upper third of the oven until a knife inserted about 2 inches from the center comes out clean, about 50 minutes. The custard should still be soft.
5. Remove the pudding pan from its water bath and cool on a rack. Serve at room temperature or while still slightly warm.

YIELD: 6 TO 8 SERVINGS.

Maggie Valley Buttermilk Pie

The South is famous for its custard pies. Melanie first tasted buttermilk pie while visiting in the Great Smoky Mountains of western North Carolina. Maggie Valley, a sleepy little town, has some excellent cooks, and one of its best served her this area specialty. It is a lovely, sweet, lemon-scented custard that has the definite tang of buttermilk. Simple to make and deceptively plain in appearance, this is one of the richest and smoothest pies you will ever encounter.

A word about pie pans—all of the same diameter are not equal. Some are shallow and some have sharply sloping sides. We usually use pie plates that are measured at the top inside diameter and are at least 1½ inches deep. If your 9-inch pie pan is smaller or shallower, then we recommend that you use a 10-inch pan. We find, in general, that Pyrex pie plates are reliable and give an evenly browned crust. Black steel tins brown the bottom crust very well and are also recommended.

PASTRY:

1¼ cups all-purpose flour

½ teaspoon salt

⅛ teaspoon double-acting baking powder

6 tablespoons unsalted butter, chilled and cut in pieces

2 tablespoons vegetable shortening, chilled

4 tablespoons ice water

¾ cup plus 2 tablespoons granulated sugar

1 tablespoon all-purpose flour

Pinch of salt

3 eggs

1 cup buttermilk

2 tablespoons lemon juice

1 teaspoon grated lemon zest

1 teaspoon vanilla extract

⅛ teaspoon nutmeg

8 tablespoons butter, melted

1. To make the pastry, sift the flour, salt, and baking powder into a mixing bowl. Cut in the butter and shortening, using your fingertips or two knives, until the crumbs are the size of small peas. Add the water, 1 tablespoon at a time, tossing lightly with a fork to moisten all the ingredients. Gather the pastry into a ball, flatten to a 5-inch disk, wrap in plastic wrap, and chill for at least 30 minutes.

The pastry may be made up to 2 days ahead and refrigerated or up to 1 month ahead and frozen.

2. On a lightly floured surface, roll the pastry into a 12-inch circle. Ease the pastry into a 9-inch pie plate. Trim the edges and crimp decoratively. Refrigerate the pastry shell for 30 minutes or place in the freezer for 10 minutes.

3. Preheat the oven to 425 degrees. Set the rack in the lower half of the oven.

4. To make the filling, whisk the sugar, flour, salt, and eggs in a large mixing bowl until thick and lemon colored. Whisk in the buttermilk, lemon juice, zest, vanilla, and nutmeg. Pour in the melted butter, stirring until the mixture is well blended and smooth. Pour into the chilled pie shell. Bake 10 minutes, then lower the oven temperature to 350 degrees and bake an additional 25 to 30 minutes, until the filling is puffed and flecked with brown, and a knife inserted 2 inches from the center comes out clean.

5. Cool the pie on a rack. Serve at room temperature.

YIELD: 8 SERVINGS.

NOTE: Leftover pie should be refrigerated and brought back to room temperature before serving.

Miss Hulling's Banana-Coconut Cream Pie

Miss Hulling's Cafeteria is a St. Louis, Missouri, institution. For those of us with school-lunch memories of rubber meat loaf with wallpaper-paste gravy, the word "cafeteria" creates less than happy culinary memories. Miss Hulling's, however, will change your mind. It is a pristine, wood-paneled, and flower-bedecked staid establishment where the food is served on real china and the napkins are stiff cloth. One does not go to Miss Hulling's without thought to dress and demeanor or else one risks being snubbed by the hostess.

However, no amount of stuffiness stops legions of downtown businessmen, shoppers, and St. Louis visitors from dining at Miss Hulling's Cafeteria. It is known far and wide that Miss Hulling's makes real mashed potatoes, pot roast better than your mother's, and pies and cakes that will make you swoon (politely, of course). Among her many famous pies, a banana-coconut cream pie with a towering meringue and toasted coconut top is indelibly imprinted in Melanie's memory. Here is our rendition. Enjoy it after a light meal—this is not a dessert for those with small appetites.

CRUMB CRUST:

8 double graham crackers
½ cup packaged flaked coconut
6 tablespoons butter, melted

FILLING:

¾ cup granulated sugar
¼ cup cornstarch
Pinch of salt
3 cups milk
1 whole vanilla bean

4 egg yolks, beaten (save the whites for the meringue)
3 tablespoons butter
1 tablespoon dark rum
2 medium bananas

MERINGUE:

4 egg whites
¼ teaspoon cream of tartar
7 tablespoons granulated sugar
⅓ cup packaged flaked coconut

1. Preheat the oven to 350 degrees.
2. To make the crust, break the graham crackers in pieces and place in a food processor along with the ½ cup coconut. Pulse to make crumbs. Turn the mixture into a 10-inch or deep 9-inch pie plate, add the butter, and mix with a spoon until well blended. Use the back of a spoon and your fingers to press the crumbs evenly onto the bottom and sides of the pie plate.

3. Bake the crust in the preheated oven until a rich golden brown, about 8 to 10 minutes. Let cool completely on a rack.

The crust may be made a day ahead and kept at cool, dry room temperature.

4. To make the pie filling, combine the sugar, cornstarch, and salt in a heavy saucepan. Slowly whisk in the milk, add the vanilla bean, and place the pan over medium heat. Cook, stirring constantly with a wooden spoon, until the mixture comes to a boil and is thickened and smooth, about 8 to 10 minutes. Boil mixture, stirring, for 1 minute. Whisk about half of the hot milk mixture into the egg yolks to temper them, then return the egg-milk mixture to the saucepan. Cook, stirring constantly, until the mixture thickens more and almost returns to a boil, about 1 to 2 mintues. Take the pan off the heat and stir in the butter and rum until smooth. Remove the vanilla bean, split it length-wise, and scrape the seeds back into the custard. Discard the vanilla bean.

5. Slice the bananas ¼ inch thick and scatter evenly over the bottom of the crumb crust. Pour the filling over the bananas.

6. Preheat the oven to 375 degrees.

7. To make the meringue, beat the egg whites until foamy. Add the cream of tartar and beat until soft peaks form. Add the sugar, 1 tablespoon at a time, until the whites are stiff and shiny, but not dry. Spread the meringue over the filling, covering it completely. Swirl the top decoratively with a small spatula. Sprinkle with the ⅓ cup coconut. Bake until the meringue is a pale golden brown and the coconut is toasted and fragrant, about 6 to 8 minutes. Watch carefully to prevent the coconut from burning and the meringue from overbrowning.

8. Completely cool the pie on a rack, then refrigerate if not serving immediately.

YIELD: 8 SERVINGS.

NOTE: The pie is best eaten within about 4 hours, but leftovers can be refrigerated.

Double Crust Apple-Quince Pie

A quince is a hard, usually spotted, unpromising-looking yellow fruit with an exquisite, intensely spicy-sweet taste when cooked. Just one chopped quince in this pie contributes an elusive yet deliciously distinctive perfume that lifts it out of the ordinary. If quince are unavailable in your area, substitute one sweeter apple, such as a Golden Delicious or a Gravenstein.

This pie pastry come from Melanie's grandmother, who always added a little vinegar to her crust. It seems to make this already tender pastry even flakier.

PASTRY:

2½ cups all-purpose flour

1 teaspoons salt

1 teaspoon granulated sugar

8 tablespoons unsalted butter, chilled and cut in pieces

6 tablespoons lard, chilled and cut in pieces

1½ teaspoons cider vinegar

5 to 6 tablespoons ice water

5 large (2 to 2½ pounds) tart apples, such as Granny Smiths

1 large (10 to 12 ounces) quince

1 cup granulated sugar

¼ teaspoon ground cinnamon

¼ teaspoon nutmeg

1 tablespoon lemon juice

½ teaspoon grated lemon zest

¼ teaspoon vanilla extract

4 teaspoons all-purpose flour

2 tablespoons butter, cut in pieces

1 tablespoon milk for brushing on top of the pie

2 teaspoons sugar for sprinkling on top of the pie

1. To make the pastry, combine the flour, salt, and sugar in the workbowl of a food processor. Pulse to blend. Add the butter and lard, and pulse until the shortening is the size of peas. Add the vinegar and 5 tablespoons of the water through the feed tube, pulsing only until the dough just begins to clump together. (To make the pas-

try by hand, sift the dry ingredients into a mixing bowl. Work the butter and lard together using your fingertips until the fat is the size of small peas. Combine the vinegar and 5 tablespoons of the ice water in a measuring cup. Sprinkle this mixture over the flour, tossing lightly with a fork.) Add another tablespoon of water if the flour is not moistened enough to clump together. Divide the dough into two parts, flatten into 5-inch disks, and wrap each in plastic wrap. Chill for at least 30 minutes.

2. To prepare the filling, peel and core the apples and slice them ¼ to ½ inch thick. Peel and core the quince, cut it into 2-inch chunks, and coarsely chop in a food processor. Combine the fruits in a large mixing bowl with the sugar, cinnamon, nutmeg, lemon juice, lemon zest, vanilla, and flour. Toss together to mix.

3. Preheat the oven to 425 degrees.

4. On a lightly floured board, roll out one disk of pastry into a 12-inch circle. Ease it into a 9-inch pie plate. Roll out the second circle of pastry and set aside to use after the pie has been filled. Pour the apple mixture into the prepared shell and dot the top with the butter. Lay the pastry over the top of the pie. Trim the edges with scissors so they extend about ¾ inch beyond the rim of the pie plate, fold them under, and crimp with your fingertips or the tines of a fork. Brush the top of the crust with a little milk and sprinkle with sugar. Cut several slashes in the crust so steam can escape.

5. Bake in the lower third of the preheated oven for 20 minutes. Reduce the temperature to 350 degrees and continue baking until the fruit is tender and the crust is a rich golden brown, about 40 to 50 minutes. Cool at least an hour before serving.

YIELD: 6 TO 8 SERVINGS.

NOTE: The pie may be made early on the day it is to be served and held at room temperature. If there are leftovers, store at cool room temperature, not in the refrigerator.

Pear Strudel

Strudels are simple, homey creations using phyllo pastry, the paper-thin leaves of dough that bake to buttery, flaky layers. The pastry is classic in many Middle Eastern, Middle European, and Greek dishes, and being able to use it is a skill well worth acquiring.

Strudels are usually shaped into rolls, either straight or curved, and may be filled with almost anything from apples to zucchini. Like crepes, strudels are well suited to roll around mixtures both sweet and savory. Here, we use pears, which make a particularly aromatic strudel. We love it as dessert, especially after an autumn supper of roast pork or chicken. But we also serve it for a special breakfast treat, with a pitcher of pouring cream.

Working with phyllo dough is daunting to the uninitiated. The fragile leaves tear and dry out before your eyes. Remember, though, that the dough is always used in buttered layers, so tears and imperfections will not show in the end product, and a subsequent layer will hide the flaws in the layer below. The dough, because it is so thin and low in fat, does dry out quickly, so it is important to have the filling and remaining ingredients nearby and ready before you unwrap the pastry package. To keep it workable, lay the leaves on barely moistened tea towels and cover the unused dough with another towel. As soon as you are finished, reroll the extra dough, wrap it well in heavy plastic or foil, and refrigerate it for about 3 days or freeze up to 3 months. The frozen dough should be placed in the refrigerator for about 3 hours to thaw before using, and it should be kept cool at all times.

About 1½ pounds ripe but firm pears, peeled, cored, and cut in ½-inch cubes (3 cups)
⅓ cup coarsely chopped walnuts
⅓ cup light brown sugar
½ teaspoon ground cinnamon
¼ teaspoon ground mace
¼ teaspoon grated lemon zest

Pinch of salt
½ teaspoon vanilla extract
4 sheets phyllo or strudel dough (each about 14 by 17 inches)
⅓ cup unsalted butter, melted and cooled
⅓ cup graham cracker crumbs
Confectioners' sugar for dusting the strudel

1. Preheat the oven to 400 degrees.

2. In a mixing bowl, gently toss together the pears, nuts, sugar, cinnamon, mace, lemon zest, salt, and vanilla.

3. Place one sheet of the phyllo, with the short end facing you, on a work surface lined with a slightly dampened tea towel. Brush with about ⅕ of the melted butter and sprinkle with about ¼ of the crumbs. Lay another sheet over the first and brush and sprinkle again. Lay the third sheet over and repeat the process. Lay the fourth sheet over, brush with half of the remaining butter and all of the remaining crumbs.

4. Spoon the fruit on the lower third of the dough, leaving a 1-inch margin all around. Beginning at the lower fruit-filled short end and using the tea towel as an aid, roll it up, tucking in the ends as you go so the filling will not escape during baking.

5. Use some of the remaining butter to brush on a rimmed baking sheet or jelly roll pan. Use the tea towel to help you invert the strudel, seam side down, onto the baking sheet. Brush the top of the strudel with the remaining butter. Score the strudel just through the top layers of pastry into 8 diagonal pieces.

6. Bake in the center of the oven for 10 minutes. Lower the temperature to 350 degrees and bake until the pastry is golden brown and crisp, an additional 20 minutes.

7. Let cool slightly on the baking sheet, then remove to a serving platter. Serve warm or at room temperature liberally dusted with confectioners' sugar.

YIELD: 8 SERVINGS.

NOTE: Strudel is wonderful served warm from the oven, but the baked strudel may be refrigerated overnight and then reheated on a baking sheet in a 300-degree oven for about 10 minutes or until warm and crisp. It may also be frozen, well wrapped, for a month or so.

Cranberry Bread Pudding with Whiskey Sauce

Cranberries contribute their beautiful color as well as a refreshingly lively flavor to this splendidly rich and custardy pudding. In New Orleans, where bread pudding is a specialty, it is always served with a sweet whiskey sauce. Though one might think that a little bit of lily-gilding, the sauce does seem to tie everything together very nicely, so we'd never refuse it. The pudding is perfectly delicious without it, though.

Serve this dessert after a not-too-rich winter dinner. When we were developing it, we tasted it first thing one morning and thought it would make a *great* breakfast. Why not?

2 teaspoons butter, softened
16 slices (8 ounces) French bread, cut ½ inch thick
1 cup cranberries, coarsely chopped
3 eggs
1 cup plus 2 teaspoons granulated sugar
2 cups half-and-half or light cream

1 cup heavy cream
2 tablespoons vanilla extract
½ teaspoon ground cinnamon
¼ teaspoon ground nutmeg
½ teaspoon grated orange zest
¼ cup orange juice

1. Use the butter to grease a shallow 2-quart baking dish. Slice the bread. Coarsely chop the cranberries either with a large knife or by pulsing them on and off in a food processor. Arrange half the bread in the bottom of the baking dish and scatter half the cranberries over the bread. Layer the rest of the bread over the cranberries and scatter the remaining cranberries over the top.

2. In a mixing bowl, whisk the eggs with 1 cup of the sugar. Whisk in the half-and-half, cream, vanilla, cinnamon, nutmeg, orange zest, and orange juice. Pour this custard mixture evenly over the bread and cranberries. Lay a sheet of plastic wrap directly on the surface of the pudding and place a slightly smaller pan on the plastic wrap. Put a couple of heavy cans into the pan to weigh it down so the bread is completely immersed in the custard. Set aside to soak for 10 minutes.

3. Preheat the oven to 325 degrees.

4. Remove the weights and the plastic wrap and place the pudding in the center of the preheated oven. Bake for 20 minutes, then remove the dish from the oven and sprinkle the remaining 2 teaspoons of sugar over the top of the pudding. Return the dish to the oven to bake for another 35 to 40 minutes, or until the top is golden and slightly caramelized and the custard is set when tested with the point of a knife about 2 inches out from the center. The very center of the pudding should be slightly wobbly since it will continue to cook a bit after it is removed from the oven. The pudding will have puffed up quite a bit and will sink some as it cools.

5. Serve the pudding hot or warm, or bake it up to about 2 hours ahead and serve it tepid. Cut the pudding into squares or use a large spoon to scoop out each portion. Pass Whiskey Sauce (see below) to be spooned over the pudding if desired.

YIELD: 6 TO 8 SERVINGS.

WHISKEY SAUCE:

⅔ cup granulated sugar

¼ cup water

4 tablespoons butter

1 egg

4 tablespoons whiskey

1. Combine the sugar, water, and butter in a saucepan. Simmer, stirring, until the butter is melted and the sugar is dissolved, about 2 minutes.

2. In a bowl, beat the egg with a whisk until light and foamy, about 1 minute. Gradually beat the hot sugar-butter mixture into the egg, whisking constantly. Stir in the whiskey. Serve at room temperature over the Cranberry Bread Pudding.

YIELD: ABOUT 1¼ CUPS.

NOTE: The sauce may be made ahead and stored at room temperature for several hours. If refrigerated, warm over hot water and stir well to return to the correct consistency.

Mocha Pudding with Coffee Cream

This chocolatey pudding might be even better than the one in your memories. A small amount of instant coffee adds the perfect bitter edge to a dessert that can sometimes be somewhat too decidedly . . . chocolate.

It's the perfect ending to many a supper. Just dig right in and please lick your spoon!

⅔ cup granulated sugar
1 tablespoon cocoa
1½ tablespoons cornstarch
1 teaspoon instant coffee, preferably instant espresso
Pinch of salt
3 cups milk
2 eggs
2 egg yolks
1 cup (6 ounces) semisweet chocolate chips or 6 1-ounce semisweet chocolate squares, chopped

1 tablespoon butter
1 tablespoon coffee-flavored liqueur (optional)
2 teaspoons vanilla extract

COFFEE CREAM:

¾ cup chilled heavy cream
½ teaspoon instant coffee, preferably instant espresso
2 teaspoons confectioners' sugar

1. To make the pudding, combine the sugar, cocoa, cornstarch, instant coffee, and salt in a heavy saucepan. Slowly stir in the milk and bring to a boil over medium heat, stirring constantly.
2. In a small bowl, whisk together the eggs and the egg yolks. Whisk in a small amount of the hot milk mixture to temper the eggs, then whisk the egg-milk mixture back into the saucepan. Cook over low heat, stirring constantly, until the mixture is the consistency of a medium-thick cream sauce and heavily coats a spoon, about 5 minutes.
3. Remove the pan from the heat and add the chocolate and the butter. Stir until the chocolate is melted and the mixture is smooth. Stir in the liqueur and the vanilla. Pour the pudding into six individual dessert dishes or stemmed glasses or 1½-quart bowl and refrigerate until firm, about 1 hour.
4. To make the coffee cream, combine the chilled cream and the instant coffee and stir until the coffee dissolves. Whip the cream, adding the confectioners' sugar as the cream thickens.
5. Serve the mocha pudding topped with a large dollop of the coffee cream.

YIELD: 6 SERVINGS.

NOTE: The pudding may be made ahead and covered when cold. It will keep, refrigerated, for up to 2 days.

Pumpkin Custard

We think that using canned pumpkin is a great deal easier than making the purée from scratch; it also has superior texture, color, and taste. Large jack-o'-lantern pumpkins are grown for size and shape rather than for taste, and the pulp obtained from such varieties is apt to be watery and flavorless.

The aroma of this sweetly spiced custard pudding will warm and tantalize the entire household as it bakes.

1¼ cups half-and-half or light cream
⅛ teaspoon salt
2 eggs
½ cup granulated sugar
⅔ cup pumpkin purée
½ teaspoon ground cinnamon
⅛ teaspoon powdered ginger
Generous pinch of allspice

Generous pinch of ground cloves
Generous pinch of ground nutmeg
1 tablespoon molasses
1 tablespoon dark rum
½ teaspoon vanilla extract
3 tablespoons chopped pecans
½ cup heavy cream

1. Preheat the oven to 325 degrees.
2. Heat the half-and-half or cream with the salt until small bubbles appear around the edge.
3. In a mixing bowl, whisk the eggs with the sugar, pumpkin purée, spices, molasses, rum, and vanilla. Gradually add the hot half-and-half to the mixture and whisk gently to combine.
4. Pour the custard mixture into an 8-inch-square baking dish, set the dish in a larger pan, and pour enough hot water into the larger pan to come halfway up the sides of the baking dish.
5. Bake in the preheated oven until a knife inserted near the edge of the custard comes out clean, about 35 to 40 minutes. The custard will be soft and the center will not be as firm as the edges, but it will continue to cook a bit after it is out of the oven. Remove the custard dish from its water bath and place on a rack to cool.
6. Toast the pecans in a 325-degree oven until they are fragrant and dark brown, about 8 minutes.
7. Whip the cream to soft peaks. Spoon it into a bowl and sprinkle with the toasted nuts.
8. Serve the pudding warm, tepid, or cool, with the cream and chopped pecans spooned over each serving.

YIELD: 4 TO 6 SERVINGS.

Candied Gingerbread with Vanilla Cream

To our minds, gingerbread must be very fragrant with spices, dark and sticky with molasses, and freshened with a hint of citrus. The texture should be cakey enough for dessert but moist enough to be a good "keeper" for snacking. With all of these prerequisites in mind, we whipped up more than a few gingerbreads before we were satisfied. But this one has become an instant tradition at both of our homes. We love it as a fall and winter dessert with softly whipped cream, sweetened and scented with vanilla. We also like it dusted with powdered sugar and straight from the pan for snacking or with a pitcher of pouring cream or a spoonful of applesauce for breakfast. It is wonderful and fragrant when fresh from the oven; it is also delicious a day or so later since it deepens in flavor and becomes more moist as it "ages."

We suggest baking a batch of this gingerbread around the first of December. The aroma wafting from the oven is guaranteed to bring the Christmas spirit to your home.

½ cup dark molasses	1½ teaspoons powdered ginger
½ cup dark corn syrup	1 teaspoon ground cinnamon
½ cup dark brown sugar	½ teaspoon ground nutmeg
8 tablespoons butter	½ teaspoon ground cloves
1 cup orange juice	2 eggs
3 tablespoons finely chopped crystallized ginger	1 cup heavy cream
	2 tablespoons confectioners' sugar
2 cups all-purpose flour	1 teaspoon vanilla extract
1¾ teaspoons baking soda	

1. Preheat the oven to 350 degrees. Grease and flour a 9-inch-square baking pan.
2. In a heavy saucepan, heat the molasses, corn syrup, brown sugar, and butter. Stir often, until the butter is melted and the mixture is bubbly. Take the pan off the heat and stir in the orange juice and crystallized ginger. Let cool slightly.
3. In a large mixing bowl, stir together the flour, baking soda, powdered ginger, cinnamon, nutmeg, and cloves. Make a well in the center of the dry ingredients and add

the eggs and molasses mixture. Using a whisk or wooden spoon, beat until smooth. (The batter will foam up and be rather thin.)
4. Pour into the prepared pan and bake in the center of the oven until a toothpick inserted in the center comes out clean, about 35 to 40 mintues. Set the pan of gingerbread on a baking rack to cool for about 10 minutes.
5. While the gingerbread is cooling slightly, whip the cream to soft peaks, add-

ing the confectioners' sugar and vanilla when the cream begins to thicken.

6. Serve warm or at room temperature, cut in 8 or 9 squares, and accompanied by generous dollops of the whipped cream.

YIELD: 8 OR 9 SERVINGS.

NOTE: The gingerbread may be made a day ahead, covered with foil, and then reheated in the foil in a 350-degree oven until just warm, about 5 minutes. Leftover gingerbread can be dusted with powdered sugar and served at room temperature as a snack. This gingerbread also freezes exceptionally well.

Wine-Washed Strawberries

When Brooke attended a cooking class taught by Paula Wolfert, one thing that really stayed in her mind was Paula's idea of washing strawberries in wine rather than in water. She pointed out that rinsing berries in water just made them waterlogged and diluted their taste, but that no one ever minded if the fruit was slightly "winelogged." The wine, in fact, really enhances the taste of the berries.

Add sugar to the sour cream according to the sweetness of the strawberries, using less if you happen to be lucky enough to have really ripe, sweet fruit. Either red or white wine is fine for the rinse, though a fruity red is slightly preferable since it seems to complement the sweetness of the berries.

1 pint strawberries
½ cup wine
½ cup sour cream

1½ to 2 tablespoons brown sugar (depending on the sweetness of the berries)

1. Leave the stems on the strawberries and trim them of any brown spots. Wash in the wine by placing them in a bowl and pouring the wine over them. Toss the berries in the wine with your fingers and remove them, shaking off the excess wine. Arrange the strawberries in a pretty glass bowl.

2. Stir the brown sugar into the sour cream. Pass at the table with the strawberries so that each person may spoon a little of the sweetened sour cream onto his plate and dip the berries into the sauce, holding them by their stems.

YIELD: 4 SERVINGS.

Purple Plum Crumble

Small purple plums, also known as Italian prune plums, appear in mid-August and are an excellent value through September. Meatier than most plums, they taste best when cooked. This crumble, which some might call a crisp or a crunch, depending upon their local culinary heritage, is a homey and delicious dessert that takes only minutes to prepare and smells heavenly while baking. The hint of orange enhances both the aroma and flavor. We love to eat the crumble while still warm with a scoop of vanilla ice cream or a mound of whipped cream on the side. We must confess, though, to more than occasional late-night spoonsful of leftovers straight out of the refrigerator.

2 pounds purple Italian prune plums, pitted and quartered (about 5 cups)
¼ cup granulated sugar
2 tablespoons Grand Marnier or other orange liqueur
2 tablespoons orange juice
⅓ cup walnut pieces
¾ cup old-fashioned rolled oats
¾ cup all-purpose flour

⅔ cup packed light brown sugar
1 teaspoon grated orange zest
1 teaspoon ground cinnamon
Pinch of salt
10 tablespoons unsalted butter, chilled and cut in pieces
Unsweetened whipped cream as an accompaniment

1. Preheat oven to 375 degrees. Butter a 9-inch-square baking dish.
2. Toss the plums with the granulated sugar, Grand Marnier, and orange juice, and place in the prepared dish.
3. To make the topping, coarsely chop the walnuts in a food processor. Add the oats, flour, brown sugar, orange zest, cinnamon, salt, and butter to the processor, being sure to disperse the butter evenly in the workbowl. Process with 6 to 8 pulses, until the butter is cut in and the mixture is crumbly. (To make the topping by hand, chop the nuts and combine with the remaining ingredients, using a pastry blender or your fingertips.) Sprinkle evenly over the plums. (The layer of topping will be ½ to ¾ inch thick.)
4. Bake in the center of the oven until the plums are tender and bubbly and the topping is crisp and browned, about 40 to 45 minutes.
5. Serve slightly warm with whipped cream.

YIELD: 6 TO 8 SERVINGS.

NOTE: This dessert may be made early on the day it is to be served and reheated, covered, in a 350-degree oven until warm, about 10 minutes.

Lemon-Blueberry Mousse

Lemon curd is one of England's best culinary ideas. In spite of its rather unappetizing name, lemon curd is one of the richest, smoothest, tartest, sweetest creations that you ever licked off a spoon. Made simply with eggs, butter, sugar, and lemon, it is actually nothing more than a stovetop stirred custard. The English use it as a condiment and breakfast spread for toast or for a teatime accompaniment to scones. But, to our minds, that only scratches the surface of its versatility.

Here, we have used the basic curd to create a simple yet satiny and sublime lemon mousse dessert that is a breeze to prepare. We fold in whole blueberries, which give a wonderful color, texture, and taste without disguising the purity of the lemon itself.

This is the perfect dessert after a meal of complex tastes.

3 whole eggs
3 egg yolks
1¼ cups granulated sugar
1 tablespoon grated lemon zest
½ cup lemon juice

⅛ teaspoon salt
4 tablespoons butter, melted
1 cup heavy cream, chilled
1½ cups blueberries

1. Whisk the whole eggs, yolks, and sugar in a heavy, nonreactive saucepan until thick and lemon colored. Whisk in the lemon zest, juice, salt, and melted butter.
2. Set the pan over medium-low heat and cook, stirring constantly with a wooden spoon, until the mixture is very smooth and thick enough to heavily coat the back of the spoon, about 6 to 8 minutes.
3. Force through a strainer into a bowl. Cover and refrigerate about 1 hour until cold.

The recipe may be prepared ahead up to this point and refrigerated for up to a week or frozen for longer storage.
4. Whip the cream and set aside about ½ cup for the garnish. Fold the remainder into the lemon curd. Set aside 18 blueberries and gently fold the remainder into the mousse. Spoon the mousse into dessert dishes or stemmed goblets or a 1½-quart serving bowl. Refrigerate until ready to serve, up to 6 hours.
5. Garnish the mousse with dollops of the reserved whipped cream and sprinkle with the reserved blueberries.

YIELD: 6 SERVINGS.

Green Tomato Cobbler

This cobbler is similar to a deep-dish pie but has a cream-enriched, shortcake biscuit crust. Green tomatoes taste something like tart apples but are juicier, creating a lot of delicious liquid to be soaked up by the crust. If green tomatoes aren't available, substitute the same quantity of peeled, coarsely chopped, tart apples. Since apples are less juicy than tomatoes, add ¼ cup apple juice or water to the fruit mixture.

About 2½ pounds green tomatoes, coarsely
   chopped (6 to 7 cups)
¾ cup granulated sugar
½ teaspoon grated lemon zest
3 tablespoons butter

COBBLER DOUGH:

1½ cups all-purpose flour
¾ teaspoon salt
2 teaspoons double-acting baking powder
1 tablespoon plus 2 teaspoons granulated sugar
3 tablespoons cold butter
¾ cup plus 1 tablespoon heavy cream

1. Preheat the oven to 400 degrees.
2. In a mixing bowl, toss the cut-up fruit with the sugar and lemon zest. Scatter the fruit over the bottom of a lightly buttered, shallow, 2-quart baking dish of any shape. Cut the 3 tablespoons butter into about 10 small chunks and scatter them over the fruit.
3. To make dough, place the flour, salt, baking powder, and 1 tablespoon of the sugar in a food processor. Pulse 2 to 3 times to blend. Add butter and heavy cream and process until a soft ball forms, then continue to "knead" by processing for about 45 seconds. (If the dough does not form a ball, add more flour, 1 tablespoon at a time, until a ball does form.) (To make the dough by hand, combine the flour, salt, baking powder, and 1 tablespoon of the sugar in a mixing bowl. Cut the 3 table-spoons of cold butter into about 5 pieces and toss it with the flour mixture, working it in with your fingertips until the butter is about the size of small peas. Make a well in the center, pour in ¾ cup of the cream, and stir with a fork or your fingertips until the dough clumps together into a ball. Do not overwork it, or the dough will be tough.)
4. On a lightly floured board, roll out the dough until it is about ¼ inch thick and slightly smaller than the interior dimensions of the baking dish. Trim the edges and crimp them with your fingertips or a fork. Place the dough over the fruit and cut several deep slashes in the cobbler top so that steam can escape. Brush with the remaining tablespoon of cream and sprinkle the remaining 2 teaspoons of sugar evenly over the crust.
5. Bake in the preheated oven until the

crust is browned and the fruit is tender, about 30 to 35 minutes. Serve warm, with softly whipped cream if desired.

YIELD: 6 SERVINGS.

Baked Amaretti Nectarines

Gorgeous, ripe fruit is sometimes the *only* way you want to end a summer supper. But if you feel like offering guests something just a little more elaborate than plain sliced fruit, try this simple method of baking nectarines. Enhanced with a touch of Marsala and topped with some Amaretti crumbs, this is a lovely way to treat a nectarine. Substitute peaches, if you like, though they should be peeled first.

6 nectarines (a total of about 1½ pounds)
¼ cup Marsala
2 tablespoons water
1 teaspoon lemon juice
1 strip lemon zest
½ teaspoon vanilla extract

3 tablespoons butter, melted
1½ tablespoon granulated sugar
About 4 1½-inch Amaretti, crushed
   (3 tablespoons)
½ cup heavy cream
¼ teaspoons almond extract

1. Preheat the oven to 375 degrees. Cut the nectarines in half, twisting gently to release the flesh from the pit. If the fruit doesn't pull apart into neat halves this way, then cut the nectarines in quarters to free them from the pits.
2. Combine the Marsala, water, lemon juice, zest, and vanilla in a measuring cup and set aside.
3. Brush a shallow 2-quart baking dish with 1 tablespoon of the melted butter and sprinkle the dish with the sugar. Arrange the nectarines, cut sides up, in the dish, and pour the prepared liquid around the fruit. Sprinkle the nectarines with the crushed Amaretti and drizzle the remaining butter over the fruit.

The recipe to this point may be prepared up to 2 hours ahead.
4. Bake, uncovered, in the preheated oven until the nectarines are soft but not mushy, about 20 minutes. If the crumbs have not browned, run the baking dish under the broiler until the top is bubbly brown and caramelized, about 30 to 60 seconds.
5. Whip the cream and the almond extract to soft peaks. Serve the nectarines while still warm, with the almond whipped cream spooned on the side.

YIELD: 6 SERVINGS.

Baked Ginger–Bay Leaf Apples

Baked apples are such a splendidly straightforward dessert that a book on Sunday suppers would not be complete without a recipe for this favorite. We have eschewed the richer raisin-nut fillings in favor of a simple sugar-butter combination flavored with a little crystallized ginger. The bay leaves infuse the syrup and also add a sophisticated touch.

Baked apples are best when made with large, juicy, very flavorful apples. Choose the variety from your area that best fits this description. Here in the eastern United States, we like to use Cortlands, Rome Beautys, or Northern Spys. Golden Delicious apples, available nationally, are also a good choice.

6 large, juicy baking apples
¼ cup light brown sugar
2 tablespoons finely chopped crystallized ginger (see note)
½ teaspoon ground cinnamon
¼ teaspoon grated lemon zest

2 tablespoons butter
1 cup water
⅓ cup honey
1 tablespoon lemon juice
3 bay leaves, each broken in half
Lightly whipped cream as an accompaniment

1. Preheat the oven to 375 degrees.
2. Core the apples and peel them about halfway down. Arrange in a buttered 9- by 13-inch baking dish. (If the apples won't stand upright, slice off a small piece to make their bottoms flat.)
3. In a small bowl, mix together the brown sugar, ginger, cinnamon, and lemon zest. Divide the sugar mixture equally among the apples, spooning it into the cavities. Cut the butter into 6 pieces and place 1 atop each apple.
4. In a saucepan, heat the water, honey, lemon juice, and bay leaves, stirring until the honey melts. Pour around the apples.

Bake in the center of the preheated oven until the apples are tender but not mushy when pierced with the point of a sharp knife, about 40 to 45 minutes. Spoon the juices over the apples every 10 minutes as they bake.

5. Remove the pan from the oven and continue to spoon the juices over the apples as they cool so that they get slightly glazed with the syrup. Serve while still warm, accompanied by lightly whipped cream, if desired. The apples may be kept warm for about an hour before serving if loosely covered with foil.

YIELD: 6 SERVINGS.

NOTE: Substitute ½ teaspooon ground ginger if crystallized ginger is unavailable.

Peanut Butter–Chocolate Chip Brownies

Surveys show that the most popular candy bar combination in America is chocolate with peanuts and that brownies are far and away the favorite bar cookie. With all of this important data in mind, we have concluded that our Peanut Butter–Chocolate Chip Brownies could be one of the few things in life that "please all of the people all of the time." At least they have pleased our family and friends for years. If cut in large bars, these can be dessert unto themselves. In small pieces, they are a wonderful accompaniment to a bowl of sliced peaches in summer or oranges in winter. We find that they are a terrific dessert for informal backyard picnics and totable lunches. They keep for a few days in a covered tin and are well suited to freezer storage, too.

1 cup all-purpose flour
1 teaspoon double-acting baking powder
¼ teaspoon baking soda
¼ teaspoon salt
⅔ cup extra-chunky peanut butter

4 tablespoons unsalted butter, softened
1 cup packed light brown sugar
2 eggs
1 teaspoon vanilla extract
1 cup (6 ounces) semisweet chocolate chips

1. Preheat the oven to 350 degrees. Butter a 9-inch-square baking pan.
2. Sift together the flour, baking powder, baking soda, and salt. Reserve.
3. In a mixing bowl, cream together the peanut butter, butter, and brown sugar until light and fluffy. Add the eggs and vanilla and beat until smooth. With the mixer at low speed, add the flour mixture, beat-ing until it is just combined. Stir in the chocolate chips by hand.
4. Scrape the batter into the prepared pan and spread evenly. Bake in the center of the oven until the surface is dry and golden, about 30 to 35 minutes. Cool completely in the pan on a rack. Cut into 16 large or 24 smaller squares.

YIELD: 16 TO 24 BROWNIES.

NOTE: The brownies may be made 3 days ahead and stored, covered, at room temperature. They may also be frozen for up to 1 month.

Mixed Fruit–Chocolate Pan Soufflé

We love chocolate soufflés, and were determined to overcome the obstacles of last-minute preparation and the high risk of failure. This is quick, easy, and sinfully chocolatey. It puffs beautifully in a pie plate every time to make an airy, hot soufflé that you can pop in the oven and bake in about the time it takes the after-dinner coffee to brew. If you want to bake it a little earlier, you can serve a cooled, incredibly fudgey and creamy baked pudding. Either way, we think this method produces the ultimate showstopping yet homey dessert. Any brand of semisweet or bittersweet chocolate can be used, but the better the quality, the better the result.

We have also made this recipe using ⅓ chopped macadamia nuts instead of the mixed fruit (adding the rum with the vanilla) with resounding success! In either case, softly whipped cream is the perfect accompaniment.

2 tablespoons dark rum
¼ cup diced mixed dried fruit
2 tablespoons butter
2 tablespoons all-purpose flour
Pinch of salt
¾ cup milk
3 egg yolks

5 tablespoons granulated sugar
2 teaspoons vanilla extract
4 ounces bittersweet or semisweet chocolate,
   chopped into small pieces
4 egg whites
½ cup heavy cream, whipped to soft peaks

1. Preheat the oven to 425 degrees. Generously butter a 10-inch pie plate or a shallow baking dish of a similar size. Sprinkle with granulated sugar.
2. Gently heat the rum and soak the fruit in it for 15 minutes.
3. In a heavy saucepan, melt the butter, stir in the flour and salt, and cook, stirring constantly, over medium-low heat for 2 minutes. Slowly whisk in the milk. Cook, stirring, until smooth, thick, and bubbly, about 3 minutes.
4. Lightly beat the yolks with 2 tablespoons of the sugar. Stir about ¼ of the hot milk mixture into the yolks to warm them, then scrape the milk-yolk mixture into the saucepan. Cook, stirring over low heat, for about 1 minute. Do not boil. Take the saucepan off the heat and stir in the vanilla, chocolate, and dried fruit along with any unabsorbed rum. Stir until the chocolate is melted and the mixture is well blended.

The recipe may be made up to 2 hours in advance up to this point and held at room temperature.
5. Beat the egg whites to soft peaks, then gradually add the remaining 3 tablespoons sugar until firm, moist peaks form. Do not overbeat. Stir a large spoonful of the

beaten whites into the chocolate custard, then fold the custard into the remaining whites using a quick, light touch.

6. Pour into the prepared pie plate and bake in the center of the oven about 10 to 12 minutes. The soufflé will be puffed but still soft and wobbly in the center.

7. To serve, spoon the soufflé on to dessert plates and spoon some whipped cream on the side.

YIELD: 4 TO 6 SERVINGS.

Hot Brownies with Brandy–Ice Cream Sauce

This dessert encourages the American childhood pastimes of sneaking the brownies hot from the pan and stirring your ice cream into soup. Both may have driven your mother up a tree, but we think even mom would approve of this adult version of those childhood habits.

Although it's great hot out of the oven, this brownie can be cut into squares when cool. The batter is especially simple to mix because it's all completed in the same saucepan in which you've melted the chocolate.

1 pint vanilla ice cream
4 tablespoons butter
2 ounces unsweetened chocolate
1¼ cups granulated sugar
2 eggs

⅔ cup all-purpose flour
⅛ teaspoon salt
1½ teaspoons vanilla extract
¾ cup chopped pecans
3 tablespoons brandy or Cognac

1. Preheat the oven to 350 degrees. Soften the ice cream for about 30 minutes in the refrigerator.

2. Melt the butter and chocolate together in a saucepan over low heat or in a large, nonmetal bowl in the microwave oven.

3. Remove from the heat and beat in the sugar, eggs, flour, salt, vanilla, and pecans. Spread into a buttered 8-inch-square pan and bake in the preheated oven until firm to the touch on top and a cake tester inserted 2 inches from the center comes out clean, about 25 minutes. The center should still be slightly underdone.

4. Whisk the brandy into the softened ice cream. With a large spoon, scoop portions of the warm baked brownies from the baking dish into dessert dishes and serve topped with the cold sauce.

YIELD: 4 TO 5 SERVINGS.

Luscious Pecan Pie Bars

The slow baking is the secret to the caramelization of these rich, dark, and addictive bars.

PASTRY BASE:

1¼ cups all-purpose flour
½ teaspoon salt
8 tablespoons chilled butter, cut in pieces
3 to 4 tablespoons ice water

PECAN TOPPING:

2 eggs
⅔ cup granulated sugar
⅔ cup dark corn syrup
1 teaspoon vanilla extract
Pinch of salt
2 cups broken pecan meats

1. To make the pastry base, combine the flour and salt in the workbowl of a food processor. Add the cold butter and pulse until the mixture resembles coarse meal. Sprinkle on the ice water and pulse 5 or 6 times until the pastry just begins to clump together. (To make the dough by hand, combine the flour and salt in a mixing bowl. Cut or rub in the cold butter until the mixture resembles coarse meal. Add the ice water, tossing lightly until the dough is evenly and lightly moistened.) Gather into a flattened square, wrap, and chill for at least 30 minutes or for up to 2 days.

2. On a lightly floured surface, roll the pastry to a 10-inch square. Ease the pastry into a 9-inch-square baking pan. The pastry should come about ¾ inch up the sides of the pan. Trim if necessary. Prick all over with a fork and place in the freezer for about 20 minutes. Preheat the oven to 450 degrees.

3. Bake the pastry base in the preheated oven until the pastry begins to color and is firm, about 10 to 12 minutes. Remove it from the oven while making the topping. Do not turn the oven off.

4. To make the topping, whisk the eggs with the sugar in a large mixing bowl. Whisk in the corn syrup, vanilla, and salt, Stir in the pecans. Pour the topping evenly over the pastry base.

5. Place in the oven and immediately turn the heat down to 275 degrees. Bake 1½ hours until the bars are a rich brown, firm, and caramelized. Let cool in the pan on a wire rack. While still slightly warm, cut into 16 bars.

YIELD: 16 BARS.

NOTE: Store the cookies in a tightly covered container for up to 3 days, or wrap well and freeze for up to 1 month.

Giant Anise Sugar Cookies

Being sugar cookie lovers from way back, our preference is for the big, soft kind. We also like them subtly flavored with ground anise seed, especially when served with sweet, juicy, ripe watermelon at a picnic on a hot day in the summer or with a mug of coffee or hot chocolate after a soup-and-sandwich supper on a snowy day in winter.

1¾ cups all-purpose flour
½ teaspoon baking soda
½ teaspoon salt
2 teaspoons anise seed
1 cup granulated sugar

8 tablespoons unsalted butter, softened
1 whole egg
1 egg yolk
1 teaspoon vanilla extract

1. Sift together the flour, baking soda, and salt and set aside. Crush the anise seed with ¼ cup of the sugar using a mortar and pestle or a small food mincer (not a standard food processor).
2. Cream the butter, anise-flavored sugar, and ½ cup of the remaining sugar until light. Beat in the egg, the yolk, and the vanilla until light and fluffy. With the mixer on low speed, beat in the flour mixture until well blended.
3. Wrap the dough in plastic wrap and chill for 1 to 2 hours or overnight. Place the remaining ¼ cup sugar in a shallow dish. Preheat the oven to 350 degrees. Grease baking sheets.
4. Divide the dough into 16 equal pieces, each about 1½ inches in diameter, and form into balls with lightly floured hands. Dredge each ball in sugar and place on the prepared baking sheets. Allow at least 3 inches in between each cookie ball and bake only 8 cookies on each sheet.
5. Bake in the center of the oven until the cookies are very lightly browned, about 18 to 20 minutes. The cookie balls will spread and the tops will crinkle. Cool completely on racks.

YIELD: 16 LARGE COOKIES.

NOTE: Store the cookies in an airtight container for up to 3 days or freeze them for up to 1 month.

Molasses-Ginger Crinkles

We have both been fond of gingersnaps since we were kids. We also like the soft, chewy molasses cookies that filled the cookie jars of our childhood homes. This recipe is an attempt to re-create the fragrant and delicious memories of both. The cookies are a breeze to make, and both the unbaked dough and the finished cookies freeze well. The cookies also keep well in a tin, although we have never been able to keep them around long enough to accurately gauge just how long they will last. Served by themselves with a cold glass of milk, they are quite nice. But put out a plate of them along with some dishes of lemon sherbet and you have a first-class dessert!

2 cups all-purpose flour
½ **teaspoon baking soda**
½ **teaspoon salt**
¾ **teaspoon ground ginger**
½ **teaspoon ground cinnamon**
½ **teaspoon ground mace**

Pinch of cloves
8 tablespoons unsalted butter
¾ **cup granulated sugar**
1 egg
½ **cup dark molasses**

1. In the workbowl of a food processor, first pulse the flour, baking soda, salt, ginger, cinnamon, mace, and cloves to "sift," then remove them to a piece of wax paper. Without washing the workbowl, cut the butter into several pieces and process along with the sugar, egg, and molasses until fluffy, about 30 seconds. Add the dry ingredients and pulse 3 or 4 times to blend well. (To make the dough by hand, sift together the dry ingredients. Reserve. Cream the butter with ½ cup of the sugar until light. Add the egg and molasses and beat until smooth. With the mixer at low speed, blend in the flour mixture.)
2. Scrape the dough onto a large piece of wax paper, flatten until about 1 inch thick, and wrap completely in the wax paper. Refrigerate at least 1 hour or up to 2 days. (The dough can also be frozen for up to 1 month.)
3. Preheat the oven to 350 degrees. Lightly grease two baking sheets. Place the remaining ¼ cup sugar in a small, shallow dish.
4. Remove half of the dough from the refrigerator. Dust your hands lightly with flour and pinch off pieces of dough about 1 inch in diameter. Roll into smooth balls with your hands and then roll each ball in the sugar. Place 2 inches apart on the prepared baking sheets. Repeat with the other half of the dough.

5. Bake, one sheet at a time, in the center of the oven until the tops are rounded and crinkled and the cookies are set, about 12 to 15 minutes. (If you want to bake both sheets at the same time, reverse their positions in the oven halfway through the baking time to ensure even baking.) Cool cookies on racks.

YIELD: 24 TO 30 COOKIES.

NOTE: Store the cookies in a tightly covered container for up to 1 week or freeze them for up to 1 month.

Cranberry-Cointreau Sundaes

This simple preparation of warm cranberry sauce is a brilliant color, texture, temperature, and flavor contrast to the smooth richness of good vanilla ice cream. A jar of this sauce would also make a nice Christmas gift.

1 12-ounce bag (3 cups) cranberries
1 cup granulated sugar
1 cup orange juice

5 tablespoons Cointreau or other orange
 liqueur
1 quart excellent-quality vanilla ice cream

1. Place the cranberries, sugar, and orange juice in a heavy, nonaluminum saucepan. Bring to a boil, stirring constantly to dissolve the sugar. Lower the heat and simmer, stirring occasionally, until all the berries have popped and the sauce is slightly thickened, about 8 to 10 minutes. Remove from the heat and stir in the Cointreau.

2. To serve, divide the ice cream among dessert bowls. Spoon the warm sauce over the ice cream.

YIELD: 6 SERVINGS (ABOUT 1¾ CUPS SAUCE).

NOTE: The sauce may be made 3 or 4 days ahead and stored in the refrigerator. Reheat gently before serving.

Tin Roof Sundaes

Tin Roof Sundaes are a fond memory from Melanie's childhood. No amount of research, though, has come up with a definitive explanation of the origin of the name. We have given up the search and just enjoy the wonderful combination of vanilla ice cream, peanuts, and chocolate. This, our contemporary and delightfully simple version, has crushed peanut brittle mixed into the ice cream. Use the best peanut brittle you can find.

We have yet to find a commercial hot fudge sauce that we like as well as our own homemade. Not only is this one a snap to prepare, but it keeps for days in the refrigerator. We think it will keep for weeks, but we aren't really sure since we have never been able to make it last even a day or two. The top always seems to mysteriously develop small road tracks that look suspiciously like finger marks running thought it—probably done at night by anonymous raiders. So, if we plan to make it in quantity to give as gifts, we either hide it in brown bags or deliver it immediately.

1 quart fine-quality vanilla ice cream
10 ounces high-quality, store-bought peanut
    brittle

HOT FUDGE SAUCE:

⅓ cup granulated sugar
⅓ cup packed light brown sugar

½ cup unsweetened cocoa, preferably Dutch
    process
¾ cup heavy cream
⅓ cup light corn syrup
Pinch of salt
½ ounce unsweetened chocolate, chopped
5 tablespoons unsalted butter
1½ teaspoons vanilla extract

1. Spoon the ice cream into a large mixing bowl and let it soften about 5 minutes. Meanwhile, coarsely crush the peanut brittle in a food processor. Measure out 1 cup of the crushed brittle and reserve the remainder for garnish.

2. Stir the 1 cup peanut brittle into the ice cream until blended. Cover the bowl with foil or repack it into the ice cream container and place in the coldest part of the freezer.

3. To make the hot fudge sauce, combine the granulated sugar, brown sugar, cocoa, heavy cream, corn syrup, and salt in a heavy, medium-size saucepan over medium heat. Bring slowly to a boil, stirring to dissolve the sugars. Lower the heat and simmer for 5 minutes, stirring often. Remove the pan from the heat and add the unsweetened chocolate and the butter. Stir until melted and smooth and then stir in the vanilla until well blended.

The sauce may be made ahead and chilled in a covered jar until ready to use. Then reheat it gently by placing the jar in a pan of hot water.

4. When ready to serve, scoop the ice cream into dessert bowls. Ladle about ¼ cup hot fudge sauce while still warm over the ice cream. Sprinkle each sundae with some of the reserved peanut brittle.

YIELD: 6 TO 8 SERVINGS.

INDEX